Cosmology Without God?

VERITAS
Series Introduction

". . . the truth will set you free" (John 8:32)

In much contemporary discourse, Pilate's question has been taken to mark the absolute boundary of human thought. Beyond this boundary, it is often suggested, is an intellectual hinterland into which we must not venture. This terrain is an agnosticism of thought: because truth cannot be possessed, it must not be spoken. Thus, it is argued that the defenders of "truth" in our day are often traffickers in ideology, merchants of counterfeits, or anti-liberal. They are, because it is somewhat taken for granted that Nietzsche's word is final: truth is the domain of tyranny.

Is this indeed the case, or might another vision of truth offer itself? The ancient Greeks named the love of wisdom as *philia*, or friendship. The one who would become wise, they argued, would be a "friend of truth." For both philosophy and theology might be conceived as schools in the friendship of truth, as a kind of relation. For like friendship, truth is as much discovered as it is made. If truth is then so elusive, if its domain is *terra incognita*, perhaps this is because it arrives to us—unannounced—as gift, as a person, and not some thing.

The aim of the Veritas book series is to publish incisive and original current scholarly work that inhabits "the between" and "the beyond" of theology and philosophy. These volumes will all share a common aspiration to transcend the institutional divorce in which these two disciplines often find themselves, and to engage questions of pressing concern to both philosophers and theologians in such a way as to reinvigorate both disciplines with a kind of interdisciplinary desire, often so absent in contemporary academe. In a word, these volumes represent collective efforts in the befriending of truth, doing so beyond the simulacra of pretend tolerance, the violent, yet insipid reasoning of liberalism that asks with Pilate, "What is truth?"—expecting a consensus of non-commitment; one that encourages the commodification of the mind, now sedated by the civil service of career, ministered by the frightened patrons of position.

The series will therefore consist of two "wings": (1) original monographs; and (2) essay collections on a range of topics in theology and philosophy. The latter will principally be the products of the annual conferences of the Centre of Theology and Philosophy (www.theologyphilosophycentre .co.uk).

Conor Cunningham and Eric Austin Lee, *Series editors*

Not available from Cascade

Deane-Peter Baker	*Tayloring Reformed Epistemology: The Challenge to Christian Belief.* Volume 1
P. Candler & C. Cunningham (eds.)	*Belief and Metaphysics.* Volume 2
P. Candler & C. Cunningham (eds.)	*Transcendence and Phenomenology*
Marcus Pound	*Theology, Psychoanalysis, and Trauma.* Volume 4
Espen Dahl	*Phenomenology and the Holy.* Volume 5
C. Cunningham et al. (eds.)	*Grandeur of Reason: Religion, Tradition, and Universalism.* Volume 6
A. Pabst & A. Paddison (eds.)	*The Pope and Jesus of Nazareth: Christ, Scripture, and the Church.* Volume 7
J. P. Moreland	*Recalcitrant Imago Dei: Human Persons and the Failure of Naturalism.* Volume 8

Cascade

[Nathan Kerr	*Christ, History, and Apocalyptic: The Politics of Christian Mission.* Volume 3][1]
Anthony D. Baker	*Diagonal Advance: Perfection in Christian Theology.* Volume 9
D. C. Schindler	*The Perfection of Freedom: Schiller, Schelling, and Hegel between the Ancients and the Moderns.* Volume 10
Rustin Brian	*Covering Up Luther: How Barth's Christology Challenged the* Deus Absconditus *that Haunts Modernity.* Volume 11
Timothy Stanley	*Protestant Metaphysics After Karl Barth and Martin Heidegger.* Volume 12
Christopher Ben Simpson	*The Truth Is the Way: Kierkegaard's* Theologia Viatorum. Volume 13
Richard H. Bell	*Wagner's Parsifal: An Appreciation in the Light of His Theological Journey.* Volume 14
Antonio Lopez	*Gift and the Unity of Being.* Volume 15
Toyohiko Kagawa	*Cosmic Purpose.* Translated and introduced by Thomas John Hastings. Volume 16
Nigel Zimmerman	*Facing the Other: John Paul II, Levinas, and the Body.* Volume 17

---

1. Note: Nathan Kerr, *Christ, History, and Apocalyptic*, although volume 3 of the original SCM Veritas series, is available from Cascade as part of the Theopolitical Visions series.

Cosmology Without God?

The Problematic Theology Inherent
in Modern Cosmology

DAVID ALCALDE

Foreword by MICHAEL HANBY

CASCADE *Books* · Eugene, Oregon

COSMOLOGY WITHOUT GOD?
The Problematic Theology Inherent in Modern Cosmology

Veritas

Cascade Books
An Imprint of Wipf and Stock Publishers
199 W. 8th Ave., Suite 3
Eugene, OR 97401

www.wipfandstock.com

PAPERBACK ISBN: 978-1-5326-3684-4
HARDCOVER ISBN: 978-1-5326-3686-8
EBOOK ISBN: 978-1-5326-3685-1

Cataloguing-in-Publication data:

Names: Alcalde, David. | Hanby, Michael, foreword.

Title: Cosmology without God? : the problematic theology inherent in modern cosmology / David Alcalde ; foreword by Michael Hanby.

Description: Eugene, OR: Cascade Books, 2019 | Series: Veritas | Includes bibliographical references and index.

Identifiers: ISBN 978-1-5326-3684-4 (paperback) | ISBN 978-1-5326-3686-8 (hardcover) | ISBN 978-1-5326-3685-1 (ebook)

Subjects: LCSH: Religion and science | Physics—Religious aspects | Cosmology | God | Metaphysics | Creation | Deism

Classification: BL265 A52 2019 (print) | BL265 (ebook)

Manufactured in the U.S.A.   November 29, 2018

Table of Contents

Foreword

THE BREAK THAT EMERGED into the open in the nineteenth century between modern science and the natural philosophy that gave it birth has left contemporary science woefully lacking in self-knowledge and even more woefully complacent about this fact. Ignorant of its own philosophical history, blind to the metaphysical and theological presuppositions inherent in its operative notions of nature and truth, and unaware of the metaphysical preconditions of its own cognitive act, both theoretically and practically, science marches on—forward, it thinks—confident that its practical success finally silences all theoretical questions. The inevitable result is a pervasive and endemic reductionism inadequate both to the richness of scientific cognition and to the world we cannot helping living in, a world that includes scientists among its many possibilities, with the reductive scientist beating a perpetual retreat to an Archimedean point outside of nature, and exempting himself from his own reductionism in the moment of his theorizing. As reason is reduced to scientific and technical reason, as scientific reason exhaustively defines what it means for us *to think,* there seem to be fewer and fewer things to think *about.* More and more dimensions of human being and experience—indeed the most fundamental dimensions—fall outside of the scientific gaze, while the ground and possibility of it all fall outside our reduced understanding of reason and thus cease to be meaningful questions. The anti-reductionism currently in vogue in the form of complex systems theories merely conceals these facts from view.

With the possible exception of Darwinian biology, bastard child of the functionalist tradition of British natural theology with its own peculiar theological history and socio-religious function, this state of affairs is nowhere more evident than in the so-called dialogue between science and religion. On the one side, there are the atheist cosmologists and public scientists, who confidently declare the death of philosophy and theology while appropriating for themselves the mantle of the public intellectual, thereby reinforcing the thoughtless pragmatism of our public reason. Their engagement in the very theological enterprise that they reject, albeit in the negative form of an intellectually lazy atheism with a cartoon God, is evident to everyone but themselves. On the other side, there are the earnest theologians and philosophers of religion, some of them former scientists, who desire to justify the ways of God to science and to preserve a viable space for theological reason in the public square. "Dialogue" is forever on their lips, but in the end only one voice is audible. They begin with the uncritical acceptance of the ontological and epistemic presuppositions of modern science, leaving its mechanistic understanding of nature untouched, and end up uncritically embracing the reduced notion of God rejected by the atheists, never quite entering into a truly critical engagement with the sciences, and never quite attaining to an intellectually rigorous engagement with the doctrines of God and creation or the claim that Christianity lays to the whole of reality in its breadth and depth.

Missing from this so-called dialogue is the awareness that science inevitably entails metaphysical and theological judgments of its own that may be subject to philosophical and theological criticism, or that science's necessary dependence upon metaphysics and theology calls into question its authority as sole arbiter of the knowledge of nature. This great authority, further legitimated by the widespread idea that religion is an irrational phenomenon concerned, at best, with the realm of private "values," absolves the scientist in his role as public intellectual of the most basic intellectual rigor or theological understanding, and leaves him free to make the most absurd and irresponsible theological pronouncements with impunity. It is fundamentally an unserious exercise. And it is a profound mistake for a Christian to engage it on its own terms. The result will tend inevitably toward an un-Christian understanding of God, creation, and nature, and reinforce the pervasive idea that Christianity has nothing of real importance to say about the nature of things. What is needed instead is a deep philosophical and theological engagement with the philosophical first principles of modern science and the conception of God, being, nature, knowledge, and truth that lay buried within it.

The present volume by Fr. David Alcalde is an important contribution to this endeavor. Fr. Alcalde brings to this work the rare perspective of one trained in both theology and astrophysics—he holds doctorates in both—and so the realms of physics and cosmology are thus his chosen terrain. Yet it is a perspective made rarer still by the fact that he, unlike others who have chosen a similar path, does not let his scientific training determine the grounds or dictate the limits of his theology. To the contrary, because he recognizes that metaphysics and theology precede the sciences in the *ordo rationis*, he begins, first, with the God revealed in Scripture as the great I AM (Exod 3:14) and reflected upon down the Christian centuries as the self-subsistent act of being (*ipsum esse subsistens*) and, second, with the understanding of *creatio ex nihilo* that follows upon the doctrine of God. He is thus able to rescue the notions of both God and creation from the "ontic" understanding of a science that takes being for granted and restore them to their proper theological and metaphysical meaning.

On this basis he is then able to critically assess the notions of God and creation at work on both sides of the "dialogue." The atheist cosmologies represented by a thinker like Stephen Hawking are then revealed to be not so much an alternative *to* theology, but an alternative theology that does not know itself, one that is deeply deficient on both doctrinal and philosophical grounds. Sadly, God's scientific defenders do not fare much better, and indeed are shown to partake of the same positivism, the same theological extrinsicism, and the same mechanistic ontology as their opponents. Along the way he debunks a number of cherished but deeply flawed notions. The idea of a methodologically pure and ontologically neutral science, free of metaphysical and theological contamination turns out to be a fiction. So too the distinction between science and scientism, designed to insulate the scientific method from its own metaphysical foundations and thus to shield the sciences from just the sort of deep philosophical criticism that Alcalde advocates. What is revealed instead is that for all the peculiarities of its methods and for all its practical and predictive success, modern science is not exempt from the necessities imposed upon thought by being and creaturehood. It cannot be liberated from its constitutive relationship to metaphysics and theology, and therefore represents one of the inevitable ways of coping with the question of God.

There remains a great deal at stake in this question. If God is indeed God, and the world is creation after all, then our failure or refusal to grasp this truth means not only a failure to apprehend God's being and nature, which is already everything, but it implies a fundamental failure (or refusal) to grasp the truth about nature and ourselves. The failure of science then to "get God right" will always mean a failure to "get the world right," its refusal to be integrated into a more comprehensive order of reason, a refusal to be less than the "lords and masters of nature" of Descartes' ambitions. This is one deep reason why science must now be said to hold forth at least as much peril as promise for the human future. This book provides grounds for the otherwise dwindling hope the promise may yet win out.

—Michael Hanby
Associate Professor of Religion and Philosophy of Science
Pontifical John Paul II Institute, Washington, DC

Acknowledgments

THIS BOOK IS A revised edition of my doctoral dissertation, which was defended in 2017 at the Pontifical John Paul II Institute for Studies on Marriage and Family at the Catholic University of America. Firstly, I want to express my earnest gratitude toward my dissertation supervisor, Michael Hanby. The work that I am presenting in this book would not have come to fruition without his invaluable help. I deeply appreciate his keen insights on the subject of my research. I also thank Conor Cunningham for his willingness to publish my book in the Veritas series, which he edits along with Eric Austin Lee. I am truly honored by being included in the prestigious Veritas book series. Finally, I am indebted to Denise Eggers for her magnificent proofreading and editing services.

Introduction

THE BEGINNING OF MODERNITY witnessed the appearance of a new idea of science which brought an unprecedented development of technology. Modern science was praised for its technological achievements and its success in understanding and manipulating the workings of nature. The exaltation of modern science reached the point of claiming science as the only access to knowledge and rejecting metaphysics and theology, a phenomenon that has since come to be known as *scientism*. This was the natural consequence of the modern idea of science, for modern science understands the world as inherently mechanistic and scientific experiments as the paradigmatic way to obtain the truth. However, though modern science claims to be able to conquer every possible area of knowledge, it cannot: it disregards metaphysical and theological knowledge and therefore is unable to integrate science into a higher order of philosophical wisdom. Therefore, the advent of modern science almost inevitably brought the eventual separation of modern science from philosophy and theology.

Aware of some of the problems of scientism, Michael Polanyi, Karl Popper, Thomas Kuhn, and other philosophers of science in the twentieth century criticized scientific positivism and paved the way for the recognition of the limitations of the scientific method and the appreciation of forms of knowledge other than science, especially metaphysics and theology. Although modern science did not abandon scientism (and it cannot avoid it inasmuch as it is part of its essence), the critique of positivism brought about a cultural change, which made possible the beginning of the dialogue between science and theology in a committed way, especially by philosophers and theologians. The starting point of this contemporary dialogue was the book *Issues in Science and Religion*, written by Ian Barbour and published in 1966.[1] Since then,

1. Smedes, "Beyond Barbour," 235.

1

the field has grown tremendously, and it is slowly reaching a state of maturity with the institutionalization of the field through academic chairs (for example at Oxford and at Princeton Theological Seminary) and the journals *Zygon: Journal of Religion and Science* and *Theology and Science*. An incredible amount of literature has appeared since the late 1960s on all kinds of topics, but most notably on the scientific worldview and the possibility of divine action (for example through quantum theory, chaos theory, and most recently emergence), evolutionary theory and the doctrine of creation, and the philosophical and theological implications of the new neurosciences.[2]

This friendly disposition towards theology is not shared by the scientific academy as a whole. In fact, there are atheistic scientists who attempt to use their scientific research to demonstrate their atheistic positions. It is worthwhile to note that evolutionary biologists have usually taken the lead on this issue. One of the most relevant figures defending atheism today is the evolutionary biologist Richard Dawkins.[3] But antagonism toward theology is not confined to the field of evolutionary biology. In the field of cosmology, atheistic scientists use their research in order to deny creation from the scientific point of view. Some of them interpret the initial space-time singularity of the Big Bang model as the beginning of the universe and the moment of divine creation, and they think that once the initial singularity is absent, creation is superfluous.

As an example, Stephen Hawking, together with James Hartle, proposed a cosmological model that eliminated the initial singularity of the Big Bang theory. Supported by this model, Hawking came to this conclusion: "So long as the universe had a beginning, we could suppose it had a creator. But if the universe is really completely self-contained, having no boundary or edge, it would have neither beginning nor end: it would simply be. What place, then, for a creator?"[4] Commenting on the story of Pierre Simon Laplace regarding God as an unnecessary hypothesis for the physical description of the universe, Hawking said the following: "I don't think that Laplace was claiming that God didn't exist. It is just that He doesn't intervene, to break the laws of Science. That must be the position of every scientist. A scientific law is not a scientific law, if it only holds when some supernatural being decides to let things run, and not

2. Smedes, "Beyond Barbour," 235–36.

3. See Dawkins, *The God Delusion*.

4. Hawking, *Brief History of Time* (1998), 146.

intervene."[5] It is pertinent here to cite the words of Dawkins regarding Hawking's book *The Grand Design*: "Darwin kicked him [God] out of biology, but physics remained more uncertain. Hawking is now administering the coup de grace."[6]

According to William Carroll, "New theories concerning what happened 'before the Big Bang' as well as those which speak of an endless series of big bangs are often attractive [to atheistic scientists] because they too deny a fundamental beginning to the universe."[7] As we can see, these scientists show an interest in creation, albeit in a negative form. However, this interest has a clear goal: to use science in order to deny any divine intervention in the universe. These scientists fail to understand that

---

5. Hawking, "Does God Play Dice?" "Laplace's argument, *I had no need of that hypothesis*, is still being used today. Hawking and Mlodinow in their book, THE GRAND DESIGN [2010], created a stir by claiming God did not exist. But their argument was just Laplace's pushed back from the beginning of the solar system to the beginning of the universe: they had no need of that hypothesis" (Jennings, *In Defense of Scientism*, 59). "One of Laplace's interests was the mathematical astronomy he found in Newton's *Principia*. In the *Principia*, Newton had been unable to account for all of the motions of the planets—this instability was literally left in God's hands as an occasional intervention was required to maintain the planets in their orbits. Laplace was able to overcome the difficulties in the Newtonian system, and in a monumental five-volume work called *Celestial Mechanics*, he presented a mathematical and physical description of the solar system with every movement completely accounted for. In fact, as the story goes, when Napoleon was presented with a copy of *Celestial Mechanics*, the emperor [sic] inquired why God was never mentioned. Laplace's rather cheeky reply was: 'I had no need of that hypothesis'" (Timmons, *Makers of Western Science*, 156). "This oft-repeated phrase [*I have no need of that hypothesis*] may not have been spoken verbatim, but Herschel's diary records an event that reports the gist of the exchange" (Hahn, *Pierre Simon Laplace*, 172). This is the entry for August 8, 1802 (Sunday) in the diary of the British astronomer William Herschel: "The first Consul [Napoleon] then asked a few questions relating to Astronomy and the construction of the heavens to which I made such answers as seemed to give him great satisfaction. He also addressed himself to Mr. Laplace on the same subject, and held a considerable argument with him in which he differed from that eminent mathematician. The difference was occasioned by an exclamation of the first Consul, who asked in a tone of exclamation or admiration (when we were speaking of the extent of the sidereal heavens): 'And who is the author of all this!' Mons. De la Place wished to shew that a chain of natural causes would account for the construction and preservation of the wonderful system. This the first Consul rather opposed. Much may be said on the subject; by joining the arguments of both we shall be led to 'Nature and nature's God'" (Herschel, *The Herschel Chronicle*, 310).

6. Dawkins, "The God Debate"; Hawking and Mlodinow, *The Grand Design*.

7. William Carroll, *Creation and Science*, 2.

creation is not a divine intervention in the universe—which is conceived as a worldly mechanism—but the giving of the universe to itself *ex nihilo*.

Additionally, there are theologians and philosophers who have striven to reject scientism, and they have insistently tried to reconcile theology with science by integrating scientific discoveries into theology. Their effort is problematic due to the scientism that underlies the modern science they accept. In spite of their honest intention, the result of their effort to reconcile theology with science is a reduction of theological categories to accommodate *neutral* scientific facts. In the end, theology's role in the science-theology dialogue consists in responding to the deliverances of science in a limited way, as it is incapable in principle of either calling the fundamental scientific principles into question or making truth claims about the natural world. Underneath these ideas there is positivism because ultimately only *scientific* knowledge is recognized as being authentic. When the participants in the dialogue use "science to counter scientistic claims" and to give theology a place in the academy, they are assuming and strengthening scientism. "By consequence, what they are doing does not constitute an attack to scientism, but merely a proposal to revise some scientistic assumptions so as to include the possibility"[8] of theology as an interlocutor with science. This approach taken by theologians and philosophers is problematic because it assumes scientistic metaphysical ideas, such as the alleged neutrality of the scientific method, which carry with them questionable theological suppositions.

Both kinds of approaches, the scientistic one and the scientific-theological one, are flawed because of the explicit (or implicit) scientism present in them. It is important to note here that scientism is itself laden with metaphysical and theological judgments. One of these is the indifference of the scientific study of nature towards God.[9] In turn, this indifference presupposes a mechanistic understanding of nature and an extrinsicist theology.[10] These two premises lead to misconceptions of

8. Smedes, *Chaos, Complexity, and God*, 186–87.

9. "For modern science the world is no longer something created: it is just Nature" (Morales, *Creation Theology*, 4).

10. "When the scientific worldview became independent of the relationship with God because of the purely mechanical description of the origin of the planetary system in the pioneering work of Kant and Laplace . . . only one approach to the reality of God was left open, namely, the contemplation of human self-consciousness and its foundation" (Pannenberg, *Toward a Theology of Nature*, 50–51). This is why "the arguments of modern atheism from Feuerbach by way of Marx and Nietzsche to Freud, Sartre,

nature and God, and the way in which they relate. These inadequate notions go unnoticed in the dialogue between science and theology, because
they are usually not questioned but simply assumed with the affirmation
of the indifference of nature towards God. This indifference can also be
formulated as *theological extrinsicism*: God is extrinsic to nature.

The theological extrinsicism present in the thought of scientists,
theologians, and philosophers is highly problematic, and these scholars are normally unaware of it. This present book aims to uncover and
criticize the incoherent theological extrinsicism inherent in a concrete
branch of modern science, which is modern cosmology.[11] The purpose of
the *first chapter* is to demonstrate that theological extrinsicism is inherent
in modern science in general. In this chapter, I will examine the radical
new concepts of nature and God that came into being with the advent of
modern science. The novel understanding of science was founded upon
the rejection of scholasticism and upon the mathematical interpretation
of the world. As stated above, modern science claims that its method,
the scientific method, is epistemologically superior to others and neutral
with regard to metaphysics and theology. I will refute that assertion about
the neutrality of science by showing that every scientific understanding
of nature presupposes metaphysical and theological ideas. This is so because science, metaphysics, and theology are intrinsically related. Therefore, the affirmation of the neutrality of science does not dispense science
from having metaphysical and theological presuppositions. These presuppositions do not cease to be present in the allegedly neutral science,
but they become invisible to the scientists using their restrictive scientific
method. However, the main problem with those metaphysical and theo-

---

and Camus are directed likewise to the thematics of the self-understanding of human
beings and not the problems of the knowledge of nature" (ibid., 50). As a consequence,
"The underlying religious interpretation of reality is taken no longer as universally
valid but as a matter of private preference, if not as superstition" (Pannenberg, "Theological Questions to Scientists," 65).

11. Modern cosmology is understood as the physical science that deals with the
universe as a whole and whose origin dates to the beginning of the twentieth century. "Modern scientific cosmology is a recent field of study, not really starting until
the early 20th century" (Liddle and Loveday, *Oxford Companion to Cosmology*, 81).
Rigorously, the adjective which should accompany the noun "cosmology" should be
"contemporary" instead of "modern." However, the current cosmologists do not use
the adjective "contemporary." The standard term is modern cosmology, and, as such,
it appears in scientific books and papers. These are some renowned textbooks about
current cosmology: Hawley and Holcomb, *Foundations of Modern Cosmology*; Liddle,
Introduction to Modern Cosmology, and Dodelson, *Modern Cosmology*.

logical presuppositions is not that they remain unconscious for the most part, but that they are deficient and untenable. These presuppositions, based on the affirmation that theology and metaphysics are extrinsic to science, are encompassed under the name of *extrinsicism*. This extrinsicism is present in varied ways in those working in science, ranging from those who reject metaphysics and theology to those who approach those subjects in a friendly manner. I will criticize these different expressions of extrinsicism and their common faulty metaphysical and theological assumptions. These defective presuppositions can be summarized as a mechanical understanding of nature and an extrinsic idea of God. These two kinds of presuppositions are inseparable because they imply each other.

In order to uncover and criticize the extrinsicism present in modern science and, more concretely, in modern cosmology, it is necessary to provide a coherent and unreduced image of God and nature, to give a better theological understanding of the relation between the world and God. This can be accomplished through a convincing doctrine of creation, for the doctrine of creation is both a doctrine of God and a conception of the world. A plausible doctrine of creation is a valuable tool to point out and overcome the problematic theological extrinsicism and mechanistic ontology present in modern science and, most particularly, in modern cosmology.[12] The goal of the *second chapter* is to lay out the doctrine of creation *ex nihilo* in its twofold sense, theological and metaphysical, in order to have a foundation for criticizing the extrinsic theology present in modern science and, more concretely, in modern cosmology. In order to deal with the doctrine of creation in its dual aspect as a doctrine both of God and of the metaphysical constitution of the world, I will lean on the works of Thomas Aquinas, because they are a philosophically precise exposition of the Christian tradition. However, my intention is not to present a treatise of the Thomistic understanding of creation but to articulate how the Christian tradition understands creation. Although Thomas is very helpful for grasping the doctrine of creation, he is not the

---

12. A cogent doctrine of creation helps us also to see that "the reality of God is a factor in defining what nature is, and [that] to ignore this fact leaves us with something less than a fully adequate explanation of things" (Pannenberg, *A Theology of Nature*, 48). Even more, this doctrine of creation allows science to be less theological and more natural. As Michael Hanby says, "Good theology liberates the sciences to be science and, moreover, performs for them a service without which they will tend to falsify themselves and their objects" (Hanby, "Saving the Appearances," 71).

only source. For this reason, I will use other authors apart from Aquinas to apprehend what creation is.

In my purpose of criticizing the extrinsicist theology of modern cosmologies, the doctrine of creation is crucially important from two perspectives. From the side of God, the doctrine of creation preserves God's transcendent otherness from the world. In other words, the doctrine of creation clearly conveys that the being of God and the being of the world are completely different, though this radical difference is itself the cornerstone of the world's analogical similarity to God. From the side of the world, the doctrine of creation clarifies that the act of creation is not a mechanical process, giving account of how the world came to be. Rather, creation is about the unasked-for gift of being to what was nothing, i.e., the giving of the world to itself. To put it in another way, to create is to make something from nothing; it is the passage from non-being to being. These reflections on the doctrine of creation will be helpful in my criticism of the misunderstanding of God and creation assumed by extrinsicist theologians and cosmologists.

The rich and profound understanding of both God and the world provided by the doctrine of creation is the counterpoint necessary to criticize the extrinsicist theology inherent in modern cosmology, which is the goal of the *third chapter*. Modern cosmology is a fitting scientific field for studying the theological and metaphysical presuppositions inherent in modern science, because this scientific branch deals with questions that were previously assumed to be purely theological. According to the theological extrinsicism present in modern cosmology, God is conceived as an external agent who is in competition with natural processes, and creation is conceived as a worldly mechanism. Immersed in this extrinsicism, atheistic cosmologists attempt to deny the existence of God, arguing that what was formerly assigned to divine action (due to scientific ignorance) can be now explained solely in scientific terms. The extrinsic understanding of God is also present in those scientists and theologians who try give scientific evidence for the existence of God (using cosmology). These scientists and theologians share the extrinsic theological assumptions of the atheistic cosmologists because they uncritically assume the metaphysical and theological presuppositions of modern science. As a result, the conception of God held by these theistic scientists and theologians is severely reduced to comply with the exigencies of scientific discoveries, which are taken as normative. They try to explain God's action in the world in reductive scientific terms, thus showing their misunderstanding of creation and divine action. In my task of criticizing the theological extrinsicism of modern cosmology, I will treat two main cosmological issues: the beginning of the universe and the finely tuned universe.

I would like to remark that the purpose of criticizing the extrinsic theology inherent in modern cosmology is not simply to rescue theology by denouncing the deficient image of God implicit in modern cosmology, though rescuing theology is part of the point. The purpose is also to indicate that there is no such thing as a truly atheistic cosmology, because a concept of God always lies at the foundation of all of these cosmological theories. The fact that some of the thinkers in question disbelieve in a defective image of God or construct their cosmologies so as to render him obsolete is beside the point. The point, rather, is this: that given the impossibility of dispensing with God in thought, atheist cosmologists should think and write about God more responsibly. This is the precondition for any genuine dialogue between science and theology.

A fruitful dialogue must recognize that science has unavoidable metaphysical and theological dimensions. This recognition is crucial for an adequate philosophical comprehension of the nature and limits of modern science. The acceptance of the inevitable metaphysical and theological presuppositions of modern science is the only way to overcome extrinsicism and thus make science more reasonable, i.e., more intellectually responsible and more serious. As we will see in the third chapter, the scientific theories proposed by some contemporary cosmologists, whose goal is to reduce or eliminate God, are not only metaphysically and theologically primitive but also scientifically unreasonable, to the point of being more science fiction than real science.

1

The Problem of Theological Extrinsicism in Modern Science

Introduction

THE GOAL OF THIS book is to uncover and criticize the theological extrinsicism inherent in modern cosmology. By *theological extrinsicism*, I mean the deficient theological understanding that conceives of God as an external agent who is in competition with natural processes and of creation as a worldly mechanism. This poor theology is present not only in modern cosmology but also in other branches of modern science, such as biology.[1] In fact, modern cosmology suffers from theological extrinsicism because it is a branch of modern science. In other words, the problem of theological extrinsicism is a problem of modern science. The goal of this initial chapter is to demonstrate that theological extrinsicism inheres in modern science. I intend to achieve this goal in a number of steps. I will start by dealing with the concept of *modern science*. I will show that the advent of modern science brought a revolutionary way of understanding nature and God, based on two pillars: (a) the rejection of scholasticism and (b) the mathematical comprehension of the world. Modern science claims that "science, metaphysics, and theology are essentially 'outside' of each other, where their relationship and their

1. See Cunningham, *Darwin's Pious Idea*, and Hanby, *No God, No Science?*

9

respective claims can be adjudicated from the neutral standpoint afforded by the empirical and experimental methods of science."[2] This claim, known as *extrinsicism*,[3] is erroneous for three reasons: (1) It falsifies the concepts of both God and nature. On the one hand, God's transcendence is lost because God is reduced to an external agent acting on the same level as any natural agent. On the other hand, nature loses its own interiority and unity; it is reduced to a mechanism composed of unrelated parts. The reduction of the image of God and the reduction of the concept of nature are inseparable because they imply each other. (2) It is self-contradictory because it pretends that science is indifferent to metaphysics and theology, but it entails metaphysical and theological ideas. (3) It makes the dialogue between science and theology completely pointless.

In the third section of this chapter, I will examine the faulty theological and metaphysical assumptions present in modern science. In spite of having deficient theological and metaphysical premises, modern scientists tend to pride themselves on having a scientific method that is neutral with regard to metaphysics and theology. This assertion is founded on modern science's own criterion of epistemological superiority and on modern science's self-imposed goal of a controlling understanding of nature. In the fourth section, I will argue that there is no such a thing as a neutral science because every understanding of science has theological and metaphysical presuppositions. This is the case because, as we will see, science, metaphysics, and theology are intrinsically related. The affirmation of a neutral science does not dispense with metaphysics and theology. The very act of affirming a metaphysically and theologically free science entails, at least implicitly, metaphysical and theological assumptions that are deficient. In the fifth section, I will criticize the concept of methodological neutrality defended by modern science. This supposed neutrality is self-contradictory and entails problematic extrinsic assumptions, both theological and metaphysical. In the final section of the chapter, I will reveal and criticize different ways that scientists defend the untenable extrinsicism. The different proposals have in common the same flawed metaphysical and theological assumptions: a mechanical understanding of nature and a reduced notion of God.

2. Hanby, *No God, No Science?* 3.

3. Hanby, *No God, No Science?* 3. Theological extrinsicism focuses on theology being "outside" of science.

Modern Science

In this section, I want to deal with the concept of *modern science*. The adjective *modern* before the noun *science* is intended to convey that its historical origin has to be located in modernity.[4] Indeed, the sixteenth and seventeenth centuries witnessed the appearance of a new and revolutionary idea of science.[5] This new understanding of science, which was named *natural philosophy* at the time,[6] entailed "a radical conceptual

4. The scientist Carl Sagan popularized the idea, common among many, that science was invented 2,500 years ago by the pre-Socratics of ancient Greece (whom he called Ionians), such as Thales and Democritus, silenced later on by Platonists and Christians, and rediscovered again in the modern era. (See Sagan, *Cosmos*, 167–94, and Sagan, *Backbone of the Night*). However, as the physicist Steven Weinberg points out, "None of the pre-Socratics . . . had anything like our modern idea of what a successful scientific explanation would have to accomplish: the *quantitative* understanding of phenomena. How far do we progress toward understanding why nature is the way it is if Thales or Democritus tells us that a stone is made of water or atoms, when we still do not know how to calculate its density or hardness or electrical conductivity? And of course, without the capacity for quantitative prediction, we could never tell whether Thales or Democritus is right" (Weinberg, *Dreams of Final Theory*, 7). From the point of view of modern science, which is intrinsically *quantitative*, "the 'physics' of Aristotle [so rejected by modern scientists] was no better than the earlier and less sophisticated speculations of Thales and Democritus" (ibid., 8). Therefore, Sagan's idiosyncratic idea of the origin of modern science is quite open to dispute. "One has only to note that many careful studies of the Scientific Revolution of the seventeenth century see it as quite original and not at all a reawakening of the Ionian Enchantment" (Giberson and Artigas, *Oracles of Science*, 142).

5. The term science, as we understand it today—knowledge of nature obtained by observation, experimentation, and mathematization—took its meaning in the nineteenth century. "By the early 1700s, when the Scientific Revolution had largely run its course, 'science' still meant natural philosophy. . . . Natural philosophy had by then shed its Aristotelian metaphysics, rejected occult qualities in explanation, adopted new standards of evidence and experiment, created entirely new sorts of instrumentation, and generally incorporated new concepts and results. This was especially the case in the exact sciences of astronomy, mechanics, and optics. Yet 'science' was just beginning to assume its modern meaning and scope; this understanding emerged more definitely between the late Enlightenment and the early twentieth century. . . . It was in the nineteenth century that . . . new terms like 'biology' and 'physics,' and 'biologist' and 'physicist,' were created to describe the new disciplines and their practitioners. . . . Certainly by the final third of the nineteenth century, one could speak legitimately, that is, in a modern sense, of 'science,' 'scientists,' and the disciplines of science" (Cahan, *From Natural Philosophy*, 4).

6. Note that the great scientist Isaac Newton gave to his most renowned scientific work the title of *Philosophiae Naturalis Principia Mathematica* (1687), translated as *Mathematical Principles of Natural Philosophy*. This masterwork deals with mechanical physics, and Newton considered this subject as *natural philosophy*. "We should not be

shift, which altered the foundations of natural philosophy as practiced for nearly the preceding two thousand years."[7] The radical shift carried out by modern science was built upon the rejection of Aristotelian natural philosophy.[8] This rejection is clear in one of the programmatic and foundational works of modern science, the *Novum Organum Scientiarum*, written by Francis Bacon and published in 1620. In this work, Bacon propounded "a system of reasoning to supersede Aristotle's, suitable for the pursuit of knowledge in the age of science."[9] The new and revolutionary idea of science dismissed the notions of being and substance,[10]

---

mislead [*sic*] by the fact that because the term 'scientist' was only introduced in the nineteenth century, therefore no activity we would want to call science could have occurred before that century simply because 'scientists' may have been called by another name: natural philosophers" (Grant, *History of Natural Philosophy*, 314).

7. Lindberg, *Beginnings of Western Science*, 365. "The most profound change in natural philosophy occurred in the seventeenth century. It involved a union of the exact sciences and natural philosophy, a phenomenon that has received relatively little attention in the vast literature about the meaning and causes of the Scientific Revolution. Without that fusion, however, it is doubtful that the Scientific Revolution could have occurred in the seventeenth century. One major result of this coming-together was that natural philosophy, once regarded as largely independent and isolated from mathematics and the exact sciences, became significantly mathematized. *In this mathematized form, natural philosophy became synonymous with the term science, which came into use in the nineteenth century*" (Grant, *History of Natural Philosophy*, xii; emphasis mine).

8. It is necessary to nuance this affirmation. "From the vantage point of the seventeenth century, the Aristotelian-Scholastic science was a barren enterprise from its outset, a dead-end. Its main concern had been with definition rather than with the precise relation between phenomena. . . . Yet ever since the creative energies of medieval thought were rediscovered by recent historians, this seventeenth-century assessment has been called into question" (Funkenstein, *Theology and Scientific Imagination*, 13). In other words, the relation between modern science and scholasticism is historically more complicated than a simple rejection (ibid., 14). In fact, the early moderns took over much from the scholastics and modified it in the course of rejecting it. For example, "Early modern physics inherited many of the medieval techniques of hypothetical reasoning that involved, in questions mechanical, the beginning of a new mathematical technique. But it gave them a concrete, new interpretation" (ibid., 17).

9. Jardine, "Introduction," xii.

10. "There is nothing sound in the notions of logic and physics: neither substance, nor quality, nor action and passion, nor being itself are good notions; much less heavy, light, dense, rare, wet, dry, generation, corruption, attraction, repulsion, element, matter, form and so on; all are fanciful and ill defined" (Bacon, *The New Organon*, 35 (I, 15)). There is also no interest in the nature of an object: "It is a mark of the highest incompetence to make a thorough investigation of some one thing by itself" (ibid., 73 (I, 88)).

so important in Aristotelian physics. Modern science also rejected the Aristotelian fourfold causality, and the concept of form ceased to be crucial for the understanding of what a being is.[11] All the above makes clear that modern science entails a radical novelty in the understanding of science.[12] Because of the intrinsic relation between science, metaphysics, and theology, this novelty in the understanding of science has a corresponding metaphysical novelty. The French philosopher Alexandre Koyré appropriately argued that "the underlying source of revolutionary [scientific] novelty in the sixteenth and seventeenth centuries . . . was metaphysical and cosmological."[13] According to David Lindberg, "The organic universe of medieval metaphysics and cosmology had been routed by the lifeless machinery of the atomists."[14]

11. "The Final [cause] is a long way from being useful; in fact it actually distorts the sciences except in the case of human actions. Discovery of Form is regarded as hopeless. And the Efficient and Material causes . . . are perfunctory, superficial things, of almost no value for true, active knowledge. Nor have we forgotten that earlier we criticised and corrected the error of the human mind in assigning to Forms the principal role in being. For though nothing exists in nature except individual bodies which exhibit pure individual acts in accordance with law, in philosophical doctrine, that law itself, and the investigation, discovery and explanation of it, are taken as the foundation both of knowing and doing. It is the law and its clauses which we understand by the term Form, especially as this word has become established and is in common use" (Bacon, *The New Organon*, 102–3 (II, 2)). Although modern science has tried to eliminate the Aristotelian fourfold causality, this is something impossible to do. As D. C. Schindler remarks, Aristotle's causes cannot be rejected, but only transformed: "The essence of the scientific revolution, viewed specifically in relation to the issue of causality, is not that it retains only some of Aristotle's causes [efficient and material] and rejects others [final and formal], but that it retains *all* of them in some sense even while it radically transforms the meaning of each. . . . This transformation is not arbitrary, but itself reflects a change in the understanding of being" (D. C. Schindler, "Historical Intelligibility," 23).

12. This is very clear in the case of physics: "By the end of the Enlightenment, experimental physics had come to mean the use of a quantitative, experimental method to discover the laws governing the inorganic world. The original meaning of the term *physics*, however, had been quite different; and as a result the word continued to be used ambiguously throughout the eighteenth century. The discipline of physics had originally been created by Aristotle, and it had nothing to do with experiment or quantitative measure, nor was it limited to the inorganic world. Aristotle's *Physics* treated form, substance, cause, accident, place, time, necessity, and motion through a priori arguments that could then be used to explain the phenomena of the world, both organic and inorganic" (Hankins, *Science and the Enlightenment*, 46).

13. Lindberg, *Beginnings of Western Science*, 364. See Koyré, "Origins of Modern Science," and Koyré, "Galileo and Plato."

14. Lindberg, *Beginnings of Western Science*, 365.

In exchange for the purposeful, organized, organic world of Aristotelian natural philosophy, the new metaphysics offered a mechanical world of lifeless matter, unceasing local motion, and random collisions. It stripped away the sensible qualities so central to Aristotelian natural philosophy, offering them second-class citizenship as secondary qualities, or even reducing them to the status of sensory illusions. In place of the explanatory capabilities of form and matter, it offered the size, shape, and motion of invisible corpuscles—elevating local motion to a position of preeminence within the category of change and reducing all causality to efficient and material causality. As for Aristotelian teleology, which discovered purpose *within* nature, defenders of this new mechanical philosophy substituted the purposes of a creator God, imposed on nature from without. The metaphysics of the mechanical philosophy reverberated through the scientific disciplines of the seventeenth century, transforming the ways of thinking about all manner of subjects.[15]

The metaphysical change of modern science is clear in Galileo Galilei, "the father of modern physics—indeed, of modern science altogether."[16] The French philosopher and mathematician Olivier Rey defends that Galileo brought a thorough change of the metaphysical framework.[17] We could say that this change is encapsulated in the following celebrated passage:

Philosophy is written in this grand book—I mean the universe—which stands continually open to our gaze, but it cannot be understood unless one first learns to comprehend the language and interpret the characters in which it is written. It is written in the language of mathematics, and its characters are triangles, circles, and other geometrical figures, without which it is humanly impossible to understand a single word of it; without these, one is wandering about in a dark labyrinth.[18]

15. Lindberg, *Beginnings of Western Science*, 365.

16. Einstein, *Ideas and Opinions*, 271.

17. Rey, *Itinéraire de l'Égarement*, 57. "*Pour Galilée, la physique aristotélicienne était encore un adversaire. Pour ses successeurs, elle était simplement absurde. En soi, elle n'avait pourtant rien d'absurde. La physique moderne ne l'a pas infirmée, elle s'est substituée à elle en vertu d'un changement de cadre métaphysique*" (ibid., 59). English translation by Aaron Riches: "For Galileo, Aristotelian physics was still an adversary. To his followers, it was simply absurd. In itself, there is nothing absurd about it. Modern physics has not overturned it; modern physics has rather replaced it with a change of metaphysical framework."

18. Galilei, "The Assayer," 183–84 (c. 6).

In this passage, Galileo "laid down a new program for science by declaring that true philosophy is inscribed in the book of nature, a book written in the language of mathematics, without which it is pointless to try to decipher it."[19] It is important to note that "the mathematical nature of the world is not a fact of experience—especially not in Galileo's day, when mathematical physics did not exist—but is rather a postulate."[20]

> When the mathematical character of the world is postulated, we move from science as confined to experience, in the Aristotelian sense of the word which consists in observing things as they appear to us, to science that has recourse to experimentation, which consists in putting into place apparatus for testing theoretical hypotheses formulated about reality.[21]

The advent of modern science redefined what counted as real. In fact, the new science considered only "the strictly quantifiable aspects of nature . . . [as] the truly and objectively real."[22] For classical Christian metaphysics, the real was considered as "the macro world presented to us by the senses and arranged in a hierarchy of being." However, the new science "rejected this entire world-view *tout court*, and counted the truly real as only the sub-sensual and sub-personal realm of sheer mathematical quantity."[23] Therefore, modern science created a rift between

19. Rey, "Science Twenty-First Century," 43.

20. Rey, "Science Twenty-First Century," 44.

21. Rey, "Science Twenty-First Century," 44. "It is not 'experience,' but 'experiment,' which played—but only later—a great positive role. Experimentation is the methodical interrogation of nature, an interrogation which presupposes and implies a language in which to formulate the questions, and a dictionary which enables us to read and to interpret the answers. For Galileo, as we know well, it was in curves and circles and triangles, in mathematical or even more precisely, in geometrical language—not in the language of common sense or in that of pure symbols—that we must speak to Nature and receive her answers. Yet obviously the choice of the language, the decision to employ it, could not be determined by the experience which its use was to make possible. It had to come from other sources" (Koyré, "Galileo and Plato," 403).

22. Chapp, *The God of Covenant*, 98.

23. Chapp, *The God of Covenant*, 100. Chapp makes a very incisive comment in this regard: "Those in the modern science and religion dialogue who want to downplay the conflict between science and the Christian faith need to take this fundamental metaphysical rupture more seriously in their historical analysis of this critical period" (ibid., 100n57). In his book *Barbarism*, originally published in 1987, the French philosopher Michel Henry noted that Galilean science (or modern science) was not neutral regarding culture. In this regard, he stated that "Galilean science does not just produce a revolution on the theoretical plane; it will shape our world by marking a

"the world which is absolute, objective, immutable, and mathematical; and that [world] which is relative, subjective, fluctuating, and sensible. The former is the realm of knowledge, divine and human; the latter is the realm of opinion and illusion."[24] Those qualities attributed to the language of mathematics were coined "primary qualities" by the English philosopher John Locke; the rest he called "secondary."[25]

The distinction between absolute and relative worlds implied a cosmological revolution. As Koyré pointed out, the founders of modern science destroyed the understanding of the cosmos and replaced it with another.[26] In other words, modern science entailed the destruction of the metaphysical concept of *cosmos*, as it was previously understood.[27]

---

new historical epoch: modernity" (Henry, *Barbarism*, xiii). In other words, the French philosopher remarked that Galilean science is the "*a priori* of modernity" (ibid., xiv). Henry also noted that Galileo, by rejecting the sensory world, proclaimed that the real world was the one "composed of un-sensed material bodies that are extended and have forms and figures" (ibid., xiii). After the Galilean revolution, the way to know the world "is not the sensibility that varies from one individual to another and thus only offers appearances, but the rational knowledge of these figures and forms: geometry. The geometrical knowledge of material nature—a knowledge that can be formulated mathematically (as Descartes demonstrated right afterward)—is the new knowledge that takes the place of all others and rejects them as insignificant" (Henry, xiii). The rejection of the sensory world "is the decision to understand, in the light of geometrical-mathematical knowledge, the universe as reduced henceforth to an objective set of material phenomena" (ibid., xiii).

24. Burtt, *The Metaphysical Foundations*, 83.

25. Locke, *Essay concerning Human Understanding*, 85–86 (II, viii, 9–10). "Primary qualities constitute the truly real and are comprised of the quantifiable aspects of matter, while the secondary qualities are the purely subjective constructions of the human mind and are, therefore, less objectively real" (Chapp, *The God of Covenant*, 98). These are Galileo's words in this respect: "I do not believe that for exciting in us tastes, odors, and sounds there are required in external bodies anything but sizes, shapes, numbers, and slow or rapid movements; and I think that if ears, tongues, and noses were taken away, shapes and numbers and motions would remain but not odors or tastes or sounds. These, I believe, are nothing but names, apart from the living animal—just as tickling and titillation are nothing but names when armpits and the skin around the nose are absent" (Galilei, "The Assayer," 311 (c. 48)).

26. Koyré, "Galileo and Plato," 405. "The dissolution of the Cosmos means the destruction of the idea of a hierarchically ordered finite world-structure, of the idea of a qualitatively and ontologically differentiated world, and its replacement by that of an open, indefinite and even infinite universe, united and governed by the same universal laws; a universe in which, in contradiction to the traditional conception with its distinction and opposition of the two worlds of Heaven and of Earth, all things are on the same level of Being" (ibid., 404).

27. Koyré, "Galileo and Plato," 403.

"The *term* [Cosmos] remains, of course, and Newton still speaks of the Cosmos and its order (as he speaks of *impetus*), but in an entirely new meaning."[28] For Koyré, "The dissolution of the Cosmos . . . seems . . . to be the most profound revolution achieved or suffered by the human mind since the invention of the Cosmos by the Greeks."[29] The replacement of the idea of cosmos came with another replacement: the natural approach of common sense was replaced by a counterintuitive approach that is anything but natural.[30]

In spite of being increasingly counterintuitive, modern science has been praised for and validated by its technological achievements and its success in understanding and manipulating nature. This is not surprising: after all, the technological achievements of modern science are its very purpose. Modern science changed the focus from the knowledge of essences to the understanding of how things work, in order to manipulate them and obtain benefits.[31] According to Joseph Ratzinger, "The truth with which man is concerned is neither the truth of being, nor even in the last resort that of his accomplished deeds, but the truth of changing the world, molding the world."[32] Using the slogan of the philosopher Hans Jonas, "The modern knowledge of nature, very unlike the classical one, is a 'know-how' and not a 'know-what.'"[33] This is due to the fact that

---

28. Koyré, "Galileo and Plato," 404n12.

29. Koyré, "Galileo and Plato," 404.

30. Koyré, "Galileo and Plato," 405. "The irony of course is that science is often portrayed in the modern Enlightenment myth as the champion of common sense whereas religion is all about pie in the sky illusion. In point of fact, however, it was modern science that seemed to be the champion of the truly bizarre and the counterintuitive, whereas religion was attempting to preserve the reality and truth-bearing content of our everyday experience of the world" (Chapp, *The God of Covenant*, 99–100).

31. In his *Novum Organum Scientiarum*, Bacon asserted that "the true and legitimate goal of the sciences is to endow human life with new discoveries and resources" (Bacon, *The New Organon*, 66 (I, 81)). For the Englishman, the success of science is given by its results: "None of the signs is more certain or more worth noticing than that from products. For the discovery of products and results is like a warranty or guarantee of the truth of a philosophy" (ibid., 60 (I, 73)). Therefore, science ceases to be contemplative and becomes radically pragmatic. There is no surprise when Bacon equates human knowledge with human power (ibid., 33 (I, 3)). and truth with usefulness (ibid., 96 (I, 124)).

32. Ratzinger, *Introduction to Christianity*, 63.

33. Jonas, "Practical Uses of Theory," 204.

"to modern theory in general, practical use is no accident but is integral to it, . . . [for] 'science' is technological by its nature."[34]

In this brief discussion about the notion of modern science, two main ideas have appeared: experimentation and mathematics. These are the two pillars of the scientific method.[35] This method is "confirmed by the success of technology."[36] Pope Benedict XVI clarifies that, in the scientific mindset, "only the kind of certainty resulting from the interplay of mathematical and empirical elements can be considered scientific. Anything that would claim to be science must be measured against this criterion. Hence the human sciences, such as history, psychology, sociology, and philosophy, attempt to conform themselves to this canon of scientificity."[37] Theologians also attempt to adapt their field of study to the scientific canon. "Science is considered a priori rational, and theology has to live up to the standards of scientific rationality if it wants to be taken seriously."[38] As a result, "theology is put on a Procrustean bed of scientific standards, which . . . results in bad theology."[39] Therefore, theology is not taken seriously and theological issues, such as creation, are treated are mere scientific problems.[40]

34. Jonas, "Practical Uses of Theory," 198.

35. "The origin of modern scientific method occurred in Europe in the 1600s: involving (1) a chain of research events from Copernicus to Newton, which resulted (2) in the gravitational model of the solar system, and (3) the theory of Newtonian physics to express the model" (Betz, *Managing Science*, 21). "Science began in that intellectual conjunction of the research of six particular individuals: Copernicus, Brahe, Kepler, Galileo, Descartes, Newton. Why this particular set of people and their work? For the first time in history, all the component ideas of scientific method came together and operated fully as *empirically grounded theory*: 1. A scientific model that could be verified by observation (Copernicus); 2. Precise instrumental observations to verify the model (Brahe); 3. Theoretical analysis of experimental data (Kepler); 4. Scientific laws generalized from experiment (Galileo); 5. Mathematics to quantitatively express theoretical ideas (Descartes and Newton); 6. Theoretical derivation of an experimentally verifiable model (Newton)" (ibid., 22).

36. Benedict XVI, "The Regensburg Address," 171. Rowland reproduces the Regensburg Address by permission of Libreria Editrice Vaticana with translation courtesy of ZENIT. See also Ratzinger, *Introduction to Christianity*, 64.

37. Benedict XVI, "The Regensburg Address," 172.

38. Smedes, "Religion and Science," 595.

39. Smedes, *Chaos, Complexity, and God*, 229.

40. Smedes, "Beyond Barbour," 246. In a very incisive way, the French philosopher Jean-Pierre Dupuy complains against treating theological issues as scientific questions: "When scientists purport to treat religion in the same way that they treat heat or electricity, there is every reason to suspect that they are constructing monuments to their

Those scholars, including theologians, who attempt to comply with the canon of scientificity are assuming the epistemological superiority of the scientific method. Notice that modern science invents and projects its own instrumental criterion of what constitutes "epistemological superiority," basing it on a pragmatic conception of truth and, consequently, a functional understanding of nature. The epistemological superiority of modern science is expressed in its role as first philosophy. Before the Scientific Revolution, metaphysics held the position of first philosophy.[41] Thereafter, natural science ceased to be the maid of metaphysics to become the mother of all sciences.[42] Metaphysics is currently relegated to being the maid of modern science, if it is not dismissed altogether. For example, Hawking boldly proclaimed the death of philosophy and the enlargement of modern science to occupy the philosophical realm:

> How can we understand the world in which we find ourselves? How does the universe behave? What is the nature of reality? Where did all this come from? Did the universe need a creator? . . . Traditionally these are the questions for philosophy, but philosophy is dead. Philosophy has not kept up with modern developments in science, particularly physics. Scientists have become the bearers of the torch of discovery in our quest for knowledge.[43]

---

own stupidity" (Dupuy, *Mark of the Sacred*, 91). The assumption is that "modern science is the way it is by some kind of necessity, while Christian theology is an altogether plastic reality capable of endless permutation" (Chapp, *The God of Covenant*, 140n3).

41. Aquinas, following the Aristotelian tradition (Aristotle, *Metaphysics*, VI, 1), distinguished three kinds of theoretical sciences: physics or natural science, mathematics, and metaphysics. This last one is "also called first philosophy, inasmuch as all the other sciences, receiving their principles from it, come after it" (Aquinas, *Super Boethium De Trinitate*, q. 5, a. 1, co. English translation taken from Aquinas, *Division and Methods*, 15). About the previous Thomistic affirmation, Armand Maurer commented: "Of course the other sciences have their own principles, which can be known without an explicit knowledge of the principles of metaphysics; they are autonomous in their own spheres. Yet the principles of metaphysics are the absolutely universal and primary principles. All the others can be resolved into them. It is in this sense that all the other sciences are said to take their principles from metaphysics, and that this science is said to explain the principles of all the other sciences" (translator note in Aquinas, *Division and Methods*, 15n21). See Wippel, *Metaphysical Thought of Aquinas*, 4–10; Marion, "The Other First Philosophy," 785–88.

42. Hanby, *No God, No Science?* 31. "The great mother of the sciences [natural philosophy] with wonderful indignity has been pressed to perform the services of a maid" (Bacon, *The New Organon*, 65 (I, 80)).

43. Hawking and Mlodinow, *The Grand Design*, 5. On the very next page after the

Philosophy is dead because it has not been able to situate itself within the strict confines of the scientific method, the only accredited path for knowledge. For Hawking, science, and most specifically physics, has become the first philosophy. In response to those who say that "the laws of nature tell us how the universe behaves, but they don't answer the *why?* questions,"[44] he replied: "We claim . . . that it is possible to answer [both] these questions purely within the realm of science."[45]

Modern science aspires to conquer every possible area of knowledge and considers any other access to truth as inferior or nonexistent. Those areas of knowledge not submitted to the mathematical rigor of the scientific method are considered not scientific and, therefore, suspicious. "Philosophical and theological understandings of nature came now to be viewed suspiciously as mystifications of a fundamentally quantitative reality that only the new science could properly understand."[46] The scientific method, and the modern science based on it, proudly boast of being free of metaphysical and theological allegiances. In other words, the scientific method is presupposed as neutral with regard to metaphysics and theology.[47] Both are considered as extrinsic to modern science.

In summary, we have seen that modern science entailed a revolutionary new way of understanding nature, based on the rejection of scholasticism and on the mathematization of the world. Among the substantive content of the new metaphysics inherent in modern science, I would like to emphasize two ideas, which have been previously

---

previous quotation, there is a cartoon by Sidney Harris which displays a scientist who is showing a mathematical formula on a blackboard to two other scientists, telling them ". . . And *that* is my philosophy" (ibid., 6).

44. Hawking and Mlodinow, *The Grand Design*, 171.

45. Hawking and Mlodinow, *The Grand Design*, 172.

46. Chapp, *The God of Covenant*, 98.

47. The neutrality of modern science makes it a transnational language able to overcome cultural biases (where religion and philosophy are included). According to Sagan, "Ethnocentrism, xenophobia and nationalism are these days rife in many parts of the world. Government repression of unpopular views is still widespread. False or misleading memories are inculcated. For the defenders of such attitudes, science is disturbing. It claims access to truths that are largely independent of ethnic or cultural biases. By its very nature, science transcends national boundaries. Put scientists working in the same field of study together in a room and even if they share no common spoken language, they will find a way to communicate. Science itself is a transnational language. Scientists are naturally cosmopolitan in attitude and are more likely to see through efforts to divide the human family into many small and warring factions" (Sagan and Druyan, *The Demon-Haunted World*, 416).

mentioned in this section. First, matter is understood as free from form and from the act of being. Because of the dismissal of being and form, matter is now comprehended in a quantitative manner, as a positive datum, without the interiority and unity provided by form. Second, truth is equated with usefulness, and thus it is verified by results. That is to say, modern science entails a functionalist notion of truth.[48] In the next section, I will explore more deeply the theological and metaphysical content of modern science, which can be summarized as theological extrinsicism and mechanistic ontology.

Theological Extrinsicism and Mechanistic Ontology

In the previous section, I noted that modern science brought with itself new theological and metaphysical postulates. These postulates meant a radical new way of understanding God and nature. Indeed, Hanby points out that the Scientific Revolution was undoubtedly "a theological and metaphysical revolution." The metaphysical and theological presuppositions that were present at the birth of modern science are still operative in science, "even though subsequent science has superseded the philosophies that gave them birth." At the heart of those presuppositions, we can find "a reduction of being from act to facticity and a theological extrinsicism which reduces God to a finite object, nature to artifice, and creation to manufacture."[49] The understanding of being as facticity implies a new "externalized" concept of matter, which is independent of form and, therefore, of being-as-act. In this section, I will develop in some detail these presuppositions and some of their implications.[50]

As we will see in the next chapter, the Christian doctrine of *creatio ex nihilo* entails not only an image of God but also an image of nature. In other words, this doctrine tells us who God is and what the world is. In this regard, Hanby says that the doctrine of "creation *ex nihilo* is simultaneously the doctrine of God and the ontological structure of the world."[51] Modern science falsifies the doctrine of creation in its dual as-

48. When scientists claim that science is true because it works, they are not giving evidence of science's truthfulness; they are just making explicit one of the presuppositions of science.

49. Hanby, *No God, No Science?* 3.

50. In this section, I will follow closely Hanby's conclusions. See Hanby, *No God, No Science?* 107–49.

51. Hanby, *No God, No Science?* 334.

pect. Let us begin with creation understood as the ontological structure of the world. Modern science can only offer a reductive understanding of the world. This is because the scientific method is unable to see "the depth dimension of being."[52] Indeed, the scientific method is based on "a primary *ontological reduction* of nature,"[53] which is "the reduction of being from act to brute facticity."[54]

This reduction of being has inevitable consequences for the understanding of matter. In modern science, "Matter becomes positive and actual in its own right prior to and outside of form, which is now consequent upon it. The positivity of matter and its independence from form, which now has no ontological toehold, is a persistent and fundamental feature of all modern permutations of the concept of matter."[55] Once matter is emptied of form, it is emptied of everything that previously characterized form, i.e., "quality, immanence, *intrinsic* intelligibility."[56] The new understanding of matter "amounts to a renunciation of the world . . . 'defined as the totality of that which is given to the mind, without any *a priori* exclusion of the conditions it requires in order to be understood' (Gilson 1965: 447). Those conditions are now conditions of ontological unmeaning. What is left of this 'residue,' then, is sheer abstract externality."[57] Externality means "the capacity for occupying space."[58] By giving the priority to externality, all matter is made homogeneous.[59] Because mat-

---

52. Balthasar, *Theo-Logic I*, 16. Balthasar references in this paragraph Pieper, *Silence of St. Thomas*.

53. Jonas, "Practical Uses of Theory," 200.

54. Hanby, *No God, No Science?* 334.

55. Hanby, *No God, No Science?* 116. "The positivity of matter and its independence from form . . . is one essential reason why modern matter in all its forms remains essentially mechanistic in spite of claims to the contrary by emergence theorists and others" (ibid.). "David Bohm, e.g., maintains that the usual interpretation of quantum mechanics remains a form of nondeterministic mechanism despite his own view that quantum physics undermines mechanism. See Bohm (1957), pp. 94–103" (Hanby, *No God, No Science?* 139n54). The reference to Bohm is the following: Bohm, *Causality and Chance*, 94–103.

56. Hanby, *No God, No Science?* 117. Matter is, "as René Guénon describes pure quantity, 'the residue of an existence emptied of everything that constituted its essence' (1953: 13)" (Hanby, *No God, No Science?* 117). The reference to Guénon is the following: Guénon, *The Reign of Quantity*, 13.

57. Hanby, *No God, No Science?* 117. The reference to Gilson is the following: Gilson, *Philosophy of Bonaventure*, 447.

58. Hanby, *No God, No Science?* 117.

59. Hanby, *No God, No Science?* 117. See Galilei, *Dialogue concerning World*

ter is essentially external, it is also essentially measurable. "Measurability, rather than the being-in-itselfness of quiddity or *esse*, now constitutes its very essence." We have here the two fundamental characteristics of matter: externality and measurability. These two characteristics are not only present at the birth of modern science, but they also "persist in all subsequent conceptions of matter (or their functional replacements) even as matter comes to be conceived in terms of energy."[60]

The advent of the twentieth century brought a significant change in the scientific understanding of matter. First, Einstein's theory of relativity affirmed the interchangeability of matter and energy. Second, quantum mechanics postulated the wave-particle duality, by which matter, e.g., an electron, can behave both as a particle and as a wave.[61] With these discoveries, "matter seemed to have been dematerialized, its mechanism dismantled and substituted by an uneasy abstraction. . . . But the same moment that matter seemed more uncontrollable and uncertain, control over it increased rather than lessened, and technology moved in directions of greater promise and power."[62] Therefore, measurability continues being part of the essence of matter. Regarding the externality of matter, it is certain that one can no longer assign an exact location to a microscopic particle, such as an electron. The microscopic particle is now described as a wave function. However, that wave function provides a definite region of space where the particle can be found. In the case of an electron in an atom, these definite regions of space are known as orbitals, which have a specific shape.[63] Therefore, subatomic particles, which are ruled by the laws of quantum mechanics, do occupy space (although in a different way than macroscopic particles). It is in this sense that we can affirm that externality is preserved, together with measurability, as intrinsic to the scientific understanding of matter.

The ontological reduction of nature brought with modern science entails the mere externality of matter being understood as something ontologically basic. Each thing is considered as *extrinsic* and *external* to the rest of things, even if that former thing never exists without other things. In the scientific framework, each object is considered as an aggregation of

---

Systems, 71–92 (first day) and Descartes, *Principles of Philosophy*, 232 (part II, 23).

60. Hanby, *No God, No Science?* 117.

61. Anastopoulos, *Particle or Wave*, 6–7.

62. Anastopoulos, *Particle or Wave*, 6–7.

63. For the first "image" of an orbital see Stodolna et al., "Hydrogen Atoms under Magnification," 213001 (1–5).

different unrelated parts (basic units).[64] "The reduction of being from act to the brute facticity of externalized matter eliminates just that unity and interiority which for Aristotle and the tradition had distinguished 'things existing' by nature from artifacts."[65] The collapse of nature into artifact is "a retreat from the *actual* world, the world of things-*in-act*."[66] The retreat from the actual world gives the primacy to a "counterfactual world of abstracted singularities which never actually exists." This counterfactual world is considered as "the theoretical and ontological *basis* of the actual world, which is now a second-order phenomenon constructed from the counterfactual."[67] As we will see in the third chapter, modern cosmology offers plenty of examples of bizarre counterfactual worlds.

The collapse of nature into artifact eventually brings also a collapse of the order of being to the order of history.[68] "The new metaphysics [brought by the Scientific Revolution] reduces being to history and process and for this very reason 'stills' the world at the same time."[69] In this new scenario, motion ceases to be an *act* and becomes a *state*.[70] Motion is understood as "mere successions of discrete events."[71] Time also loses its actuality and is conceived as "a linear series of 'nows' extrinsic and contiguous to each other and following densely upon one another in close succession."[72] This reductive conception of time permeates modern

64. Hanby, *No God, No Science?* 118.

65. Hanby, *No God, No Science?* 118. "Descartes is quite explicit about this. 'For I do not recognize any difference between artifacts and natural bodies except that the operations of artifacts are for the most part performed by mechanisms which are large enough to be easily perceived by the senses (Descartes, *Principles*, IV, CSM, 288)'" (Hanby, *No God, No Science?* 118). This is the reference of the Cartesian text: Descartes, *Principles of Philosophy*, 288 (part IV).

66. Hanby, *No God, No Science?* 118.

67. Hanby, *No God, No Science?* 116.

68. Hanby, *No God, No Science?* 197. The reduction of the order of being to the order of history was not an immediate result of the seventeenth-century Scientific Revolution, although it was implicit in it. This reduction began to take shape in the eighteenth century and came to fruition in the different versions of historicism of the nineteenth century. In the field of biology, it was Darwin who brought this reduction fully to the fore (ibid.). Hanby defends that "the conflation of nature and art eliminated self-transcending form," and that "entailed the reduction of the order of being to the order of history" (ibid.).

69. Hanby, *No God, No Science?* 140n69.

70. Hanby, *No God, No Science?* 119.

71. Veatch, *Two Logics*, 262.

72. Hanby, *No God, No Science?* 197.

science, and it makes cosmologists unable to understand creation as the transition from non-being to being. Cosmologists are only able to conceive of creation as a question of temporal origins, as I will discuss in the following chapters.

Modern science, in its effort to ignore or even reject creation, perpetuates a deficient understanding of creation, reducing it to just a natural event within the world, in competition with other natural events. This is the result of conceiving divine causality as a kind of natural causality. Divine and natural causality are no longer located on different ontological levels but on the same level and, therefore, they are made competitors. The reduced sense of causality follows logically from the metaphysical assumptions of modern science. As previously indicated, Bacon rejected the Aristotelian fourfold causality.[73] Then later, Galileo defined cause as that "which is always followed by the effect, and which when removed takes away the effect."[74] This definition of cause represented a radical departure from Aristotelian metaphysics. For Aristotle, cause was "the source of responsibility for anything." It is important to note that cause is always a source "rather than the nearest agent or instrument that leads to a result," and it refers "more to responsibility for a thing's being as it is than for its doing what it does."[75] In other words, cause "accounts for a thing's being the way it is."[76] However, "Cause for Galileo is not what accounts for an effect, but what produces an effect, and indeed does so wholly through direct, material contact. Moreover, the only relationship that holds in an essential way between cause and effect is temporal succession."[77] Galileo realized that "this view of causality—which to be sure unlocks the door

---

73. "The Final [cause] is a long way from being useful; in fact it actually distorts the sciences except in the case of human actions. Discovery of Form is regarded as hopeless. And the Efficient and Material causes . . . are perfunctory, superficial things, of almost no value for true, active knowledge. Nor have we forgotten that earlier we criticised and corrected the error of the human mind in assigning to Forms the principal role in being. For though nothing exists in nature except individual bodies which exhibit pure individual acts in accordance with law, in philosophical doctrine, that law itself, and the investigation, discovery and explanation of it, are taken as the foundation both of knowing and doing. It is the law and its clauses which we understand by the term Form, especially as this word has become established and is in common use" (Bacon, *The New Organon*, 102–3 (II, 2)).

74. Galilei, "The Assayer," 219 (c. 14).

75. Sachs, *Aristotle's Physics*, 245; See Aristotle, *Metaphysics*, V, 1, 1013a17.

76. D. C. Schindler, "Truth and Christian Imagination," 524.

77. D. C. Schindler, "Truth and Christian Imagination," 534.

to a new character of the material world, namely, one that, in its predict-ability, allows a kind of mastery never before possible—comes at the price of renouncing insight into the essence of things."[78]

In the context of modern science, "Efficient causes are taken to be the only real forms of causation and any appeal to metaphysical notions of final or formal causation are taken to be philosophically illegitimate attempts to reintroduce supernaturalism through the back door."[79] After being is reduced to pure facticity, efficient causality is "no longer under-stood to be the communication of act in the constitution of a being, and . . . [comes] to be understood, rather, as the initiation of a displacement by impulse."[80] Because being is emptied of any interiority, efficient cau-sality is misunderstood as merely physical force.[81] Notice that "force is precisely an *extrinsic* imposition of determination."[82]

For classical metaphysics, causality reflects the communication of form. Communication implies something shared between the cause and the effect. However, nothing is shared in the scientific concept of causal-ity. According to this concept, "The only thing joining cause and effect . . . is succession in time and space. Physical motion (mechanistically understood) by its nature is not something that can be shared; it is atom-istic of its essence."[83] Accordingly, "The connection between them [cause and effect] is only *extrinsic*; it is the nature of force to operate from the outside."[84]

---

78. D. C. Schindler, "Truth and Christian Imagination," 535. For example, "Ac-cording to Galileo, we know nothing about the inner nature or essence of force, we only know its quantitative effects in terms of motion" (Burtt, *The Metaphysical Foun-dations*, 102).

79. Chapp, *The God of Covenant*, 1. Material causality is "taken for granted in connection with all natural happenings—though with a definitely non-Aristotelian meaning, since in the modern world view matter is essentially the subject of change, not 'that out of which a thing comes to be and which persists'" (Bunge, *Causality and Modern Science*, 32. The inside quotation is from Aristotle, *Physics*, II, 3, 194b24, translated by Robert P. Hardie and Russell K. Gaye).

80. Schmitz, *The Gift*, 122.

81. Dodds, *Unlocking Divine Action*, 50. Efficient causality came to mean "an active force or impulse that initiated change by transfer of energy to another, resulting in a displacement of particles in a new configuration and with an accelerated or deceler-ated rate of motion among the particles" (Schmitz, *The Texture of Being*, 34).

82. D. C. Schindler, "Historical Intelligibility," 20 (emphasis mine).

83. D. C. Schindler, "Truth and Christian Imagination," 535.

84. D. C. Schindler, "Truth and Christian Imagination," 534 (emphasis mine).

Until now we have been discussing the main assumptions of the new ontology brought by modern science. Being is no longer understood as act but as brute facticity. As a consequence, there is a positive and quantitative concept of matter, a functionalist idea of truth, and a priority of quantity and force. These assumptions, "which take their classical form in the seventeenth century and which can aptly be termed *mechanistic*, continue to shape the interpretations of twentieth-century physics, despite a widespread claim by physicists and others that this is not so."[85] For the physicist David Bohm, the mechanistic order "has been, for many centuries, basic to all thinking in physics."[86] When I refer to the mechanistic understanding of nature, I refer to the assumptions mentioned above. Bohm summarized them as follows:

(i) The world is reduced, as far as possible, to a set of basic elements. Typically, these have been taken as particles, such as atoms, electrons, protons, quarks, etc., but to these may be added various kinds of fields that expand continuously through space, e.g., electromagnetic, gravitational, etc.

(ii) These elements are basically *external* to each other, not only in being separate in space, but more important, in the sense that the fundamental nature of each is independent of that of the other. Thus, the elements . . . may be compared to parts of a machine, whose forms are determined externally to the structure of the machine in which they are working.

(iii) . . . The elements interact mechanically, and are thus related only by influencing each other externally, e.g., by forces of interaction that do not affect their inner natures.[87]

I have previously said that modern science falsifies the doctrine of creation in its dual aspect, as a doctrine of God and as a metaphysical

85. David L. Schindler, "Beyond Mechanism," 186 (emphasis mine). David L. Schindler is expressing in this quotation David Bohm's views, especially those appearing in his book *Wholeness and the Implicate Order*, published in 1980. These are the words preceding the quoted words: "Bohm, long recognized as one of the world's leading theoretical physicists, has in his writings, most recently in *Wholeness and the Implicate Order*, continuously challenged the assumptions which have prevailed in modern physics. His view is that those assumptions . . . " (David L. Schindler, "Beyond Mechanism," 186).

86. Bohm, *Wholeness and Implicate Order*, 223.

87. Bohm, "The Implicate Order," 14–15.

conception of nature. We have seen that modern science entails an ontological reduction of nature. Let us now deal with the defective image of God inherent in modern science. Hanby points out that "conceptions of God and nature are correlative as a matter of principle."[88] This is the case because "the distinction between God and nature is an irreducibly theological distinction. It is impossible to specify nature in distinction from God without simultaneously giving specification to the God from whom nature is distinguished."[89] In other words, the treatment of nature requires a demarcation of what is not the world, i.e., God. Therefore, the study of nature presupposes a relation between nature and God, even if that relation is conceived negatively or indifferently. When the idea of God is denied by atheism, this system is parasitic upon the notion of God that it is denying.[90] Even when there is an indifference towards God, this implies a certain notion of God. It is not simply, as Hans Urs von Balthasar said, that from the nature of being is derived the idea of divine being.[91] There has to be a conception of God already inherent and operative within the conception of being. In other words, every concrete metaphysics of nature implies a concrete image of God.[92]

Because the image of nature correlates with the image of God, a conception of God will be defective if its correlative conception of nature is defective. Let us illustrate this affirmation with a historical example. For Galileo, nature was "a simple, orderly system, whose every proceeding is thoroughly regular and inexorably necessary."[93] In this regard, Galileo asserted that nature "is inexorable and immutable; she never transgresses the laws imposed upon her, or cares a whit whether her abstruse reasons and methods of operation are understandable to men."[94] This mathematical necessity of nature was intrinsically related to an un-

88. Hanby, *No God, No Science?* 334.

89. Hanby, *No God, No Science?* 121.

90. "Atheism's dismissal of the subject of God is only apparent, that in reality it represents a form of man's concern with the question of God, a form that can express a particular passion about this question and not infrequently does" (Ratzinger, *Introduction to Christianity*, 104).

91. "Philosophy discovers the presuppositions of that function of reason which considers the nature of universal being. From this latter there arises the idea of the absolute or divine Being, and thus philosophy necessarily borders on religion" (Balthasar, *Science, Religion and Christianity*, 4).

92. Hanby, *No God, No Science?* 121.

93. Burtt, *The Metaphysical Foundations*, 74.

94. Galilei, "Letter to Duchess Christina," 182.

derstanding of God as "a geometrician in his creative labours [because] he makes the world through and through a mathematical system."[95] For Galileo, the real world was *"a world of mathematically measurable motions in space and time."*[96] The world was pictured "as mechanical rather than teleological."[97] As a consequence, God was "relegated to the position of first cause of motion, the happenings of the universe then continuing *in aeternum* as incidents in the regular revolutions of a great mathematical machine."[98] The intrinsic relation between God and the world is clear: a geometrical world only allows the understanding of God as geometrician.

The deficient metaphysics of modern science inevitably entails a deficient theology. Once the concept of being is reduced from actuality to facticity, God is reduced "from *ipsum esse subsistens* [self-subsisting being] to a finite object juxtaposed to and in competition with the world."[99] There is a true theological reduction because God becomes a being within a more comprehensive order of being that is taken for granted but never thought through or explicated (i.e., positivism). Once God and the world are considered as objects, because of a univocal application of the concept of being, analogy no longer expresses the infinite distance between God and the world; instead, it "comes to express a simple likeness or parallelism differentiated by a difference of magnitude."[100]

I will offer now a couple of historical examples of the parallelism cited above. For Galileo, "the distinction between his [God's] knowledge of things and ours is that his is complete, ours partial; his immediate, ours discursive."[101] These are Galileo's words: "As to the truth of the knowledge which is given by mathematical proofs, this is the same that Divine wisdom recognizes; but . . . the way in which God knows the infinite propositions of which we know some few is exceedingly more excellent than ours. Our method proceeds with reasoning by steps from one conclusion to another, while His is one of simple intuition."[102] As Burtt pointed out,

95. Burtt, *The Metaphysical Foundations*, 82.

96. Burtt, *The Metaphysical Foundations*, 93.

97. Burtt, *The Metaphysical Foundations*, 113.

98. Burtt, *The Metaphysical Foundations*, 113.

99. Hanby, *No God, No Science?* 334.

100. Hanby, *No God, No Science?* 123.

101. Burtt, *The Metaphysical Foundations*, 82.

102. Galilei, *Dialogue Concerning World Systems*, 119 (first day).

"God knows infinitely more propositions than we, but yet in the case of those that we understand so thoroughly as to perceive the necessity of them, *i.e.*, the demonstrations of pure mathematics, our understanding equals the divine in objective certainty."[103] In Galileo's words, "With regard to those few [mathematical propositions] which the human intellect does understand, I believe that its knowledge equals the Divine in objective certainty, for here it succeeds in understanding necessity, beyond which there can be no greater sureness."[104] Descartes provided us with another example of parallelism. According to the French philosopher, divine will is like human will, but more excellent: "For although God's will is incomparably greater than mine, both in the virtue of the knowledge and power that accompany it and make it more firm and efficacious, and also in virtue of its object, in that it ranges over a greater number of items, nevertheless it does not seem any greater than mine when considered as will in the essential and strict sense."[105]

The parallelism referred to in the preceding paragraph is a consequence of the univocal understanding of being. This understanding erases the distinction between primary and secondary causes, and thus God is considered as the first efficient cause (the greater) among many efficient causes (the lesser).[106] Therefore, God is, in the end, a particular being (although a very important one) within the comprehensive order of being, which is described in physical terms such as power and force.[107] Within the modern scientific framework, the divine concept suffers from objectivization. Once metaphysics is rejected, "and without a theologically adequate sense of analogy, it is inevitable that God will be reimagined fundamentally as a problem for physics and natural science, which given its ontology of extensive quantity, means that God will be reduced *ipso facto* to an object."[108] Hence, there is no surprise in Newton's affirmation that "to treat of God from phenomena is certainly part of natural philosophy."[109]

103. Burtt, *The Metaphysical Foundations*, 82.

104. Galilei, *Dialogue Concerning World Systems*, 118 (first day).

105. Descartes, *Meditations on First Philosophy*, 40 (part IV).

106. Certainly, I do not want to deny that God is the efficient cause of the world. The problem is the way in which God is conceived as the efficient cause after the Scientific Revolution.

107. Hanby, *No God, No Science?* 123–24.

108. Hanby, *No God, No Science?* 124.

109. Newton, *Principia*, 943 (General Scholium).

With the replacement of being-as-act by sheer positivity, "God is included univocally as an object falling under the facticity of being." This is evidenced by Newton, when he "conceives of God's existence as a *quantity in relation* to absolute space and time. Indeed, Newton conceives of God's existence as a quantity precisely because he has already brought God into 'real relation' with the world. Space and time are the 'measurement' of God's existence."[110] Newton understood space and time as mathematical realities able to be measured. These two are absolute and true compared with relative space and time. Absolute time and space are postulates, not perceived by the senses, presupposed as "infinite, homogenous, continuous entities, entirely independent of any sensible object or motion by which we try to measure them; time flowing equably from eternity to eternity; space existing all at once in infinite immovability."[111]

It is very interesting to note here that "space and time were not merely entities implied by the mathematico-experimental method and the phenomena it handles; they had an ultimately religious significance which was for him [Newton] fully as important; they meant the omnipresence and continued existence from everlasting to everlasting of Almighty God."[112] Hanby remarks that "God's dependence upon creation is *manifest* in the role absolute space plays in permitting God to exercise his dominion. Absolute space is the receptacle for the divine will, the medium through which God can establish his dominion."[113] For Newton, "Space and time are explicatory predicates to God's omnipresence and eternity."[114] This is why Newton said that God "endures always and is present everywhere, and by existing always and everywhere he constitutes duration and space."[115] Amos Funkenstein noticed that "the presence of God in space allowed him not only to act in space . . . but to be the actual carrier, or subject, of forces between bodies. And finally, space is indeed a *sensorium Dei*, a 'sense organ' of God." Therefore, "The relationship between God and entities in space (creatures) is analogous to that between the sensing subject and his sensations."[116]

---

110. Hanby, *No God, No Science?* 126.

111. Burtt, *The Metaphysical Foundations*, 247–48.

112. Burtt, *The Metaphysical Foundations*, 257.

113. Hanby, *No God, No Science?* 127.

114. Funkenstein, *Theology and Scientific Imagination*, 96.

115. Newton, *Principia*, 941 (General Scholium).

116. Funkenstein, *Theology and Scientific Imagination*, 96.

In that situation, "God becomes another 'individual thing' whose quantity of existence happens to be 'eternal' and 'infinite,' relative to time and space, but his is still an existence dependent upon the *extensivities* of time and space."[117] According to Newton, "Space is a disposition of being *qua* being. No being exists or can exist which is not related to space in some way."[118] Because God is taken as a being among beings, "if ever space had not existed, God at that time would have been nowhere; and hence either he created space later (in which he was not himself), or else, which is less repugnant to reason, he created his own ubiquity."[119]

Once the difference between God and the world is eclipsed, divine transcendence is compromised and God is brought into a "real relation" to the world.[120] With the objectification of God, not only is his transcendence from the world lost, but also his immanence through the act of being. God is no longer most intimately present in beings. His relation to the world is "that of two entities of the same order extrinsically juxtaposed to one another and conjoined through a relationship of power whereby one acts *upon* the other."[121] According to this theological extrinsicism, God can only relate externally to nature, in the same way forces act upon things. This extrinsic God is the craftsman of the artifact of nature, and he relates to the world as a designer who imposes meaning through laws. "Whereas in a Trinitarian understanding of God, the relations between the persons are the eternal basis of God's relation to creation . . . , for Newton [and subsequent science] there is no such eternal relation with the One: divine relationality, by which God is known, is only temporal and exists within a univocity between God and creatures."[122]

---

117. Hanby, *No God, No Science?* 127. "'The quantity of God's existence is eternal,' it would seem, because he exists *at all times*, and infinite because his being extends endlessly in all directions. But of course this is nothing like what the tradition had meant in ascribing infinity to God. It is what Hegel called a 'bad infinite.' The infinity of God is unity beyond number, a fullness of actuality that is, as such, utterly simple" (ibid., 126–27). "It is of an entirely different order and indeed transcends all orders as the source of their limited and participated actuality. . . . Endless extension, by contrast, is only infinite 'by addition' and endlessly divisible into innumerable finite parts, which is to say that it is not properly infinite at all" (ibid., 127).

118. Newton, *Unpublished Scientific Papers*, 136.

119. Newton, *Unpublished Scientific Papers*, 137.

120. Hanby, *No God, No Science?* 127.

121. Hanby, *No God, No Science?* 128.

122. Oliver, *Philosophy, God and Motion*, 161.

Hanby remarks that modern science is premised not only upon a *finitization* of God but also upon a *detrinitization*.[123] As we will see in the third chapter, the theology inherent in modern science is ultimately untrinitarian, most explicitly in its atheistic forms. The positivistic understanding of being, which is endemic in modern science, prevents scientists from thinking properly about the Trinity. "The theological emphasis . . . veers away from a concept of God as a loving series of personal relations and toward a voluntaristic conception that emphasizes omnipotence and the divine will as primary."[124] We can see in Newton that, once the difference between God and the world is gone, the mystery of the Incarnation collapses. There cannot be consubstantiality between the Father and the Son. "Rather, the Son is a mere creature, albeit the highest creature, who carries out the divine will."[125] Newton considered the trinitarian faith as an idolatry "of the fourth century onwards," a "relapse of the pure ancient Noachian faith," and a "fall away from a true natural philosophy." According to the uncorrupted faith, Christ should be understood as "an exalted and yet created mediator between God and the universe."[126] Rejecting the trinitarian dogma, Newton "saw the divine as utterly remote and acting through Christ as an intermediary. God and Christ were not one in substance, but one in unity of will and dominion."[127]

To summarize, modern science entails a theological understanding which is deficient merely because God is reduced to an object among objects. Both divine transcendence and immanence disappear, and the result is a conception of God that is utterly extrinsic to the world. This theological understanding is known as *theological extrinsicism*. In this theological scenario, God makes no difference to what remains an

123. Hanby, *No God, No Science?* 122. The finitization and the detrinitization of God are, says Hanby, the indispensable conditions of the mechanistic conception of nature.

124. Chapp, *The God of Covenant*, 89. "In the Trinitarian conception, divine freedom is a function of the relation between the Father and the Son, which is to say that it is fundamentally an expression of *love* and inseparable from all the other predicates with which it is convertible. In the unitarian doctrine of this new secular theology, divine freedom becomes a matter of power, unqualified by goodness, beauty, or truth, closely akin if not indeed identical to the concept of force" (Hanby, *No God, No Science?* 121).

125. Chapp, *The God of Covenant*, 89.

126. Oliver, *Philosophy, God and Motion*, 158.

127. Oliver, *Philosophy, God and Motion*, 172.

essentially mechanistic understanding of nature. In other words, the world is indifferent to God.

As I end this section, I can affirm that an extrinsicist theology and a mechanistic understanding of nature inhere in modern science. These metaphysical and theological presuppositions are erroneous because they falsify the concepts of God and nature. On the one hand, God's transcendence is lost because God is reduced to an external agent acting on the same level as any natural agent. On the other hand, nature loses its own interiority and unity; it is reduced to a mechanism composed of unrelated parts. Matter is understood in a positive and quantitative way. Once the key concepts of immanence, interiority, indivisible unity, and intelligibility are lost, the description of reality is severely reduced, and thus full of gaps. Therefore, the mechanistic conception of nature is unable to describe reality in its fullness. The reduction of the image of God and the reduction of the concept of nature are inseparable because they imply each other. Modern science does have a metaphysical and theological content; this is *unavoidable* because, as I will show in the next section, every conception of science harbors metaphysical and theological presuppositions, even when those presuppositions are denied.

An Intrinsic Relationship

In the second section, I dealt with the novelty of the scientific method. As stated above, modern science carried with it a radical change in the understanding of nature and in the role of metaphysics. Almost a century ago, the philosopher Edwin Burtt pointed out that modern science, more concretely modern physics, has metaphysical foundations.[128] The American philosopher stated that "there is no escape from metaphysics."[129] "Even the attempt to escape metaphysics is no sooner put in the form of a proposition that it is seen to involve highly significant metaphysical postulates."[130] When modern science prides itself on being free of metaphysical presuppositions, it is opting for a concrete kind of metaphysical postulate. Of course, that "metaphysics will be held uncritically because it is unconscious; moreover, it will be passed on to others far more readily than your other notions inasmuch as it will be propagated by insinuation

128. See Villemaire, *Burtt, Historian and Philosopher*, 247.

129. Burtt, *The Metaphysical Foundations*, 227.

130. Burtt, *The Metaphysical Foundations*, 228.

rather than argument."[131] For example, when students of Newtonian classical mechanics fail to recognize the metaphysics implied in that body of knowledge, they are giving "an exceedingly interesting testimony to the pervading influence, throughout modern thought, of the Newtonian first philosophy."[132]

The French philosopher Jean-Pierre Dupuy emphasizes that the metaphysics entailed by modern science's affirmation of neutrality is erroneous: "Those who deny metaphysics simply render it invisible, and it is very likely that their hidden metaphysics is bad or inconsistent."[133] Additionally, he thinks that "reconceiving technology and science . . . in purely positivistic or scientific terms, stripped of all metaphysics and ideology, is exactly . . . both impossible and . . . futile."[134] In other words, "There is no science without metaphysics."[135] Science and metaphysics cannot be completely isolated from each other. Dupuy also insists that an immanent science, a science free of religious transcendence, is impossible and futile.[136] Although modern science feels proud of not being "infected with the sepsis of theological bacilli,"[137] it cannot help but be a

131. Burtt, *The Metaphysical Foundations*, 229.

132. Burtt, *The Metaphysical Foundations*, 229.

133. Dupuy, "Do We Shape Technologies?" It is interesting to read the quotation in its previous context: "Precisely, what I see as the major driving force is a set of ideas, worldviews, corresponding to what Karl Popper used to dub a 'metaphysical research program.' The positivist philosophy that drives most of modern science (and much of contemporary philosophy) takes 'metaphysics' to be a meaningless quest for answers to unanswerable questions, but Popper, following the lead of Emile Meyerson, showed that there is no scientific (or, for that matter, technological) research programme that does not rest on a set of general presuppositions about the structure of the world. To be sure, those metaphysical views are not empirically testable and they are not amenable to 'falsification.' However, that does not imply that they are not interesting, substantial, and that they do not play a fundamental role in the advancement of science" (ibid.). Dupuy makes this reference to Meyerson in the previous text: "*L'homme fait de la métaphysique comme il respire, sans le vouloir et surtout sans s'en douter la plupart du temps*" (Meyerson, *De l'Explication*, 6). English translation: "Man does metaphysics as he breathes, involuntary and, above all, usually without realizing it" (Meyerson, *Explanation in the Sciences*, 11).

134. Dupuy, *Mark of the Sacred*, 57. In this regard, Pope Francis states that "science and technology are not neutral; from the beginning to the end of a process, various intentions and possibilities are in play and can take on distinct shapes" (Francis, *Praise Be to You*, 82 (paragraph 114)).

135. Dupuy, *Mark of the Sacred*, 90.

136. Dupuy, *Mark of the Sacred*, 56–57.

137. Chapp, "Intelligibility of Modern Science," 287.

"theology in spite of itself."[138] In this regard, Funkenstein remarked upon the theological conceptions of modern science.[139] A clear—but flawed— illustration of the relation between science and theology is provided by Newton. As we saw in the previous section, the English physicist postulated the existence of an absolute space, which has a crucial role in his mechanics and his theology. For Newton, absolute space is the *sensorium Dei*, the medium that God needs to exercise his dominion. Regarding Newton's position, Simon Oliver incisively points out that "because Newton maintains an Arian, non-Trinitarian position, he is unable to find a source and ground for a relational cosmos at the highest ontological level." Then, Oliver asks, "How can a motionless God, construed by Newton in voluntaristic terms, now be related to a cosmos in motion?" And he answers, "Newton conceives of an absolute space begotten of God (the infamous *sensorium dei*) in and through which God creates and acts in the world."[140]

The previous remarks offer strong indications of theological and metaphysical presuppositions inherent in modern science. The *Communio* scholars have recognized those presuppositions, and they have gone deeper into the subject.[141] In this regard, Hanby appropriately argues that "science is constitutively and intrinsically related to metaphysics and theology, and that metaphysical and theological judgments enter into the conception of the basic units of scientific analysis and into the notion of method itself."[142] The claim that science is intrinsically related to metaphysics and theology is actually "three claims which cannot be deduced nor inferred from one another as a matter of positive theological thinking. Though they form a comprehensive whole when taken together, illuminating and deepening each other, each stands on its own without reference to the other two, and they could thus be articulated in any order."[143] The senses of the claim are theological, philosophical, and historical.[144] Regarding the theological sense of the claim, Hanby

138. Dupuy, *Mark of the Sacred*, 54.

139. See Funkenstein, *Theology and Scientific Imagination*.

140. Oliver, *Philosophy, God and Motion*, 6. Oliver argues that "this absolute space takes on the characteristics of a more orthodox Christ in Newton's theology" (ibid.).

141. Another prominent group of scholars insisting on the theological and metaphysical presuppositions of modern science is the Radical Orthodoxy group.

142. Hanby, *No God, No Science?* 3.

143. Hanby, *No God, No Science?* 18.

144. Hanby, *No God, No Science?* 18–19.

points out that "science's constitutive and inexorable relation to theology is but the cognitive expression of being's constitutive and inexorable relation to God. It follows, in other words, from a proper understanding of creation understood (in its passive sense) precisely *as a relation*."[145] I would like to note that I will deal with the notion of creation as relation in the second chapter. Regarding the philosophical sense of the claim, Hanby affirms that "this philosophical argument does not require one to assent to Christian faith or the doctrine of creation *ex nihilo* in order to recognize its force." The philosophical argument is based on the fact that "every account of scientific knowledge necessarily presupposes an account of being *qua* being that mediates both the content of science and the relation to theology."[146] Regarding the historical sense of the claim, Hanby asserts that "what is true in principle in the orders of being and thought we should expect to see enacted in history. Because science cannot do without judgments of an irreducibly metaphysical and theological nature, modern science . . . [has] never in fact done without them."[147]

It is important to understand that the intrinsic relationship between science, metaphysics, and theology "does not compromise the legitimate autonomy of science so much as clarify what this autonomy consists in."[148] The fact that science is intrinsically related to theology does not mean that science can be simply inferred from theology. "Inasmuch as creation is the gratuitous gift of being to a world that is *not* God, and inasmuch as the being of the world is therefore irreducible to the being of God, it follows that the sciences are irreducible to theology."[149] It is erroneous to affirm that "scientific conclusions can simply be deduced from theological premises or that properly theological conclusions can simply be inferred from scientific or empirical starting points."[150] It is not, then, the business of theology to dictate to science how to do its job. To give an example, theology cannot and must not tell cosmologists to accept a concrete cosmological model.

It is thus certain that science and theology should deal only with their own fields of competence. However, this cannot be taken to mean that there is no relation between the two. As I have been defending,

145. Hanby, *No God, No Science?* 18.
146. Hanby, *No God, No Science?* 19.
147. Hanby, *No God, No Science?* 19–20.
148. Hanby, *No God, No Science?* 3.
149. Hanby, "Saving the Appearances," 66–67.
150. Hanby, "Saving the Appearances," 67.

science is intrinsically related to theology. "Maintaining distinctions and keeping within limits cannot mean that theology and the sciences are only extrinsically and accidentally related to each other, or that theology and metaphysics deal with the whole and the sciences only with a part."[151] By dealing with an aspect of reality, the sciences deal with the whole because of the unity of creation. It should also be noted that the world's autonomy is not in spite of, but because of, its constitutive relation to God. The world's autonomy is not affirmed by denying the relation to God. This relation does not diminish the creature's autonomy; rather, it is the condition of possibility for autonomy. In creation, God gives the entirety of being at once, letting the creature be according to its own nature. "The creature's relation to God is the necessary condition for realizing the proper integrity of creaturely identity and power: that the former relation, in other words, is directly not inversely related to the latter integrity."[152] The world is not reducible to God, but the world's autonomy is granted due to its relation to God. "Worldly realities find their true meaning, precisely as worldly—or indeed 'natural'—in their character simultaneously and intrinsically as epiphanies of God."[153] Therefore, the proper understanding of the relation between the world and God allows and guarantees a real distinction between theology and science.

Before finishing this section, I would like to comment briefly on the role of metaphysics as mediator between science and theology. Norris Clarke defended that "the most basic and indispensable mediator between the realm of revealed knowledge, grasped by faith, and that of all other natural knowledge, in particular the natural sciences, is *metaphysics*."[154] Clarke described the double role of metaphysics as mediator in this way:

(1) a negative role of monitoring the statements of scientists that would exclude integration into an integral Christian wisdom, either as incautious interpretations of authentic scientific findings or as explicit contradictions of something already in the legacy of revelation.

(2) a positive role of discerning the implications of authentic scientific findings for shedding new light on the content already in place in the treasury of Christian wisdom.[155]

151. Hanby, "Saving the Appearances," 67.
152. David L. Schindler, "Trinity, Creation," 428.
153. David L. Schindler, "Trinity, Creation," 409.
154. Clarke, "Metaphysics as Mediator," 465.
155. Clarke, "Metaphysics as Mediator," 485–86.

In my opinion, Clarke's description of the mediation of metaphysics is reasonable, but it needs to be completed by affirming the intrinsic relationship between science, metaphysics, and theology. If this intrinsic relationship is not taken into account, metaphysics will be considered as something external to science. And if this is the case, metaphysics will have a role only after the scientific work is done because it will be assumed that science is free of metaphysics in its inner core. Therefore, the metaphysical mediation will be unable to expose and question the presuppositions, both theological and metaphysical, of modern science.

Because of the inexorable relationship between science, metaphysics, and theology, "science cannot determine for itself its relation to theology [and metaphysics] . . . without effectively *doing* theology [and metaphysics], without saying, explicitly or implicitly where to draw the line, or how to characterize the difference between God and the world."[156] Let us remember extrinsicism holds that "science, metaphysics, and theology are essentially 'outside' of each other, where their relationship and their respective claims can be adjudicated from the neutral standpoint afforded by the empirical and experimental methods of science."[157] Extrinsicism, defended by modern science, is self-contradictory due to the intrinsic relationship between science, theology, and metaphysics. Indeed, the affirmation of a neutral science does not dispense with metaphysics and theology. The very act of affirming a metaphysically and theologically free science entails, at least implicitly, metaphysical and theological assumptions that are deficient and go unnoticed. These defective assumptions, which were described in the previous section, adulterate the concepts of God and nature. As previously shown, being is reduced from actuality to facticity and the concept of form is rejected. As a consequence, matter is understood positively and quantitatively, void of the unity and intelligibility provided by form. This new idea of matter is indifferent to God, who becomes an object among other objects. Divine transcendence is lost, and thus divine immanence disappears.

The incomplete presuppositions present in modern science are a consequence of modern science's self-conception: science is essentially free of metaphysics and theology. Therefore, the scientific method is assumed to be neutral. In the next section, I will deal with the alleged neutrality of the scientific method.

156. Hanby, *No God, No Science?* 14.
157. Hanby, *No God, No Science?* 3.

Methodological Neutrality

Modern science claims that "the empirical and experimental methods of scientific analysis are ontologically neutral precisely as *method*, and thus stand essentially *outside* of metaphysics and theology."[158] However, this notion of methodological neutrality betrays itself because it presumes metaphysical and theological judgments, namely, that whether or not God exists makes no difference to the world. Therefore, the world is basically indifferent to God and, if God exists, he can only be extrinsically related to the world. Consequently, the methodological neutrality claimed by modern science—the assertion that the scientific method is free of metaphysical and theological presuppositions—rests upon an unacknowledged extrinsicism.

We have already seen that extrinsicism is problematic because it falsifies and reduces both God and nature, and because it contradicts science's self-understanding as indifferent to both metaphysics and theology. However, these are not the only reasons it is problematic. Chapp remarks that the dialogue between theology and science is governed by an unquestioned dogma: methodological neutrality.[159] The defense of a neutral method implies unrecognized theological and metaphysical presuppositions that are defective. The reduced notions of God and nature assumed by the dialogue prevent a real and fruitful communication between science and theology. If the dialogue wants to seek the truth—the truth of the relationship between science and metaphysics, the truth of science's self-understanding, the truth of the world—it is absolutely necessary to affirm the inevitable relationship of the world with God. Therefore, extrinsicism is also problematic because it makes an intellectually serious dialogue impossible. There is plenty of frivolous dialogue, as I will show in the third chapter.

Directly related to the concept of methodological neutrality is the term *methodological naturalism*, which is broadly used in the dialogue between science and theology. The proponents of methodological naturalism defend a neutral scientific method regarding theological matters.

158. Hanby, *No God, No Science?* 11.

159. Chapp, "Intelligibility of Modern Science," 285. Chapp adds that "many of the leading lights in the science and religion dialogue from the theological end of the equation (Ernan McMullin, Howard Van Till, Ian Barbour, Arthur Peacocke, John Polinghorne, et al.) continue to labor under its [methodological neutrality's] influence and are deeply critical of anyone, especially those from the theological side of the question, who would dare call it [methodological neutrality] into question" (ibid.).

To put it in another way, methodological naturalism means by definition that "scientists should not appeal to supernatural entities when they
explain natural phenomena."[160] After methodological naturalism is defined, it is usually contrasted with the notion of *ontological naturalism*,
also known as philosophical or metaphysical naturalism. This kind of
naturalism claims that "there is nothing outside of nature that can affect
it."[161] The vast majority of the participants in the dialogue between science and theology point out that "methodological naturalism does not
entail ontological naturalism. One can accept the former but reject the
latter without any logical inconsistency."[162]

> Methodological naturalism basically leaves God and "the super-
> natural" aside, not because it disavows the divine, or denies its
> fundamental importance, but simply because it is not relevant
> or helpful to the methods being used and questions being in-
> vestigated. The natural sciences clearly espouse a methodologi-
> cal naturalism. They do not as such—though many scientists
> may—espouse a metaphysical naturalism, which affirms that
> there is nothing that could be called God and nothing in all of
> reality that can be described as supernatural.[163]

When modern scientists support methodological naturalism, they claim
that they are neither denying nor opposing the supernatural, but only
ignoring it for methodological reasons.[164] At the heart of the distinction between methodological naturalism and ontological naturalism,
there is an emphasis on a method that does not entail any theological

---

160. Draper, "God, Science, and Naturalism," 279. In other words, the main idea
of methodological naturalism "is that science must proceed . . . without any . . . reference to supernatural design, causation or activity in its formal scientific descriptions,
explanations and theories" (Ratzsch, *Science and Its Limits*, 122). It is supposed that
"science, properly so-called, cannot involve religious belief or commitment" (Plantinga, "Methodological Naturalism?" 341). Notice that there are metaphysical judgments
already implicit in the terms that methodological naturalism uses to understand itself,
e.g., "supernatural design."

161. Draper, "God, Science, and Naturalism," 291.

162. Stenmark, *Scientism*, 96–97. "Those who embrace both science as currently
practiced and some form of supernaturalistic religion [claim] that science is naturalistic methodologically but not metaphysically" (Draper, "God, Science, and Naturalism," 279).

163. Auletta and Stoeger, "Highlights," 11.

164. Scott, "Darwin Prosecuted," 43.

assumptions.[165] Therefore, the scientific method is supposed to be compatible with whatever theological ideas the scientist could have.[166]

Methodological naturalism assumes that it is possible to bracket out theological presuppositions in the scientific endeavor. But the very assumption that theological presuppositions can be excluded from the description of nature entails concrete ideas about God and nature. More specifically, nature is assumed to be indifferent to God, and thus God has no bearing on the intelligibility of nature or what it means to think. That is, thinking itself is not determined by the exigencies of being a creature. Thinking is just another brute fact. As explained earlier, these extrinsic notions of God and nature are deficient. Methodological naturalism could only succeed in its self-understanding if being related to God had no bearing on and made no difference to the intelligibility of the world. Given that the opposite is true—that being is constitutively and inexorably related to God—methodological naturalism is, accordingly, untenable.

I will finish this section by rejecting the supposed difference between methodological and ontological naturalism. The point in making this distinction is to deny that the scientific method is filled with theological

---

165. "Methodological naturalism does not restrict our study of nature; it just lays down which sort of study qualifies as *scientific*. If someone wants to pursue another approach to nature—and there are *many* others—the methodological naturalist has no reason to object. Scientists *have* to proceed in this way; the methodology of natural science gives no purchase on the claim that a particular event or type of event is to be explained by invoking God's creative action directly. Calling this *methodological* naturalism is simply a way of drawing attention to the fact that it is a way of characterizing a particular *methodology*, no more. In particular, it is not an ontological claim about what sort of agency is or is not possible. Dubbing it 'provisional atheism' seems to me objectionable; the scientist who does not include God's direct action among the alternatives he or she should test scientifically when attempting to explain some phenomenon is surely not to be accused of atheism!" (McMullin, "Plantinga's Defense," 57).

166. "The central idea, here, is that science is objective, public, sharable, publicly verifiable, and equally available to anyone, whatever their religious or metaphysical proclivities. We may be Buddhist, Hindu, Protestant, Catholic, Muslim, Jew, Bahai, none of the above—the findings of science hold equally for all of us. This is because proper science . . . is restricted to the deliverances of reason and sense (perception) which are the same for all people. Religion, on the other hand, is private, subjective, and obviously subject to considerable individual differences. But then if science is indeed public and sharable by all, then of course one can't properly pursue it by starting from some bit of religious belief or dogma. One root of this way of thinking about science is a consequence of the modern foundationalism stemming from Descartes and perhaps even more importantly, Locke" (Plantinga, "Methodological Naturalism?" 343).

judgments. As stated above, this is impossible to deny. The affirmation of methodological neutrality entails unacknowledged theological and metaphysical judgments that are unsustainable. As Hanby points out, "There is simply no such thing as a methodological naturalism that is not also an ontological naturalism. And ontological naturalism is, at bottom, a bad theology that does not know itself."[167]

In this section I have demonstrated that there is no such neutrality of the scientific method. The affirmation of a neutral science entails the assumption of theological and metaphysical judgments that are extrinsic. In the next section, I will address different ways in which extrinsicism is present in modern science.

Extrinsicism in Modern Science

Extrinsicism appears in various forms in modern science. Let us begin with the most explicit one. *Scientism* holds that "any question that can be answered at all can best be answered by science."[168] Therefore, "Science can in principle explain all phenomena occurring within the world."[169] Scientism suffers from "a certain blindness to the primordial value of being. This sick blindness is called Positivism, and it arises from regarding reality as raising no questions, being 'just there'—for the phrase 'the

167. Hanby, *No God, No Science?* 35. The theologian Wolfhart Pannenberg warned that "the so-called methodological atheism [or methodological naturalism] of modern science is far from pure innocence" (Pannenberg, "Theological Questions to Scientists," 66). Another theologian, Alan Padgett, remarks that "there is no such thing as a merely methodological naturalism in the sciences" (Padgett, *Science and the Study*, 78). Specifically, "Padgett's position is that so-called methodological naturalism almost inevitably degenerates into a form of metaphysical naturalism, perhaps giving an indication that the putative neutrality of methodological naturalism needs to be called into question in the first place as a thinly veiled atheism" (Chapp, "Review Essay: Alan Padgett," 367). Finally, Adrian Walker emphasizes that methodological naturalism entails ontological naturalism: "The distinction between methodological naturalism and ontological naturalism doesn't help deal with this problem. 'Methodological naturalism,' after all, can only really be just a shorthand for this: Science constitutes its domain of inquiry by setting up as its formal object (of which the following is admittedly only a partial description) 'whatever can be sufficiently explained *as if* materialistic naturalism *were* a true account of the being of the world.' But what counts as a 'sufficient explanation' here? Without substantial things as an acknowledged criterion, how do we prevent this sufficiency from drifting in the direction of an ontological naturalism?" (Walker, "Theses on Scientism.")

168. Stenmark, *Science and Religion*, 30.

169. Walker, "Theses on Scientism."

given' already says too much, since there is no one who 'gives.'" Therefore, there is a dismissal of the significance of being, and fundamental concepts are taken for granted. Within positivism, "The only question that arises is: 'What can we do with this material?' When men are blind to the further question, it signifies the death of philosophy and even more the death of theology."[170] Scientism not only considers metaphysics and theology as extrinsic to science, but also it declares them useless and sterile lucubrations.

Hawking is an explicit exemplar of scientism. As indicated previously, the cosmologist boldly proclaimed the death of philosophy and the enlargement of modern science to occupy the philosophical realm. This is the case because modern science has already *decided in advance* what kind of things exist: external objects able to be measured. It is appropriate now to add Hawking's scientistic reflections on the existence of God. The English cosmologist claimed that physics had made a creator a superfluous hypothesis: "Over the centuries many . . . believed the universe had a beginning, and used it as an argument for the existence of God. The realization that time behaves like space presents a new alternative. It . . . means that the beginning of the universe was governed by the laws of science and doesn't need to be set in motion by some god."[171] Assuming that the initial space-time singularity of the Big Bang model is the beginning of the universe and the moment of divine creation, Hawking concluded that the act of creation and the presence of a creator were not necessary,

---

170. Balthasar, *Theo-Drama II*, 286. "For philosophy begins with the astonished realization that I am this particular in being and goes on to see all other existent entities together with me in being; that is, it begins with the sense of wonder that, astonishingly, I am 'gifted,' the recipient of gifts. As for theology, born of the knowledge that eternal freedom eternally gives itself away and thus generates the Son, it begins when, addressed as 'thou,' I hearken to the One who thus addresses me" (ibid.).

171. Hawking and Mlodinow, *The Grand Design*, 135. These are other similar quotations from Hawking: "Many people through the ages have attributed to God the beauty and complexity of nature that in their time seemed to have no scientific explanation. But just as Darwin and Wallace explained how the apparently miraculous design of living forms could appear without intervention by a supreme being, the multiverse concept can explain the fine-tuning of physical law without the need for a benevolent creator who made the universe for our benefit" (ibid., 165); "Because there is a law such as gravity, the universe can and will create itself from nothing. . . . Spontaneous creation is the reason there is something rather than nothing, why the universe exists, why we exist. It is not necessary to invoke God to light the blue touch paper and set the universe going" (ibid., 180). I will deal with Hawking in more detail and I will explain his scientific terms in the third chapter. The intention here is just to present the problem of extrinsicism in general, and scientism in particular.

because science showed that there is no initial singularity. Metaphysics and theology only offer unnecessary (and untestable) hypotheses. They are external and alien to the scientific enterprise. We have here a plain case of extrinsicism: to Hawking, God is an agent extrinsic to the world who is in competition with natural processes, and creation is a worldly mechanism. There is here a clearly inappropriate use of the philosophical and theological terms in dispute. Hawking's theological extrinsicism demonstrates the inevitability of theology and yet absolves him from having to think rigorously about it. This fact clearly exposes the unreasonable character of scientism.

Modern science cannot get rid of its scientism because it is inherent to it. This is so because modern science has reduced the understanding of being from actuality to facticity. As a consequence, there is a new concept of positive quantitative matter, free of form, and free from the distinction between act and potency. There is also a new functionalist notion of truth: truth is equated with usefulness and verified by results. As a result, modern science is incapable of being integrated into a more comprehensive order of knowledge or recognizing any access to truth other than via the scientific method. It is, then, not surprising when scientists, e.g., Hawking, consider science, especially physics, as the first philosophy, and claim that science should expand itself in order to conquer every possible area of human knowledge, dismissing everything that cannot be subjected to the self-imposed rigor of the scientific method.[172] Because the ontology of modern science precludes the integration of scientific reason into a more comprehensive understanding of reason, the distinction between *science* and *scientism* is facile and untenable.[173]

Earlier, I explained that some scientists had tried to reject the positivistic and reductive epistemological interpretation given by scientism. Undoubtedly, these scientists are heirs of Polanyi, Popper, Kuhn, and other philosophers of science of the twentieth century, who criticized scientific positivism and paved the way for the recognition of the limitations of the scientific method and the appreciation of forms of knowledge other than science, especially metaphysics and theology.[174] These scien-

172. "Scientific inquiry does not depend upon any form of rationality 'higher' than itself but it is rather the final basis upon which other forms of rationality, including one's initial metaphysical assumptions, may ultimately be justified" (Hanby, *No God, No Science?* 10).

173. Hanby, *No God, No Science?* 2. See Hutchinson, *Monopolizing Knowledge.*

174. See, for example, Polanyi, *Personal Knowledge*; Popper, *Logic of Scientific*

tists, who intend to appreciate metaphysics and theology, make different proposals in their attempts to avoid scientism. As we are going to see, these proposals are ultimately extrinsic and thus unconvincing.

One of these proposals, and perhaps the most extreme, was presented by the evolutionary biologist Stephen Gould. In his book *Rocks of Ages*, Gould offered "a blessedly simple and entirely conventional resolution to . . . the supposed conflict between science and religion."[175] For this purpose, the author characterized both science and religion as magisteria. A magisterium is defined as "a domain where one form of teaching holds the appropriate tools for meaningful discourse and resolution."[176] According to this definition,

> The net, or magisterium, of science covers the empirical realm: what the Universe is made of (fact) and why does it work in this way (theory). The magisterium of religion extends over questions of ultimate meaning and moral value. These two magisteria do not overlap, nor do they encompass all inquiry (consider, for example, the magisterium of art and the meaning of beauty). To cite the old clichés, science gets the age of the rocks, and religion the rock of ages; science studies how the heavens go, religion how to go to heaven.[177]

Discovery; and Kuhn, *Structure of Scientific Revolutions*.

175. Gould, *Rocks of Ages*, 3. As previously mentioned, science cannot help but be a theology. In the last centuries, that theology inherent in modern science has clashed with Christian traditional theology. Nevertheless, a fairly standard way of carrying out the dialogue between science and theology—which Larry Chapp calls the "Templeton Paradigm" because it has emerged from "the financial trough of the Templeton Foundation" (Chapp, "Review Essay: Alan Padgett," 364)—mostly argues "in favor of the thesis that the so-called conflict between science and religion is a fiction, an intellectual urban legend, and that the true history of the much more irenic and symbiotic relationship between religion and science in general, and Christianity and Western science in particular, is just being told" (ibid., 365). Although the Templeton Foundation is a remarkable promoter of the Templeton Paradigm thanks to its munificent funding, the approach promoted by the foundation is shared broadly by scholars not related to it. In fact, the Templeton Paradigm is not simply the product of a foundation, but the natural outgrowth of deeper metaphysical and theological presuppositions built into modern science itself and modern culture, which are permeated by a positivistic metaphysics.

176. Gould, *Rocks of Ages*, 5.

177. Gould, *Rocks of Ages*, 6.

Gould used the term "NOMA," which stands for "NonOverlapping MAgisteria,"[178] to characterize the proper relationship between the two magisteria or domains of science and religion.[179] NOMA rests upon two claims: "First, that these two domains hold equal worth and necessary status for any complete human life; and second, that they remain logically distinct and fully separate in styles of inquiry, however much and however tightly we must integrate the insights of both magisteria to build the rich and full view of life traditionally designated as wisdom."[180] As we can see, NOMA radically insists on the equal status of science and religion and their separate domains: physical facts for science and values for religion. Therefore, the magisterium of religion is circumscribed to values, and the magisterium of science is confined to the natural world.[181]

Gould's definitions of magisterium and science have built into them naïve and question-begging concepts of nature, truth, and explanation. Nature is confined to the realm of physical facts. This presupposes a dismissal of being as act and an understanding of being as mere facticity. Truth and explanation are conceived in a functionalist manner. Notice that a magisterium is aimed at resolution. This functionalist understanding assumes that matter is emptied of form. Although the previous metaphysical judgments shaped Gould's thought, he was unaware of them. This lack of self-awareness is characteristic of modern scientists.

The theological assumptions of Gould's NOMA can be exposed and criticized by examining NOMA's first commandment: "Thou shalt not mix the magisteria by claiming that God directly ordains important events in the history of nature by special interference knowable only through revelation and not accessible to science."[182] When NOMA prohibits some kinds of God's intervention, not only is it placing boundaries between God and the world, but also it is presupposing a certain notion of

178. Gould, *Rocks of Ages*, 5.

179. Gould, *Rocks of Ages*, 6.

180. Gould, *Rocks of Ages*, 58–59.

181. Gould's treatment of the issue of monogenism vs. polygenism illustrates his conception of the separate domains of the magisteria: "If Pius [XII] is arguing [in *Humani Generis*] that we cannot entertain a theory about derivation of all modern humans from an ancestral population rather than through an ancestral individual (a potential fact) because such an idea would question the doctrine of original sin (a theological construct), then I would declare him out of line for letting the magisterium of religion dictate a conclusion within the magisterium of science" (Gould, "Nonoverlapping Magisteria," 22).

182. Gould, *Rocks of Ages*, 84–85.

divine action, which is undoubtedly extrinsic. God's causality is imagined on the model of natural causality, conceived of as a transaction between two externally juxtaposed agents or entities. As a result, God's transcendence and infinity are severely compromised. All of this is a function of the way nature is conceived, i.e., as sheer facticity, emptied of the unity and intelligibility given by the act of being. In the end, nature is indifferent to God. Therefore, the notion of God that is supporting NOMA is extrinsic. Notice that it does not matter whether Gould or other scientists *believe* the theology implicit in their work. What matters is that it is there. NOMA only allows a concept of God who acts in the world according to our scientific knowledge and who, therefore, does not really act as God at all. NOMA then opts for a notion of God that is subject to the dictates of the sciences.[183]

An explicit example of the extrinsicism entailed by NOMA was given by Gould when he stated that a scientist could be pious and devout, but he or she should hold a concrete idea of God,[184] namely, "an imperial clockwinder at time's beginning."[185] Only that notion of God "leaves science entirely free in its own proper magisterium."[186] "In theological terms, according to Gould's NOMA-principle, a *deistic* concept of God is the only one allowed."[187] The concept of God as clockwinder corresponds with the particular view of nature as analogous to a clock. This example illustrates the point that the concept of nature governs how one thinks about God and vice versa. Indeed, the ideas of God and nature are intrinsically related, so they cannot be separated from each other. The extrinsic conception of God held by NOMA (an imperial clockwinder at the beginning of time) is directly related to the mechanistic conception of nature held by NOMA (a clock, which is an artifact made up of unrelated parts). Because nature is considered as an artifact, God cannot be immanent in nature or even really transcendent to it. God's role is reduced to turning on the mechanism of nature.

---

183. Allen Orr describes this subjection in a very incisive way: "Gould's position is not therefore so much, 'Render to Caesar the things that are Caesar's, and to God the things that are God's' as 'Render to Caesar the things that are Caesar's, and to God the things that Caesar says he can have'" (Orr, "Gould on God," 37).

184. Smedes, "Streams of Wisdom?" 95; Gould, *Rocks of Ages*, 22 and 84.

185. Gould, *Rocks of Ages*, 22.

186. Gould, *Rocks of Ages*, 22.

187. Smedes, "Streams of Wisdom?" 95.

THE PROBLEM OF THEOLOGICAL EXTRINSICISM 49

The deistic image of God present in Gould's NOMA and the religion originating from this image are very deficient. "In the end it is hard to resist the conclusion that Gould has lifted the word 'religion' and grafted it onto a toothless, hobbled beast incapable of scaring the materialists. And he seems strangely untroubled by the fact that few religious folk resemble the creature. But surely it is obvious that Gould's religion is a close cousin of secular humanism."[188] This deistic image of God is the result of a domestication process carried out by science and, in the end, it is "a scientific hypothesis"[189] itself. The atheist Massimo Pigliucci recognizes that "NOMA applies to the very special concept of God that a deist would feel comfortable with, not to what most people think of as 'God.'"[190] Finally, Dawkins states that NOMA pares religion down to "some sort of non-interventionist minimum: no miracles, no personal communication between God and us in either direction, no monkeying with the laws of physics, no trespassing on the scientific grass. At most, a little deistic input to the initial conditions of the universe so that, in the fullness of time . . . planets develop, and life evolves."[191]

Although NOMA wants to be theologically neutral, it entails a theology that becomes quite explicit when Gould talks about God and the limits under which God is placed. Gould opted for an extrinsic theology by excluding theology from science and, therefore, he violated his own concept of NOMA. This is because science, from the very beginning, is bound up with metaphysics and theology. Science cannot help but contain within itself a certain conception of being and God—specifically, a positivistic concept of being, an idea of matter emptied of form, and a deistic image of God. This is the inconsistency of NOMA: the distinction between science and religion defended by NOMA is violated by NOMA itself. According to Hanby, Gould "unwittingly bears witness to the true nature of the relation between theology and science by violating his own proposal and trespassing into theological doctrine in the very act of articulating it."[192] Therefore, NOMA is unsustainable not only because of its

188. Orr, "Gould on God," 37.

189. Dawkins, *The God Delusion*, 61.

190. Pigliucci, "Personal Gods," 42.

191. Dawkins, *The God Delusion*, 60.

192. Hanby, *No God, No Science?* 37n9. Hanby concedes that there is a basic truth in NOMA: "There is a distinction to be maintained [between science and theology] and areas of inquiry proper to each, but Gould's proposal amounts to little more than a warmed-over representation of the 'fact-value' distinction" (ibid.). According to

defective theological and metaphysical presuppositions, but also because it is logically incoherent.

Apart from the extreme extrinsicism proposed by Gould with his NOMA, there is a milder form of extrinsicism present in the dialogue between science and theology. This softer form, as Hanby points out, acknowledges that science cannot do without metaphysics, not even, perhaps, without theology. However, this way of conceiving the nature of metaphysics and theology is problematic because it preserves the idea that science stands outside metaphysics and theology. Only after the scientific work supposedly has been neutrally done, are a metaphysical and a theological system recognized. This mild extrinsicism can recognize without any problem the metaphysical and theological assumptions present at the historical origins of the modern sciences. However, these assumptions, because they are essentially external to science, can apparently "be safely 'bracketed out' from the strictly scientific work of testing hypotheses through empirical or experimental methods."[193]

A good historical example of mild extrinsicism is provided by Georges Lemaître, a mathematician, astronomer, and Catholic priest, who in 1931 proposed the theory of the "primeval atom," later known as the Big Bang. Lemaître claimed his theory was neutral regarding religion, saying, "As far as I can see, such a theory remains entirely outside any metaphysical or religious question."[194] A contemporary illustration of mild extrinsicism is provided by the cosmologist, philosopher, and Catholic priest, Michael Heller. This is what he affirms: "I do not say that metaphysics and theology are insignificant or meaningless; I am only arguing that they should not interfere with science. The best way of doing science is to stop thinking directly about any metaphysical preconditions or implications."[195] Heller's extrinsicism, as would be expected, is

---

NOMA, "Science is devoted to the facts, data, and the 'scene' of 'how' while metaphysics and religion are consecrated to the values, the ultimate meanings, the 'foundation,' of the 'why,' according to specific research protocols" (Ravasi, "Foreword," 17).

193. Hanby, *No God, No Science?* 10.

194. Lemaître, "The Primaeval Atom Hypothesis," 7. "Lemaître was careful not to mix his religious convictions with his work as a scientist. He emphasized that, just as there is no Christian way of running or swimming, there is no Christian way of doing science" (Heller, *Creative Tension*, 71).

195. Heller, *Creative Tension*, 8. There is a sense in which metaphysics and theology do not interfere with science. Remember what I have previously said about the legitimate autonomy of science. In the third chapter, I will defend that autonomy when I argue that the various physical cosmologies do not directly touch the question of

linked with his assumption that science is neutral: "Scientific theories or models are per se neutral with respect to theological or philosophical interpretation."[196] As was previously explained, methodological neutrality is pregnant with prior unarticulated judgments, both theological and metaphysical, which are unsustainable. However, Heller has no real sense of how his own work is affected by such judgments. In fact, the lack of philosophical self-awareness about metaphysical and theological presuppositions is one of the results of extrinsicism.

An illuminative example of mild extrinsicism is provided by John Polkinghorne, the Anglican priest and former theoretical elementary particle physicist.[197] He believes that science has the "ability to pursue

------

God. The legitimate autonomy of science follows theologically from the nature of God and creation, and not from the alleged self-completeness of science.

196. Heller, "Cosmological Singularity," 679. Heller is an adjunct scholar of the Vatican Observatory. The neutrality of science is a common feature among the members of the Vatican Observatory. George Coyne, who served as director of the Vatican Observatory for twenty-eight years, states that "science is completely neutral with respect to philosophical or theological implications that may be drawn from its conclusions" (Coyne, "Evolution and Intelligent Design," 718). William Stoeger, who was Staff Cosmologist of the Vatican Observatory Research Group, expressed the neutrality of science in this way: "The natural sciences are mute with regard to the ultimate sources of existence and order" (Stoeger, "Reductionism and Emergence," 236). Additionally, he said: "In order to do good science, we do not need religion, theology, or religious faith" (Stoeger, "Responses to Questions," 204).

197. Polkinghorne has been involved intensively in the dialogue between science and theology. He is one of the most recognized figures in this dialogue and he has written and edited more than thirty books in the area of the science-theology dialogue. Finally, Polkinghorne's work was endorsed by the Templeton Foundation when he was awarded the Templeton Prize in 2002. The initiator of the Templeton Foundation was Sir John Templeton (1912–2008), stock investor and philanthropist. He established the Templeton Prize in 1972. This prize honors people who have contributed to the affirmation of spiritual dimension. Note that the monetary amount of the Templeton Prize is set to exceed the money of the Nobel Prize (£1,100,000 sterling for Templeton Prize in 2018). After the establishment of the price, the Templeton Foundation was created in 1987. This foundation strongly supports and funds mutual dialogue between the experts of science and religion. Templeton's dream was "to see experts in science and religion making new discoveries in religion, as revolutionary as the discoveries that have been made during the last century in science" (Dyson, A Many-Colored Glass, 133). "Each year, it [the foundation] doles out some $70 million in grants, more than $40 million of which goes to research in fields such as cosmology, evolutionary biology and psychology" (Waldrop, "Religion: Faith in Science," 323). One of the initiatives of the foundation is the Templeton Press, which has published about two hundred volumes. (Sources: www.templeton.org, www.templetonprize.org, and www.templetonpress.org). All the previous numbers give an idea of the powerful influence of the foundation in the dialogue between science and theology.

its investigations *etsi deus non daretur*, as if God did not exist."[198] He also believes there must be a neutral scientific method because there is a pure science. In this regard, he speaks about "the manifest success of a *methodologically* atheistic natural science."[199] Once the scientist leaves the supposedly neutral domain of science, "theology has a right to contribute to the subsequent metascientific discourse."[200] In Polkinghorne's view, metaphysics and theology should commence only *after* science has laid its foundation. He considers that the way to proceed from physics to metaphysics and theology "is first to abstract from science a metascientific view of aspects of the physical process, then to incorporate this view within an appropriately extended wider metaphysical scheme, and finally to correlate with the latter a consonant theological understanding."[201] He goes, then, from science to metascience, then to metaphysics, and finally to theology.

Let's look at an example of how Polkinghorne moves from science to metaphysics and theology. At the level of physics, Polkinghorne states that "contemporary understanding of physical process detects within it a considerable degree of intrinsic unpredictability, both within quantum theory and within chaos theory."[202] In the second level, the metascientific one, "ontological significance" is assigned to the physical fact.[203] Following his axiom "epistemology models ontology,"[204] Polkinghorne affirms that "intrinsic unpredictability is to be treated as the signal of an underlying ontological openness."[205] It is only on the third level that Polkinghorne recognizes the metaphysical contribution: "This option presents a metaphysics of dynamical becoming, in contrast to one of static being.

---

198. Polkinghorne, *Faith, Science and Understanding*, 159.

199. Polkinghorne, *Faith, Science and Understanding*, 158. Discussing the Galileo case, Polkinghorne affirms that "theology was making unwarranted claims to pronounce upon questions which were both posable and answerable in *purely scientific terms*—the nature of motion and the structure of the solar system" (Polkinghorne, *One World*, 75; emphasis mine). In addition, he says that "Darwin offered a healthy corrective to unjustified claims that the Bible had foreclosed the answers to *purely scientific questions*" (ibid., 77; emphasis mine).

200. Polkinghorne, *Theology in the Context*, 12.

201. Polkinghorne, *Faith, Science and Understanding*, 131.

202. Polkinghorne, *Faith, Science and Understanding*, 147. Polkinghorne references here Gleick, *Chaos*.

203. Polkinghorne, *Faith, Science and Understanding*, 147.

204. Polkinghorne, "Physics and Metaphysics," 34.

205. Polkinghorne, *Faith, Science and Understanding*, 147.

The future is not up there waiting for us to arrive; we play our part in bringing it about, for it is contingent upon our executed intentions as well as on the operation of other causalities and agencies."[206] The last level is the theological one. At this stage, Polkinghorne asserts that "the theological picture consonant with this option [Polkinghorne's metaphysical option] is one that sees in the divine nature a temporal pole of engagement with creation as well as, of course, an eternal pole corresponding to the steadfastly unchanging benevolent nature of God."[207]

In assuming the neutrality of science, Polkinghorne renegotiates and reduces the concepts of nature and God, concepts that are present in both the idea and the content of science from the very beginning. However, these concepts are not perceived as deficient, because of the refusal of metaphysical mediation in science. In the case of the dipolar God, who has a temporal pole and an eternal pole, Polkinghorne uses *time* and *eternity* without explaining them. There is a lack of real engagement with the way these questions have already been thought through, for instance in Thomistic thought. For Thomas Aquinas, time and eternity are foremost a function of the understanding of being: eternity is related to the divine being and time to finite beings.[208] Furthermore, Thomas understood God as the fullness of being and finite beings as participants in the divine being.[209] Therefore, God is immutable because he is pure act.[210] When God is said to be outside time, this does refer to God's transcendence of time but also to God's interiority with time. Polkinghorne does not comment on any of this. The physicist simply makes becoming the opposite of being. He never considers a classic approach to being, such as the Aristotelian philosophy of act, but just assumes being as brute facticity.

Indeed, Polkinghorne affirms that theology and metaphysics have to take "the laws of nature that science has to treat as simply given brute fact."[211] However, the notion of brute fact is not metaphysically innocent because it is pregnant with metaphysical considerations. The acceptance of brute fact requires the rejection of the Aristotelian notions of form and act, in order to restrain facts to pure empirical data that can be quantified

206. Polkinghorne, *Faith, Science and Understanding*, 150.

207. Polkinghorne, *Faith, Science and Understanding*, 151.

208. Aquinas, *Summa Theologiae*, I, q. 10, a. 4, co.

209. Aquinas, *Summa Contra Gentiles*, lib. 2, cap. 52, n. 8.

210. Aquinas, *Summa Theologiae*, I, q. 9, a. 1, co.

211. Polkinghorne, *From Physicist to Priest*, 137.

and reproduced through experiment. There is a clear decision regarding what counts as "real." This decision reproduces the modern project of "self-imposed limitation of reason to the empirically falsifiable,"[212] so that "only the kind of certainty resulting from the interplay of mathematical and empirical elements can be considered scientific. Anything that would claim to be science must be measured against this criterion."[213]

Notice how intrinsically related are Polkinghorne's image of nature (characterized by chance and necessity), his metaphysical understanding of becoming as opposite of being, and his theological idea of the dipolar God. Again, the inevitable relationship between science, metaphysics, and theology keeps appearing. With his idea of a dipolar God, Polkinghorne breaks the divine concept into two poles, temporal and eternal, thus destroying the mystery of the eternal God who relates to a changing creation. The point here is not that theology is handcuffed, but that the mild extrinsicism defended by Polkinghorne imposes, from the beginning, deficient theological and metaphysical concepts, which have been isolated from critique by the notions of brute facticity and methodological neutrality.

For mild extrinsicism, metaphysics and theology allegedly have nothing to say to science, because the core of science excludes metaphysics and theology by presupposing that the world is indifferent to God. Because science, metaphysics, and theology are inherently related, this mild extrinsicism is ultimately untenable. Metaphysics and theology cannot be "merely *presupposed* at the origins of scientific inquiry where they may thereafter be bracketed out . . . [because] they permeate the entire enterprise."[214] In the end, the difference between strong and mild extrinsicism is minimal because "they share in the more basic assumption that, whatever other methodological peculiarities may be proper to its 'essence,' science is science not least because its 'essence' excludes metaphysics and theology."[215]

In this initial chapter, I have argued that modern science operates under extrinsicist theological and metaphysical presuppositions. This is

---

212. Benedict XVI, "The Regensburg Address," 173.

213. Benedict XVI, "The Regensburg Address," 172.

214. Hanby, *No God, No Science?* 17.

215. Hanby, *No God, No Science?* 10. "In other words, it is here at the point of their mutual exclusivity that the distinction, which is really a wall of separation, is to be drawn between science on the one hand, and metaphysics or theology on the other" (ibid.).

so because nature is assumed from the beginning to be essentially indifferent to God. Whether God exists or not makes no difference to the natural world. Therefore, God is presupposed in such a manner that he can only be extrinsically related to the world. This presupposition is the core idea of methodological naturalism, which is accepted by virtually every scientist. The extrinsicism present in modern science is wrong for several reasons. First, it falsifies both the concept of God and the concept of nature. On the one hand, God's transcendence is lost because God is reduced to an external agent acting on the same level as any natural agent. On the other hand, nature loses its own interiority and unity; it is reduced to a mechanism composed of unrelated parts.[216] Second, it contradicts science's self-understanding as indifferent to both metaphysics and theology because science is indeed intrinsically related to metaphysics and theology. Third, it makes the dialogue between theology and science impossible because of the reduced notions of God and nature assumed.

Theological extrinsicism can be seen everywhere, from the theologians using science to give scientific evidence for the existence of God to the atheistic scientists using their science to negate the existence of God. Hanby has shown and criticized this problematic theological understanding present in the field of biology. Both the theologian William Paley and the atheistic scientist Charles Darwin shared the same defective image of God.[217] As Hanby notes, "Darwin basically takes over Paley's theology in negative form, thus making the theological and ontological assumptions of Paley's theology endemic to the subsequent Darwinian tradition."[218] In the third chapter, I will reveal and criticize the theological extrinsicism present in both the theologians who use modern cosmology to offer scientific proof for the existence of God and the atheistic cosmologists who use their science to reject the idea of God. In order to accomplish the task of criticizing the erroneous theological assumptions of modern cosmology, it is necessary to overcome the false doctrine of creation they are based upon. This can only be achieved by retrieving a coherent and solid doctrine of creation able to recover "the ontological question sup-

---

216. The falsification of nature eliminates from its domain features of reality that are a necessary part of our lived experience and that form the starting point of scientific inquiry. This elimination is done either by ignoring those features of reality or by explaining them away in an attempt to reduce them to a materialist denominator.

217. Hanby, *No God, No Science?* 150–249.

218. Hanby, *No God, No Science?* 4.

pressed by positivistic science and its reduction of being from act to brute facticity." By retrieving this cogent doctrine of creation, I will be able, "on the one hand, to retrieve the doctrine of God from the idolatrous natural theology presupposed by modern science in its founding gesture . . . [, and on the other,] to retrieve the world from the endemic reductionism of a pervasive mechanistic ontology."[219] The retrieval of this cogent doctrine of creation will be the goal of the next chapter. This coherent doctrine of creation will serve as the foundation for the critique of the theological extrinsicism of modern cosmology that I will carry out in the third chapter.

219. Hanby, *No God, No Science?* 324.

2

The Doctrine of *Creatio ex Nihilo*

Introduction

THE GOAL OF THIS book is to uncover the extrinsic theology that is inherent in modern science and, more concretely, in modern cosmology. Theological extrinsicism conceives God as an external agent who is in competition with natural processes and creation as a worldly mechanism. Immersed in theological extrinsicism, atheistic cosmologists attempt to deny the existence of God, arguing that the origin of the universe can be explained solely in scientific terms. The extrinsic understanding of God is also present in those scientists and theologians who try to give scientific evidence for the existence of God. These scientists and theologians share the extrinsic theological assumptions of the atheistic cosmologists because they uncritically assume the metaphysical and theological presuppositions of modern science. As a result, the conception of God held by these theistic scientists and theologians is severely reduced to comply with the exigencies of scientific discoveries, which are taken as normative. They try to explain God's action in the world in reductive scientific terms, thus showing their misunderstanding of creation and divine action.

All these scientists, who range from atheists to defenders of religion, and all these theologians share a common problem: their extrinsic theology. However, their scientific assumptions blind them to their extrinsic

57

theology and the problems that come with it. In order to uncover and criticize the extrinsicism present in modern science, and, more concretely, in modern cosmology, it is necessary to provide a coherent and unreduced image of God and nature, to give a better understanding of the relation between the world and God. In other words, the doctrine of creation is required to assess the problems of extrinsic theology and to show the erroneous conception of creation held by extrinsicist scientists and theologians.

The doctrine of creation can help to overcome the extrinsicism that understands creation as a divine mechanism in competition with natural operations. The doctrine of creation *ex nihilo* is first and foremost a doctrine of God, which rescues the image of God from its extrinsicist confinement. Because theology and metaphysics are intrinsically related, the conception of God correlates with the conception of nature. The doctrine of creation expresses not only an image of God but also an image of nature. This doctrine tells us who God is and what the world is. Therefore, "Creation *ex nihilo* is simultaneously the doctrine of God and the ontological structure of the world."[1] These two aspects of creation were formulated by Aquinas as the active and passive senses of creation, respectively.[2] According to the universal doctor, creation, in its active sense, "is the divine substance" because "creation signifies the divine operation, which is [nothing but] His essence with a certain relation."[3] Therefore, "when God makes something to exist by creating it, God 'does' nothing other than to be God."[4] If, however, creation is taken passively, then "creation is in the creature [relation], and is a creature."[5] In this chapter, I will explore the meaning of the doctrine of creation in its passive and active senses.

In fact, the goal of this chapter is to lay out the doctrine of creation *ex nihilo* in its twofold sense, in order to have a foundation for criticizing

---

1. Hanby, *No God, No Science?* 334.

2. Hanby, *No God, No Science?* 5.

3. Aquinas, *Scriptum Super Libros Sententiarum*, lib. 2, d. 1, q. 1, a. 2, ad 4. (English translations of *Scriptum Super Libros Sententiarum* are taken from Aquinas, *Aquinas on Creation*). Aquinas specified that the relation "is not a real but only a logical relation" (*De Potentia Dei*, q. 3, a. 3, co.; English translations of *De Potentia Dei* are taken from Aquinas, *On the Power of God*). I will deal with this issue later on.

4. Wilhelmsen, "Creation as a Relation," 111.

5. Aquinas, *Summa Theologiae*, I, q. 45, a. 3, ad 2. (English translations of *Summa Theologiae* are taken from Aquinas, *Summa Theologica*).

the extrinsic theology present in modern science and, more concretely, in modern cosmology. According to this extrinsicist theology, creation is conceived as "a free standing cosmology or a 'mechanical' explanation of how the world came to be."[6] In order to deal with the doctrine of creation in its dual aspect as a doctrine both of God and of the metaphysical constitution of the world, I will lean on the works of Thomas Aquinas. As Walker recognizes, Thomas remains the central figure for Catholics because "he remains the *doctor communis*, the universal doctor."[7] The works of Aquinas are a philosophically precise exponent of the Christian tradition. However, my intention here is not to present an exposition of the Thomistic understanding of creation but to express how the Christian tradition understands creation. Although Thomas is very helpful in grasping the doctrine of creation, he is not the only reference. For this reason, I will use other authors apart from Aquinas to understand what creation is. More specifically, I will engage with scholars who creatively developed Thomistic thought, particularly Balthasar.

As formerly shown, the doctrine of *creatio ex nihilo* is, first of all, a doctrine of God. The doctrine of creation presupposes and gives expression to the Christian understanding of God. I will dwell now on Aquinas to explain briefly the doctrine of God that is supported by the doctrine of creation. Speaking from the continuous Christian tradition, the universal doctor recognized that "God is absolutely immutable, He is eternal, lacking all beginning or end."[8] Because God is immutable, there cannot be any potency in God. As Aquinas stated, "The being whose substance has an admixture of potency is liable not to be by as much as it has potency; for that which can be, can not-be. But, God, being everlasting, in His substance cannot not-be. In God, therefore, there is no potency to being."[9] Therefore, God can be characterized as "pure act, without the admixture of any potentiality."[10] There cannot be any composition in God because "in every composite there must be act and potency," and "in God there is no potency."[11] The lack of composition in God refers to the ultimate simplicity and unity of God, two aspects of God always defended

6. Hanby, *No God, No Science?* 5.

7. Walker, "Personal Singularity," 461.

8. Aquinas, *Summa Contra Gentiles*, lib. 2, cap. 15, n. 2. (English translations of *Summa Contra Gentiles* are taken from Aquinas, *Summa Contra Gentiles*).

9. Aquinas, *Summa Contra Gentiles*, lib. 2, cap. 16, n. 2.

10. Aquinas, *Summa Theologiae*, I, q. 9, a. 1, co.

11. Aquinas, *Summa Contra Gentiles*, lib. 2, cap. 18, n. 2.

by the Christian tradition.[12] The fact that there is no composition in God allowed Thomas to conclude that God is his own essence. This is the Thomistic reasoning: "If some thing were not its essence, there should be something in it outside its essence. Thus, there must be composition in it. Hence it is that the essence in composite things is signified as a part, for example, humanity in man. Now, it has been shown that there is no composition in God. God is, therefore, His essence."[13] Because God is his own essence, God's essence is his own existence (*esse*). "If . . . the divine essence is something other than its being, the essence and the being are thereby related as potency and act. But we have shown that in God there is no potency, but that He is pure act. God's essence, therefore, is not something other than His being [*esse*]."[14] Finally, because God's essence is his own existence, God can be called "subsisting being itself [*ipsum esse subsistens*]."[15]

The Absence of Compulsion in the Act of Creation

As stated above, God is the *ipsum esse subsistens*, the plenitude of being, the *actus purus* [pure act], without any composition or potency. As a consequence, "nothing in God is due to coaction."[16] Therefore, the act of creation, which is nothing else but God's essence and a certain relation, cannot actualize any passive potency in God. In other words, creation cannot entail any coercion of God, either external or internal.[17] It is important to note that the doctrine of creation *ex nihilo*, as a doctrine of God, primarily expresses the absoluteness of God as first principle. The lack of compulsion for God in the act of creation is an immediate consequence of the fullness of the divine being.[18] Although God's being and his freedom must be ontological convertible, the question of the absolute aseity of God is logically first. Making the absoluteness of divine freedom

12. See Hanby, *No God, No Science?* 314.

13. Aquinas, *Summa Contra Gentiles*, lib. 1, cap. 21, n. 2.

14. Aquinas, *Summa Contra Gentiles*, lib. 2, cap. 22, n. 7.

15. Aquinas, *Summa Theologiae*, I, q. 4, a. 2, co.

16. Aquinas, *Summa Contra Gentiles*, lib. 1, cap. 19, n. 3.

17. "The plenitude of divine being, on any adequate thought of the matter, must be free of two kinds of compulsion, 'external' and 'internal'" (Hanby, *No God, No Science?* 310).

18. I use the term 'compulsion for God' to refer to anything, internal or external, that would force God to create; that is, anything that would take away God's freedom.

the central issue at stake in creation would be a voluntarist resolution of the problem. Emphasizing the theological character of the doctrine of creation, Gerhard May affirmed that "Church theology wants through the proposition *creatio ex nihilo* to express and safeguard the omnipotence and freedom of God acting in history."[19] In other words, "The doctrine of *creatio ex nihilo* proclaims in the most pointed manner the absolutely unconditioned nature of the creation and specifies God's omnipotence as its sole ground."[20]

It is important to note here that the doctrine of creation is not a free-standing cosmology, as many cosmologists think, but firstly a doctrine of *God*.[21] It is true that cosmological implications follow from the doctrine of creation, but this doctrine is not primarily an attempt to solve the problem of the origin of the universe.[22] From the historical point of view, "the doctrine of *creatio ex nihilo* does not emerge from a kind [of] cosmological curiosity somehow outside Christian theological convictions, and it is not a freestanding hypothesis devised to explain cosmological origins."[23]

As I have just explained, the doctrine of creation, as a doctrine of God, primarily expresses the absoluteness of the divine being, and then, as a consequence, the absence of compulsion for God in the act of creation. In this section I will deal with both external and internal compulsion, paying attention at the end to the problem of divine voluntarism. Let us begin with the lack of external compulsion. For this purpose, the Thomistic definition of creation is very appropriate. For Aquinas, to create is "to produce a thing into being (*esse*) according to its entire substance (*substantia*)."[24] In the act of creation, "God at the same time gives being (*esse*) and produces that which receives being (*esse*)."[25] Therefore,

19. May, *Creatio ex Nihilo*, 180. As an example, "the conception so emphatically declared by Justin of the unlimited creative power of God and the thought that God, as the sole unoriginate being stands over against the originate, the creation, are mutually supportive in their bearing and seem to urge the doctrine of *creatio ex nihilo*" (ibid., 132).

20. May, *Creatio ex Nihilo*, xi.

21. Hanby, *No God, No Science?* 3.

22. Hanby, *No God, No Science?* 164.

23. Hanby, *No God, No Science?* 79. See May, *Creatio ex Nihilo*, 28.

24. Aquinas, *Scriptum Super Libros Sententiarum*, lib. 2, d. 1, q. 1, a. 2, co.

25. Aquinas, *De Potentia Dei*, q. 3, a. 1, ad 17. In relation to this passage, Kenneth L. Schmitz commented: "The creative communication endows act absolutely: to be rather than not. Yet its product is not simply act: it is an ontological composite, a

God produces at the same time the *substance* that is going to receive existence and *existence itself*. In other words, "Creation should not be seen as a double act of producing a recipient of being and granting being to it. 'That which is' is created by the fact that being is attributed to it."[26] Hence, creation "presupposes nothing in the thing which is said to be created."[27] Therefore, creation, the bringing of something into existence (*esse*), is done "without any pre-existing matter."[28] The existence of coeval matter would challenge God's absoluteness because there would be something outside of God for which he was not responsible. God then could not be God. Consequently, a coeval principle would challenge God's rulership, placing restrictions on God's act of creation. "The unbegottenness of matter would reflect upon and compromise the absolute sovereignty of the divine creative power, setting at least passive limits to its exercise. It would require the divine will to rely upon something that lay in some sense outside its province, determining it in the way a precondition functions."[29] As Schmitz graphically described, if unbegotten matter could speak, "it would cry out: Without me, nothing can be made! Moreover, there would be an aspect in creatures themselves that they did not owe to their God, even though that element were merely the capacity to be formed by God."[30]

Because of the absence of preexisting matter in creation, to create is to "make a thing from nothing [*ex nihilo*]."[31] Aquinas explained that "creation is the proper act of God alone" because "creation is not from anything presupposed, which can be disposed by the action of the instrumental agent. So therefore it is impossible for any creature to create, either by its own power or instrumentally—that is, ministerially."[32] The idea of *nihil* expresses the gratuity of creation. In the act of creation there is nothing due to or owed by God, there is nothing expected from God "because there is no subject to which to refer the dueness, no subject to give rise to the expectation. And so, the fulfillment of the absent good

---

being. In endowing act, the creator also endows the conditions for the reception of its own communication" (Schmitz, *The Gift*, 126).

26. Velde, *Participation and Substantiality*, 158.

27. Aquinas, *Scriptum Super Libros Sententiarum*, lib. 2, d. 1, q. 1, a. 2, co.

28. Aquinas, *Summa Contra Gentiles*, lib. 2, cap. 16, n. 13.

29. Schmitz, *The Gift*, 27.

30. Schmitz, *The Gift*, 27.

31. Aquinas, *De Potentia Dei*, q. 3, a. 1, co.

32. Aquinas, *Summa Theologiae*, I, q. 45, a. 5, co.

is absolutely gratuitous, is strictly speaking: not called for."[33] The act of creation is an utterly free and generous act in which no creature can lay a claim on God. There is nothing external to God that can impose any limitation on God. Hanby explains that the concept of *nihil* in creation has the function of removing any external limitations in the act of creation.[34] The *nihil* of the doctrine of *creatio ex nihilo* does not mean a previous pre-existing matter called "nothing."[35] As Thomas clarified, "Nothing does not hold the position of patient."[36] Nothing is literally "nothing outside being thought."[37] Therefore, "The creature is said 'out of nothing' because it is 'not from something pre-existing.'"[38] The concept of *nihil* is a very difficult one to think about, "for it is virtually impossible to think of 'the nothing' without hypostasizing it into something."[39]

The idea of *nihil* is very relevant to the purpose of this book because it shows the defective theological presuppositions of modern cosmologists when they think about the origin of the universe. In an attempt "to interpret Big Bang cosmology in a way which precludes the notion of creation and a creator," some atheistic cosmologists "account for the Big Bang in terms of fluctuation in a primal vacuum known as 'quantum tunneling' from nothing, from which the universe expanded according to what is known as inflation theory."[40] As we will see in the next chapter, their idea of "nothing" is quite distant from the *nihil* referred to in the concept of *creatio ex nihilo*. "The alleged nothing [as understood by contemporary cosmologists] turns out to be a complex reality of ordering principles without which there would be no uniformity in nature and no scientific study of natural phenomena would be possible."[41] Therefore, "Contemporary cosmological speculation seems magically to reify the *nihil*."[42] Cosmologists do not think properly about the idea of *nihil* because they do not think about God's absoluteness and transcendence

33. Schmitz, *The Gift*, 31–32.

34. Hanby, *No God, No Science?* 310.

35. Schmitz, *The Gift*, 29.

36. Aquinas, *De Potentia Dei*, q. 3, a. 1, ad 4.

37. Wilhelmsen, "Creation as a Relation," 115.

38. Aquinas, *Scriptum Super Libros Sententiarum*, lib. 2, d. 1, q. 1, a. 2, co.

39. Hanby, *No God, No Science?* 310; Heidegger, "What Is Metaphysics?" 92–96.

40. Oliver, "Physics, Creation and Trinity," 182.

41. Życiński, "Metaphysics and Epistemology," 279.

42. Oliver, "Physics, Creation and Trinity," 183.

and otherness radically and thoroughly enough. As Hanby notes, "The difficulty in thinking of the *nihil* is really but the reverse side of difficulty in thinking of God alone as *ipsum esse subsistens*."[43] It is also the case that cosmologists do not think about being but they presume it, and so being does not appear as mysterious or even as a question.

Up to this point, I have been showing that there is a lack of external compulsion for God in creation because there is nothing external constraining God's action. As Rudi te Velde points out, "Creation is meant to express an absolute beginning without any pre-existing condition."[44] In other words, the doctrine of *creatio ex nihilo* presupposes nothing outside or other than God himself. In the act of creation, there is an absence not only of external compulsion, but also of internal compulsion. Let us now turn to the lack of internal compulsion for God in the act of creation.

The act of creation is an act of radical divine freedom. However, we have to take into account an important nuance about divine freedom: it "is fundamentally an expression of *love* and inseparable from all the other predicates with which it is convertible [i.e., goodness, beauty, and truth]."[45] Therefore, divine freedom cannot be abstracted "from the divine nature of triune love revealed historically in Christ, as well as its corollary, the convertibility of goodness, beauty, and truth in God's triune essence."[46] In other words, divine freedom is not independent from God's nature. Divine freedom is conditioned by the goodness, beauty and truth of God's own nature as trinitarian love. It is then erroneous to defend that divine freedom is absolutely presuppositionless. That kind of freedom would be voluntaristic and arbitrary. "But an arbitrary freedom, one which is not *responsive* to the solicitations of goodness and beauty, is both unintelligent and ultimately *unfree*; for it fails to connect the act with its motive and therefore fails to show how the action is an expression of the agent's desire. Such indeterminate spontaneity is more like a spasm than an act of volition."[47]

The act of creation is an act of divine freedom, but not of a voluntaristic freedom, because both freedom and nature are integrated in God through love. "God must create freely . . . and yet, at the same time and

43. Hanby, *No God, No Science?* 310.

44. Velde, *Participation and Substantiality*, 155.

45. Hanby, *No God, No Science?* 121.

46. Hanby, *No God, No Science?* 108.

47. Hanby, *No God, No Science?* 311.

for the same reason, . . . God must create 'naturally' [i.e., according to his nature]."[48] This dual aspect of creation (God creates both freely and according to his nature) is something defended by the Christian tradition. Let us see how Augustine expresses it:

> And by the words, "God saw that it was good," it is sufficiently intimated that God made what was made not from any necessity, nor for the sake of supplying any want, but solely from His own goodness, that is, because it was good. And this is stated after the creation had taken place, that there might be no doubt that the thing made satisfied the goodness on account of which it was made.[49]

Augustine affirms that God must create freely ("God made what was made not from any necessity, nor for the sake of supplying any want") but also that he must create according to his nature ("solely from His own goodness, i.e., because it was good").[50] Following the Christian tradition, Aquinas affirmed that God creates "not by necessity of His nature, but by the free choice of His will."[51] In the act of creation, God does not act "for the acquisition of some end; He intends only to communicate His perfection, which is His goodness."[52] In fact, "He alone is the most perfectly liberal giver, because He does not act for His own profit, but only for His own goodness."[53] Therefore, "We can posit no motive for creation beyond sheer generosity and the delight that God takes in his own beauty as Trinity."[54]

The fact that God does not create by necessity of his nature does not mean that God creates without any presupposition, not taking into account his own nature. The divine nature is the presupposition of creation but this does not mean that God creates against his will. As we already know, there is an integration of freedom and nature in God through love. "Insofar as creation is free, it must be 'unnecessary' and 'spontaneous,' a matter of gratuitous 'decision.' It cannot simply follow 'naturally' from the

48. Hanby, *No God, No Science?* 311. See Augustine, *De Civitate Dei*, XI, 24.

49. Augustine, *City of God* (2013), 331 (XI, 24).

50. Augustine, *City of God* (2013), 331 (XI, 24); Hanby, *No God, No Science?* 311.

51. Aquinas, *Summa Contra Gentiles*, lib. 2, cap. 23, n. 1.

52. Aquinas, *Summa Theologiae*, I, q. 44, a. 4, co.

53. Aquinas, *Summa Theologiae*, I, q. 44, a. 4, ad 1.

54. Hanby, "Creation without Creationism," 692.

superabundance of the One as in the case of Plotinus."[55] In creation there is an internal presupposition, which is God's own nature. However, this internal presupposition does not compel God to make creation something other than an act of love. "There can be no 'motive' for creation beyond the sheer goodness that God is."[56]

We have seen that there is no internal compulsion in the divine creative act. Hanby clarifies that this affirmation "follows from the fact that God's superabundant fullness can admit no lack."[57] The absence of internal constraint does not mean that creation is without presuppositions. As we already know, the act of creation is radically free, but it is also conditioned by the goodness, beauty, and truth of God's own nature as trinitarian love. "Creation thus implies a paradoxical coincidence of volition, nature, and being in the unity of God's simplicity."[58]

The Real Distinction in Its Negative Sense

We saw in the previous section that the doctrine of creation *ex nihilo* mainly expresses the absoluteness of God as first principle, and then, as a consequence, the absence of both external and internal compulsion for God in the act of creation. God is totally unconditioned in the act of creation except by his own nature. God is the *ipsum esse subsistens*, the one whose essence is his own existence. God is the only one who exists necessarily. In contrast, created beings are contingent: they do not exist necessarily. That they exist is due only to God's utter generosity. The existence of creatures does not belong to their essences. There is then a distinction in creatures between their essences and their existence. This distinction is known as the *real distinction* between *esse* (being) and essence.[59] This real distinction, which I will further explain momentarily, is very important

---

55. Hanby, *No God, No Science?* 311. "[In the doctrine of creation *ex nihilo,*] goodness is now understood not simply as superabundant necessity, the One 'spilling over' by nature, as it were, but as the coincidence, indeed the convertibility, of superabundant nature and infinite generosity: *bonum diffusivum sui* (Ps.-Dionysius, *Div. Nom.*, IV, 717c; Aquinas, *ST*, I.73, a.3, obj. 2)" (Hanby, *No God, No Science?* 311).

56. Hanby, *No God, No Science?* 311. See Augustine, *De Civitate Dei*, XI, 24.

57. Hanby, *No God, No Science?* 311.

58. Hanby, *No God, No Science?* 311.

59. There is an additional argument for the real distinction: that every creature is a mixture of potency and act, and so no creature possesses the whole of its being perfectly all at once.

for the purpose of this chapter because, as Hanby recognizes, the real distinction "renders intelligible the structure of worldly reality."[60] Therefore, the real distinction is key to understanding creation in its passive sense.

We have arrived at the real distinction from the contingency of the world. Hanby affirms that Christianity arrived at the real distinction not only "negatively from the contingency and thus nonnecessity of the world," but also "positively from the recognition of an act-of-existing—of 'having,' in persons—that is not simply reducible to the act of 'being a human being,' or a tree, or a stone, and so on but is incommunicably peculiar to being *this* person or *this* tree."[61] In other words, the act of being, *esse*, cannot be reduced to an essence or a form, because it is radically peculiar to each thing. The contingency of the world, on the one hand, and the ineffable peculiarity of each thing granted by *esse*, on the other hand, is what Hanby refers to as the negative sense and the positive sense of the real distinction between *esse* and essence.[62] In this section, I will treat the real distinction and its negative sense. I will deal with the positive sense in the next section. Here, and in the following sections, I will dwell not only on Aquinas, but also on other authors, such as Balthasar, who creatively developed what is implicit in Thomistic thought.

As stated above, Aquinas described God as *ipsum esse subsistens*. From this understanding of God, he concluded that "all beings apart from God are not their own being, but are beings by participation. Therefore it must be that all things which are diversified by the diverse participation of being, so as to be more or less perfect, are caused by one First Being, Who possesses being most perfectly."[63] Creaturely beings receive the same being from God but in a different way "in the sense that they participate in being in a more or less perfect manner according to their distance from the First Being who is most perfect."[64] According to Aquinas, "Whenever something is predicated of another in the manner of participation, it is necessary that there be something in the latter besides that in which it participates. And therefore, in any creature the creature itself which has being [*habet esse*] and its very being [*ipsum esse*] are other."[65] Hence, as

60. Hanby, *No God, No Science?* 354.

61. Hanby, *No God, No Science?* 337.

62. See Hanby, *No God, No Science?* 337; 351; 354.

63. Aquinas, *Summa Theologiae*, I, q. 44, a. 1, co.

64. Velde, *Aquinas on God*, 131.

65. Aquinas, *Quodlibetal* II, q. 2, a. 1, co. (English translations of *Quodlibetal* are taken from Aquinas, *Quodlibetal Questions*).

Velde states, "Participation goes together with the distinction in each creature between essence and *esse*. Each creature is being (*ens*) in a different way according to how it differently relates to the *esse* it has received from the First Being."[66] Therefore, "In each thing besides God there is a difference to be noted between the thing itself—that is, the essence or nature—and its being (*esse*)." Furthermore, "Participation goes together with the language of composition: the thing is composed of itself with the being it participates."[67] As explained earlier, the distinction between essence and *esse* is known as the real distinction.[68] We have arrived at this distinction through a Thomistic argument based on participation. However, this is not the only way used by Aquinas to justify the real distinction. In fact, John Wippel lists six of them.[69] At any rate, all of them speak about a "composition of essence and *esse* in beings other than God."[70]

66. Velde, *Aquinas on God*, 131–32.

67. Velde, *Aquinas on God*, 140.

68. "Of course whether that distinction is 'real' or merely 'conceptual' is a question of long-running dispute, both with respect to Thomas and more generally" (Hanby, *No God, No Science?* 369n47). Velde notes that "although Thomas himself seldom speaks of a 'real' distinction in contrast with a distinction made by reason, most interpreters put particular weight on the real character of the distinction because, in their view, it is only as really distinct from the *esse* it receives that the principle of essence can account for the limitation of the *esse* in each particular thing." However, Velde doubts if "one should say that the *esse* is limited *by* the receiving principle of essence" (Velde, *Aquinas on God*, 145n47). At any rate, agreeing with Hanby, "I will simply take it for granted that Thomas took the distinction to be real" (Hanby, *No God, No Science?* 369n47).

69. Wippel, *Metaphysical Thought of Aquinas*, 132–76. Perhaps the most famous, albeit polemical, way is what Wippel calls the *intellectus essentiae* argument, present in chapter 4 of Aquinas' *De Ente et Essentia* (ibid., 137–50). One significant paragraph of this chapter is the following: "Everything that does not belong to the concept of an essence or quiddity comes to it from outside and enters into composition with the essence, because no essence can be understood without its parts. Now, every essence or quiddity can be understood without knowing anything about its being [*esse*]. I can know, for instance, what a man or a phoenix is and still be ignorant whether it has being in reality. From this it is clear that being [*esse*] is other than essence or quiddity, unless perhaps there is a reality whose quiddity is its being" (Aquinas, *De Ente et Essentia*, cap. 4. English translation taken from Aquinas, *On Being and Essence*, 55). "Variations of the same argument can be found in *In I Sent.* d.8, q.5, a.2 and *In II Sent.* d.3, q.1, a.1" (Velde, *Participation and Substantiality*, 71n11).

70. Wippel, *Metaphysical Thought of Aquinas*, 137. "In substances composed of matter and form there is a twofold composition of act and potentiality: the first, of the substance itself which is composed of matter and form; the second, of the substance thus composed, and being; and this composition also can be said to be of that which is and being, or of that which is and that by which a thing is" (Aquinas, *Summa Contra Gentiles*, lib. 2, cap. 54, n. 9).

We have just seen that Aquinas arrived at his understanding of the real distinction "via a metaphysical induction from the structure of finite *ens*."[71] It is certain that the real distinction reaches its highest and most precise formulation in Thomas Aquinas. Nevertheless, the real distinction between essence and *esse* "is implicit in the doctrine of creation itself and its task of securing the transcendent plenitude of divine being."[72] Therefore, it can be said that the real distinction has already been present since the beginning of the doctrine of creation, even though it took some time for this distinction to be fully unfolded. The distinction between essence and existence is also implicit in the theological understanding of Jesus Christ as true man and true God. "The distinction between *hypostasis/persona* and *natura* . . . implied the as yet unarticulated real distinction (*distinctio realis*) between being (*esse*) and essence (*essentia*)."[73] Balthasar gave witness to the same fact: "The real distinction between essence and existence is already the implied foundation of this Christology, and its concepts are moving toward this invisible point of convergence, without yet standing expressly under its normative power."[74]

In this section I want to focus on the real distinction in its negative sense. For this reason, it is necessary to deal now with the non-subsistent character of *esse*. Although *esse* is "the act which makes substance *be* in the first place (absolutely) . . . *esse* at the same time nonetheless does not subsist—which is to say, it in some way itself 'depends' for its own existence on the very substance it makes be."[75] Aquinas recognized that

71. Hanby, *No God, No Science?* 354. "This metaphysical induction is important, because for Thomas no less than for Balthasar, the *distinctio realis* is not simply a justification for the doctrine of creation; rather, it renders intelligible the structure of worldly reality, a structure that makes its phenomenal appearance, in the latter case, in the primal experience of a child" (ibid.). See the fourfold difference in Balthasar, *Glory of the Lord V*, 613–27. The rendering of the Balthasarian fourfold difference can be found in different authors: D. C. Schindler, *Hans Urs von Balthasar*, 31–58; Healy, *Eschatology of Balthasar*, 60–72; Chapp, *The God of Covenant*, 157–62; and Hanby, *No God, No Science?* 349–52.

72. Hanby, *No God, No Science?* 336.

73. Hanby, *No God, No Science?* 336.

74. Balthasar, *Cosmic Liturgy*, 215.

75. David L. Schindler, "The Person," 176n2; Aquinas, *De Potentia Dei*, q. 1, a. 1, co. Precisely because *esse* is "the act which makes substance *be* in the first place (absolutely); and . . . *esse* at the same time nonetheless does not subsist—which is to say, it in some way itself 'depends' for its own existence on the very substance it makes be," *esse* should be "understood in a significant sense—and however paradoxically—as *both* prior *and* posterior to substance" (David L. Schindler, "The Person," 176n2).

"'to be' itself [*ipsum esse*] is not signified as the subject of 'being,' just as 'to run' is not signified as the subject of 'running.' Hence, just as we cannot say 'to run itself runs,' so we cannot say 'to be itself is'; rather, 'that-which-is' is signified as the subject of 'being,' just as 'that which runs' is signified as the subject of 'running.'"[76] D. C. Schindler remarks upon the paradoxical character of *esse*: "While *esse* is in a certain respect what makes all things be, it itself is *nothing* in the sense that it does not subsist in itself, but only inheres in *that which* exists."[77] Indeed, existence in creatures is conceivable only as the existence of a substance. However, this existence which makes substances to be is not due to them. Each finite being does not exist necessarily; rather, it has existence from God. "Created substances are not self-derived, but owe their very existence to God's liberal bestowal of *esse* in creation."[78] Existence comes from God who is the only one who exists necessarily. As outlined above, in God there is no difference between essence and existence because "God's being [*esse*] is His essence."[79] God is the "essentially self-subsisting Being."[80]

With the previous affirmations about God's being, Aquinas was reinstating the doctrine of divine simplicity. Before Thomas, this doctrine had been defended by the Christian tradition for centuries. For example, the Nicene Creed clearly confessed the simplicity of divine unity when it referred to Jesus Christ: "God from God, Light from Light, true God from true God, begotten, not made, consubstantial with the Father." Augustine, in books VI and VII of his *De Trinitate*, explored "the divine unity through articulating the Nicene language of Light from Light and God from God against the background of the divine simplicity."[81] Moreover, Augustine expressed forcefully the doctrine of divine simplicity in his denial of "any real ontological distinction between God's substance and His attributes." For the bishop of Hippo, the doctrine of divine simplicity "rallies around the claim that God *is* what He *has* (*hoc est quod habet*)."[82]

76. Aquinas, *De Hebdomadibus, lect.* 2. (English translation taken from Aquinas, *An Exposition*, 17).

77. D. C. Schindler, "What's the Difference?" 19.

78. Walker, "Personal Singularity," 472.

79. Aquinas, *Summa Contra Gentiles*, lib. 1, cap. 22, n. 8.

80. Aquinas, *Summa Theologiae*, I, q. 44, a. 1, co.

81. Ayres, *Augustine and the Trinity*, 221.

82. Rosheger, "Augustine and Divine Simplicity," 72; Augustine, *De Civitate Dei*, XI, 10. "For we do not say that the nature of the good is simple, because the Father alone possesses it, or the Son alone, or the Holy Ghost alone; nor do we say, with the

Returning to our point that *esse* is not subsistent, Hanby remarks that the non-subsistence of *esse* "protects both the transcendent fullness of God and the difference between *ipsum esse subsistens* and *esse creatum* [created being]." Regarding God's transcendence, "God remains all: the fullness of subsistent being to whom nothing can be added and from whom nothing can be subtracted." Regarding the difference between created being and self-subsisting being, "*esse creatum* is doubly distinguished from the *ipsum esse subsistens* of God by virtue of both its nonsubsistence and its subsequent dependence upon the beings whose being it is."[83] Because *esse* is not subsistent, "God can no longer in any way be regarded as the being of things." Therefore, in a radical way "God is placed over and above all cosmic being. . . . He is indeed 'the Wholly Other.'"[84]

We have seen in this section that the real distinction between *esse* and essence expresses the contingency of the world. As we already know, this is the negative aspect of the real distinction. I have explained in this section that *esse creatum* is not subsistent, because it depends on the *ipsum esse subsistens*. Because *esse creatum* is not subsistent, creation "does not explain its own existence."[85] If the world exists at all, it is due to God's generosity. The existence of the world is radically and ultimately gratuitous. Before turning to the positive aspect of the real distinction in the next section, I will discuss briefly some aspects regarding unity that follow from the consideration of being as gift.

As Hanby recognizes, "Being is gift in its inner structure" because "it is freely given by God" and because "it is given by the God whose being is his *essence* and whose essence is love." Furthermore, "Being only *is* itself in—or rather *as*—letting *another be itself*. And in the very act of letting another be (the act by which the other is), it simultaneously binds that

---

Sabellian heretics, that it is only nominally a Trinity, and has no real distinction of persons; but we say it is simple, because it is what it has [*quod habet hoc est*], with the exception of the relation of the persons to one another. For, in regard to this relation, it is true that the Father has a Son, and yet is not Himself the Son; and the Son has a Father, and is not Himself the Father. But, as regards Himself, irrespective of relation to the other, each is what He has [*hoc est quod habet*]; thus, He is in Himself living, for He has life, and is Himself the Life which He has" (Augustine, *The City of God* (2013), 318–19 (XI, 10)).

83. Hanby, *No God, No Science?* 357.

84. Balthasar, *Glory of the Lord IV*, 393–94.

85. Hanby, *No God, No Science?* 337.

other into community with all other things."[86] A similar point is made by Walker when he says that "to have a share in *esse commune* is at once to give oneself, and one's giving, to oneself and to others—and to receive oneself, and one's giving, from others."[87] Therefore, "Creatures are one, not because they fuse into sameness, but because their exercise of being, their self-constitution as subsistents, coincides with their involvement in a network of mutual giving and receiving."[88] There is truly a *uni-verse* because all beings participate in *esse commune*.[89] The concept of the universe is challenged by scientists with their alternative of multiverse. As Hanby remarks, the concept of multiverse is senseless because "inasmuch as other 'universes' are or were, they would belong to the one order of being (and causality) and thus would not truly be alternative universes, but simply heretofore unknown parts of the one universe. If they did not so belong, there could be no possibility of ever knowing about them."[90] I will discuss more thoroughly the question of the multiverse hypothesis in the next chapter.

The Real Distinction in Its Positive Sense

In this section I will continue discussing the real distinction, focusing on the positive aspect of it. As we already know, the positive sense of the real distinction can be characterized as the ineffable peculiarity of each thing granted by *esse*. The positive sense of the difference can be restated by saying that "*esse* is not just an empty facticity but an act or, rather, the act of all acts really distinct from form."[91] It is then fitting to start this section about the positive sense of the real distinction with the understanding of being as act. As discussed earlier, *esse* is not subsistent, because it needs a substance. In this sense, *esse* can be understood as an accident of a substance. However, the angelic doctor said that *esse* cannot be considered as an accident "as though related accidentally to a substance, but as the actuality of any substance."[92] In this regard, Chapp remarks that "although

86. Hanby, *No God, No Science?* 381.

87. Walker, "Personal Singularity," 473.

88. Walker, "Personal Singularity," 474.

89. Hanby, *No God, No Science?* 340 and 362.

90. Hanby, *No God, No Science?* 44–45n83.

91. Hanby, *No God, No Science?* 337.

92. Aquinas, *Quodlibetal* II, q. 2, a. 1, ad 2.

essence and existence are distinct, existence is not added to essence like an extrinsic accident. Existence inheres in its essential determination as the most interior act of the finite thing."[93]

The gift of existence (*esse*) given in the act of creation is not something given a posteriori to the essence. It is not the case that "a preexisting *essentia* is created and then put together with *esse*."[94] In fact, essence does not exist at all without *esse* or existence. "In no case does an essence conceived as possible have the ability as such to realize itself."[95] Hence, "Essence is a potency that awaits actualization in the act of existence."[96] Therefore, "There is a metaphysical priority or primacy of being over essence; this primacy cannot be temporal because we experience no existence or 'is' without some determined essence or nature."[97] This relates to the distinction between ontological and temporal origins. As indicated in the first chapter, cosmologists conceive of creation only as a question of temporal origins. These scientists conflate temporal and ontological origins, as we will see in the third chapter. This conflation prevents cosmologists from properly understanding what creation is.

The primacy of *esse* does not mean that it is the end of creation. Aquinas remarked that "*esse* is not what is created, it is not the subject of creation; instead, the terminus of the act of creation is the concretely subsisting *ens*."[98] However, "Substances do not procure *esse* for themselves out of their essences, but are created out of nothing as the subjects of *esse* at the very 'moment' that they receive it."[99] Only the reception of *esse*, "the act principle (*actus essendi*)," can make a "concrete entity (*ens*) to be realized in actuality."[100]

As Aquinas stated, *esse* is "the actuality of all acts, and therefore the perfection of all perfections." Therefore, "Being [*esse*] . . . signifies the highest perfection of all" because "act is always more perfect than potentiality."[101] The act of being (*actus essendi*) possesses "a simple and

---

93. Chapp, *The God of Covenant*, 154.

94. Bieler, "*Analogia Entis*," 325.

95. Balthasar, *Epilogue*, 45.

96. Chapp, *The God of Covenant*, 154.

97. Wilhelmsen, *Paradoxical Structure of Existence*, 47.

98. D. C. Schindler, "What's the Difference?" 19; Aquinas, *Summa Theologiae*, I, q. 45, a. 1, ad 2; ibid., I, q. 45, a. 4, ad 1.

99. Walker, "Personal Singularity," 468n11.

100. Wippel, *Metaphysical Thought of Aquinas*, 123.

101. Aquinas, *De Potentia Dei*, q. 7, a. 2, ad 9.

unlimited fullness. There is a plenitude and generosity in being, a 'more' which overflows both every particular being, and the totality of beings together." Therefore, "Being itself, as distinct from any particular being, appears as limitless source and ground."[102]

Hanby points out that, although *esse* is participated in by every entity, *esse* is nonetheless what ultimately makes every thing to be radically unique: "It is this maximum of ontological concreteness that is the particularity of the living *ens* . . . that led us to characterize *esse* not as mere facticity but as the act-fullness—the 'izzing'—operative in all subsequent acts that follow upon being."[103] Therefore, the doctrine of creation recognizes the particularity of every creature in the world. This recognition is particularly important for our modern world because it "has lost sight of the deep mystery that is the existence of each individual object. Under the sway of a mechanistic view of nature the individual objects of our world are reduced to metaphysical flat realities whose full depth of meaning as concrete individuals is swallowed up by the world of cold abstraction." Due to the empiricism governing our modern world-view, "the mystery and beauty of concrete entities is bleached white by the typological imperative of scientific classification, e.g. this particular daisy is merely an example of 'type A daisies' and this type of dog is merely an example of its species and so forth."[104] However, as Balthasar said,

102. Healy, "The World as Gift," 398.

103. Hanby, *No God, No Science?* 351. Scholasticism has maintained that Aquinas defended *signate matter* as the principle of individuation. However, this affirmation has been questioned among modern scholars in recent years. For example, Joseph Owens has defended *esse* as the principle of individuation in Aquinas (Owens, "Thomas Aquinas," 173–94). Montague Brown criticizes Owen's position and defends *form* as the principle of individuation in Aquinas (Brown, "Aquinas and Individuation," 167–85). According to Hanby, the incommunicable uniqueness of every creature cannot be attributed solely to its matter, not even to its form. "It must be attributable, ultimately to . . . [its] being, though the paradoxical relation of being to essence . . . does not deny matter or form their particularizing roles" (Hanby, *No God, No Science?* 351). "Since *esse* does not subsist (in us) outside of the form-matter composite, its primary place of individuation does not take place outside of that composite and thus does not deny either form or matter its role in individuating the creature. If form, matter, and *esse* are not elements but principles that only 'are' in and as a composite through their mutual relation to the others, then all three are involved in individuation and the question becomes one of relative priority" (ibid., 369n48).

104. Chapp, *The God of Covenant*, 201. As discussed earlier, modern science loses sight of the interior horizon of things. This is slightly different from individuality though related to it.

If each and every thing were nothing more than an "instance of
..." or a kind of algebraic "x" that could be exchanged for other
entities without loss, then things would possess absolutely no
intrinsic value of their own as individuals. By the same token,
they would have no claim whatsoever to any sphere that might
be their own by right or reserved to them alone. Any knower
who grasped the essence of the species of which they are exem-
plars would immediately comprehend at the same time every
individual entity that fell under it. . . . In a world such as this,
existence would no longer have any meaning, for being would
have lost the property that alone gives the possession of being its
desirability: unrepeatability and, therefore, interiority.[105]

The previous section showed that *esse commune* is responsible for
the unity of all things. We have just seen that *esse commune* is the ultimate
source of the peculiarity of each thing. Therefore, "*Esse commune* has the
paradoxical quality of being common to all things and most peculiar to
each thing, making it simultaneously responsible for what Adrian Walker
calls 'personal singularity' and the ground for the unity of the cosmos."[106]
Hanby explains that causality requires the two paradoxical aspects of *esse*:
unity and peculiarity.[107] "In order for a causal transaction to occur, there
must not only be a shared order of being between cause and effect; there
must also be a genuine existential *difference* between them." Therefore,
"Effects must represent a real novelty over and above their causes, not
simply in virtue of the formal distribution of their material elements
[modern science does not go beyond this point] but in virtue of their
being at all."[108]

Balthasar emphasized that the gift of *esse* granted by creation makes
every creature a bottomless mystery because *esse*, most proper to a thing,
is grounded in God. Every created being "is groundless to the extent
that it does not have its ground in itself, to the extent, in other words,
that it breaks through its own ultimate ground into the depth of God's
ultimately inexhaustible mystery."[109] Therefore, "Things are always more
than themselves, and their constantly self-surpassing transcendence
opens ultimately onto an idea that is, not the things themselves, but God

105. Balthasar, *Theo-Logic I*, 81.

106. Hanby, *No God, No Science?* 340; Walker, "Personal Singularity," 458–59n3.

107. Hanby, *No God, No Science?* 340.

108. Hanby, *No God, No Science?* 341. See ibid., 342–44.

109. Balthasar, *Theo-Logic I*, 231.

and their measure in God."[110] Because of this, Balthasar remarked that every worldly being is an epiphany of God. "Along with their own being, God has given to all created things their own operation, and this includes a spontaneity in manifesting themselves outwardly, an echo, however distant, of his infinite, majestic freedom."[111] According to David L. Schindler, "Worldly realities find their true meaning, precisely as worldly—or indeed 'natural'—in their character simultaneously and intrinsically as epiphanies of God."[112]

The bottomless mystery implied in every creature cannot be avoided by the natural sciences, because "at the heart of each thing is the mystery of being, and at the heart of the mystery of being is the mystery of God."[113] The bottomless character of being is always presupposed by science and it is the continuing positive source of scientific activity. Science can never get to the bottom of reality because it is bottomless. The depth dimension of being "ensures that the task of the sciences is interminable."[114] Therefore, the idea of a final exhaustive theory of everything "is ruled out by the nature of being as such."[115] Even more, "The scientific goal of exhaustive intelligibility and comprehensive command appears not only as hopeless but as *contra naturam*."[116] Although the depth dimension of being cannot be avoided by science because it is interminable, science is unable to see the depth dimension of being because of its "ideal of exhaustive intelligibility in the form of mathematical analysis and experimental control."[117] Because of that ideal, science cannot help "knowing the individual . . . [as] a matter of an endlessly repeatable application of knowledge of the universal, in the same way that a mathematical theorem

110. Balthasar, *Theo-Logic I*, 59.

111. Balthasar, *Theo-Logic I*, 82.

112. David L. Schindler, "Trinity, Creation," 409. "Schmemann, in agreement with the argument of Henri de Lubac (for example, in *Corpus Mysticum*), points out how Christian theology . . . has itself contributed to the draining of the world of its structurally 'symbolic' character. . . . See Schmemann, *For the Life of the World*, 128–129" (David L. Schindler, "Trinity, Creation," 409n11).

113. Hanby, *No God, No Science?* 363.

114. Hanby, *No God, No Science?* 381.

115. Hanby, *No God, No Science?* 382.

116. Hanby, *No God, No Science?* 363.

117. Hanby, *No God, No Science?* 385.

can be applied to a number of objects or a cookie cutter can be used to make as many cookies as one wants."[118]

As we have seen, the gift of existence given by the creator to every creature is a manifestation of divine generosity. This gift of existence is something visible in the creature. *Esse* cannot help but be visible in the mere act of being (*actus essendi*). This *actus essendi* "is the source of everything that is in the creature"[119] and it is manifested in every action of the creature because the creature *is* always. Balthasar stated that every being, just by the fact of existing, makes an ontological confession.[120] This aspect could be called the cataphatic aspect of the mystery of being. The luminous manifestation of being is, at the same time, mysterious and does not ever allow us full apprehension of the creature. "Existence is being's most irrefutable revelation, yet, because existing is such a marvel, it is at the very same time being's most impenetrable veil."[121] The concrete act of being is not reducible or communicable. A creature cannot be replaced by anything else. "The truth of any being will always be infinitely richer and greater than the knower is capable of grasping."[122] The inexhaustibility of the mystery of being will be referred to as the apophatic aspect of the mystery of being.[123] Balthasar affirmed that the apophatic character of creation is more apparent as we ascend in the scale of being: "The worthier and weightier existing things become, the more they are surrounded by a protective veil that withdraws them, like something sacred, from the grasping hands of the profane."[124]

118. Balthasar, *Theo-Logic I*, 81.

119. Schmitz, *The Gift*, 109.

120. "A dog, a cat, and even a human being confess their essence simply by existing: they cannot elude this ontological confession. Insofar as they exist, insofar as their essence appears, they are summoned and incited to a confession that has always already begun and that they have only to continue through spontaneous vital or spiritual acts" (Balthasar, *Theo-Logic I*, 207).

121. Balthasar, *Theo-Logic I*, 107.

122. Balthasar, *Theo-Logic I*, 88.

123. The cataphatic and apophatic characters of the mystery of being proceed from the cataphatic and apophatic discourse of the mystery of God. It is interesting to note that the divine doctrine is not apophatic because "of some false Kantian humility about the limits of reason but because of the *kataphatic* fullness of divine being, which remains forever in excess to what can be thought or said about it" (Hanby, *No God, No Science?* 321). To put it another way, "*apophatic* clarifications are not simple negations of course. Rather, they are the reverse side of the corresponding *cataphatic* assertion of God's superabundant fullness" (ibid., 307).

124. Balthasar, *Theo-Logic I*, 102.

Chapp, describing Balthasar, remarks that the mystery of being should not lead "to a radical agnosticism about the possibility of knowing and understanding existence."[125] This is the case because "in every existent ... the deep incommunicability of its inward interiority is further characterized by an *eros* toward exteriorization and communication."[126] That which is communicated in the exteriorization of the existent is connected with its interiority. "For Balthasar, there is a deep interconnection between the interior essence of a thing and its outward appearance, between its interiority and its exteriorization." Although "the appearance is not merely identical with the essence, ... what appears is a reliable guide to knowing the inner essence of an object." Furthermore, "The appearance is not an epiphenomenon of no importance to our knowledge of the object."[127] Therefore, "The habit of modern science since Newton and Galileo to divide reality into primary and secondary qualities is a violation of being. The dualism between what I perceive with my senses and apprehend with my intellect and the way reality is in itself leads directly to the modern reductionist world-view where nothing is truly real unless it is quantifiable."[128] As we saw in the first chapter, scienticism offers a falsified image of nature. We will have the opportunity to notice this in the third chapter, when I describe some bizarre and unintelligible cosmological theories.

In this section I am dealing with the positive aspect of the real distinction. Up to this point, I have shown that the gift of being (*esse*) speaks about the ontological constitution of the world. More concretely, we have seen that each being is intelligibly unique, irreplaceable, a bottomless mystery that, although it communicates itself by the mere act of existing, cannot be exhausted by our apprehension. Each being is granted a certain depth by the mere act of existing.

125. Chapp, *The God of Covenant*, 202; Balthasar, *Theo-Logic I*, 85.

126. Chapp, *The God of Covenant*, 202; Balthasar, *Theo-Logic II*, 228–32. In his explanation of Balthasar, Chapp points out that "*co-extensive* with the erotic drive of nature to move from interiority to an exteriorization of appearance in a variety of forms, there is also what can only be characterized as a kenotic, agapic, oblate side of nature. Each existent thing may exist for itself but this should not be read in a monadic, self-enclosed manner. Lower forms of existence are taken up and integrated into higher levels, and all of nature's forms, including human beings, pass away into the dissolution of death, making way for new forms to arise" (Chapp, *The God of Covenant*, 206; Balthasar, *Theo-Logic II*, 229).

127. Chapp, *The God of Covenant*, 202–3.

128. Chapp, *The God of Covenant*, 203.

The scientific method is unable to see "the depth dimension of being"[129] because it is based on "a primary *ontological reduction* of nature,"[130] which is "the reduction of being from act to brute facticity."[131] As a result, modern science can only offer a reductive understanding of the world. It is important to notice that this reductive understanding correlates to the reductive image of God entailed in theological extrinsicism. This extrinsicism reduces "God from *ipsum esse subsistens* to a finite object juxtaposed to and in competition with the world."[132]

As outlined above, at the center of the real distinction "is the theological awareness of a fundamental distinction between God and the world."[133] Before finishing this section, I want to explain how the real distinction conveys not only the radical difference between God and creation but also the analogical likeness between them. For this purpose, I need to deal with the richness and poverty of being. Balthasar summarized these two aspects in this way: "Being itself . . . is the most comprehensive and thus richest of all concepts, fullness pure and simple (since nothing except nothingness can come from nothing), while, on the other side, it is the poorest, because every determination seems to be lacking to it."[134] By now, it is clear that "although each existent depends on being for its entrance into reality, there is a reciprocal dependence of being upon the existent to attain subsistence."[135] In this regard, Balthasar also said that "the fact that an existent can only become actual through participation in the act of Being points to the complementary antithesis that the fullness of Being attains actuality only in the existent."[136] Therefore, *esse* "is simultaneously rich and poor; rich in its fullness which continually overflows the limits of every existent, and poor in that it stands in need of the limited existent to attain reality."[137]

The affirmation of the richness and poverty of *esse* is linked with the Thomistic affirmation of *esse* as "something complete and simple,

---

129. Balthasar, *Theo-Logic I*, 16. Balthasar references in this paragraph Pieper, *Silence of St. Thomas*.

130. Jonas, "Practical Uses of Theory," 200.

131. Hanby, *No God, No Science?* 334.

132. Hanby, *No God, No Science?* 334.

133. Chapp, *The God of Covenant*, 153.

134. Balthasar, *Epilogue*, 45.

135. Healy, "The World as Gift," 398.

136. Balthasar, *Glory of the Lord V*, 619.

137. Healy, "The World as Gift," 398–99.

yet non-subsistent [*aliquid completum et simplex sed non subsistens*]."[138] This characterization of *esse* is used by Ferdinand Ulrich to describe *esse* as both rich and poor. The German philosopher relates the *completum et simplex* aspect with ontological wealth, and the *non subsistens* aspect with ontological poverty. These two aspects "do not contradict each other. They are, rather, the two necessary aspects of a single phenomenon. The nonsubsistence of *esse* shows that it is always, already poured out into substantial beings, and it is poured out as a *completum et simplex*, as what is common to all that exists."[139] *Esse* is perfect, but it "has its perfection only in that which is other than itself, i.e., in the beings it makes be. Its own perfection is always already given away, or more adequately, possessed as having been given away. Thus, the perfect wealth of *esse* is coincident with a complete poverty."[140] In the unity of wealth and poverty, "*esse* reflects in the end the life of the Trinity, in which each person possesses the fullness of the divine nature (wealth) only in ecstatic and 'kenotic' openness (poverty) toward the other two persons."[141] Balthasar, too, had already insisted on this aspect:

> God-given Being is both fullness and poverty at the same time: fullness as Being without limit, poverty modelled ultimately on God Himself, because He knows no holding on to Himself, poverty in the act of Being which is given out, which *as* gift delivers itself without defence (because here too it does not hold on to itself) to the finite entities. But equally, the created entities are simultaneously fullness and poverty: fullness in the power to shelter and to tend (as "shepherd of Being") the gift of fullness of Being within themselves, however "poor" they may be on account of their limitation, and poverty again in a double sense in as much as the container experiences its inability to scoop out the whole ocean with its small bowl and, instructed by this experience, comprehends the letting-go of Being—as letting-be and letting stream, handing on further—as the inner fulfilment of the finite entity.[142]

We can see now how the real distinction shows not only the radical difference between God and creatures but also an analogical likeness

---

138. Aquinas, *De Potentia Dei*, q. 1, a. 1, co.

139. Bieler, "*Analogia Entis*," 322–23.

140. D. C. Schindler, "What's the Difference?" 19.

141. Bieler, "*Analogia Entis*," 323.

142. Balthasar, *Glory of the Lord V*, 626–27.

between God and creatures. In its unity of wealth and poverty, *esse* is an image of the life of the Trinity. The very distinction whereby creatures are differentiated from God as not being their being is also, paradoxically, an image of God as the Trinity, where unity and differentiation coincide.[143] Hanby also remarks that, "while there is no 'real distinction' in the simplicity of God, the distinction in creatures is not simply negative, but a positive image of the *identity* of essence and existence, unity and difference, in the divine being understood as triune love."[144] That is to say, "The world is an image of the God who is love . . . in its ever-greater difference *from* God," because "the unity of essence and existence in God is most profoundly reflected in creatures for whom the real *distinction* between essence and existence is greatest."[145]

The Constitutive Relation of Creation

The real distinction between essence and existence entails creatures' radical dependency on God; for all created beings participate in God's existence. Thomas stated that "everything other than God . . . must be referred to Him as the cause of its being [*causam essendi*]."[146] Therefore, the existence of every creature points towards God and relates it to him. This is ultimately why creation was characterized by Aquinas as "the very dependency of the created act of being [*esse creati*] upon the principle from which it is produced. And thus, creation is a kind of relation; so that nothing prevents its being in the creature as its subject."[147] This concept of relation is very important for the study of creation as a doctrine of God; the concept also gives us an understanding of the ontological constitution of the world. For this reason, in this section I will deal with the concept of relation and two aspects related to it: creaturely autonomy and causality.

Thomas clearly noted that the relation between the creator and creatures is not symmetrical: "Since therefore God is outside the whole order of creation, and all creatures are ordered to Him, and not conversely, it is manifest that creatures are really related to God Himself; whereas in

143. Hanby, *No God, No Science?* 362.

144. Hanby, *No God, No Science?* 364n5.

145. Hanby, *No God, No Science?* 365n6.

146. Aquinas, *Summa Contra Gentiles*, lib. 2, cap. 15, n. 6. *Essendi* is the genitive case of *essendus*, which is the gerundive (working as a gerund) of *esse*.

147. Aquinas, *Summa Contra Gentiles*, lib. 2, cap. 18, n. 2.

God there is no real relation to creatures, but a relation only in idea [rational relation], inasmuch as creatures are referred to Him."[148] The fact that "God is not really related to the creature" is due to the fact that "God does not depend upon the creature in any way, nor is He affected by the creature." On the contrary, a creature is really related to God because it is "completely and constantly dependent upon the creator."[149] The Thomistic distinction between real and rational relation is intended to protect God's absoluteness and immutability.[150] In other words, the point is to

148. Aquinas, *Summa Theologiae*, I, q. 13, a. 7, co. Thomas used in *Scriptum Super Libros Sententiarum* (lib. 1, d. 30, q. 1, a. 3, ad 3) an analogy from knowledge to explain that the relation of creation is real in the creature, but only logical in God. "Knowledge is real in the knower but rational or logical in the known because the *esse spirituale* in which the relation of knowledge is founded is in the knower but not in the known" (Wilhelmsen, "Creation as a Relation," 109). Wilhelmsen added that "the foundation for my being related to the wall I know is not the wall as knowable prior to my knowing it. There is nothing in the wall which could found a relation of *my* knowing it. The foundation must be located in the knower, in my power of intellection. In turn, the wall remains unaffected or unaltered in my knowing it; the wall, not being the foundation but rather the term of a relation, is not really related to me as knower" (ibid., 109–10).

149. William Carroll, "Aquinas on Creation," 80. "In the creature, the real relation to the Creator has two elements: it is *ad aliud*, i.e., dependent upon God, and it is an attribute inhering in the creature as in a subject" (ibid.). Therefore, "the fact that creation is a real relation in the creature . . . indicates both that creation is prior to the creature and that creation is posterior to the creature." On the one hand, "creation is prior to the creature, for the creature's relation *ad aliud* is a relation of complete dependence upon the Creator, and such dependence is absolutely prior to everything else in the creature." On the other hand, "creation is posterior to the creature, for creation inheres in the creature like an essential attribute" (ibid., 80n42).

150. Nicholas Healy questions the denial of God's real relation to the world, "*not* by denying the perfect fullness of divine being which the denial of real relation is supposed to protect, but by asking whether 'receptivity' can be included among those perfections" (Hanby, *No God, No Science?* 326n20; Healy, *Eschatology of Balthasar*, 19–90). In the book just mentioned, Healy concludes that receptivity is "an analogous perfection of God" (ibid., 213). However, "the idea that receptivity is also a divine perfection . . . is made difficult by the fact that the philosophical tradition stemming from Aristotle has tended to conflate receptivity and passive potency. On this supposition, receptivity is excluded by definition from the *ratio* of the *actus essendi*" (ibid, 75). Hanby explains that, "by explicating the divine essence as love, the doctrine of the Trinity reforms the Greek conception of act, making it at once self-contained and transitive, active and receptive, without compromising its immutable simplicity" (Hanby, *No God, No Science?* 318). In this regard, Healy remarks that, "insofar as the perfections of the *actus essendi* are revealed in a communion of love, receptivity is intrinsic to the fullness of act" (Healy, *Eschatology of Balthasar*, 185).

assert that creatures have their origin absolutely in God and that God does not need the world in order to be God.[151]

The divine transcendence clearly establishes that God is not a part of the world. Thomas affirmed that, although God is not part of a creature's essence, he is nonetheless present in every creature through being (*esse*). "As long as a thing has being, God must be present to it, according to its mode of being. But being is innermost in each thing and most fundamentally inherent in all things since it is formal in respect of everything found in a thing. . . . Hence it must be that God is in all things, and innermostly."[152] Therefore, God "is in all things as the cause of the being of all things."[153] God is the cause of being of a creature, not only "at the beginning of the creature's duration" but also "all throughout its duration. The creature is always of itself literally nothing and therefore is in constant need of being created out of nothing."[154] Consequently, the relation of creation is not only significant at the beginning of existence but also during the whole existence of every creature. There is no distinction between creation and conservation because "God does not create things by one action and preserve them by another. . . . God's action which is the direct cause of a thing's existence is not distinct as the principle of its being and as the principle of its continuance in being [*principium essendi et essendi continuationem*]."[155] In order to highlight the distinctive character of the relation of creation, Aquinas compared it to the relation a house has with its builder, which is an artificial relation.[156] "Once the coming-to-be of the house is complete, the house ceases to have any relation of dependence upon its builder; the builder could die, and the house would continue to stand." However, if the relation of a creature with God were to cease, the creature would end its own existence. "The Creator's causality

---

151. Hanby affirms that, "in order ultimately to secure transcendence, it is necessary to reconcile the perfection of act, its unity and indivisibility, so as to render it both 'transitive' and self-contained at once, so that it *includes* infinite difference, and indeed receptivity, within infinite perfection, unity, and simplicity" (Hanby, *No God, No Science?* 313; see Healy, *Eschatology of Balthasar*, 15–90).

152. Aquinas, *Summa Theologiae*, I, q. 8, a. 1, co.

153. Aquinas, *Summa Theologiae*, I, q. 8, a. 1, ad 1.

154. Baldner and William Carroll, "Analysis of Aquinas' Writings," 42–43; Aquinas, *Scriptum Super Libros Sententiarum*, lib. 1, d. 37, q. 1, a.1, co.

155. Aquinas, *De Potentia Dei*, q. 5, a. 1, ad 2.

156. Aquinas, *Scriptum Super Libros Sententiarum*, lib. 1, d. 37, q. 1, a.1, co.

must be continual, and of the same kind, all throughout the creature's existence."[157]

Because "God is the source of my being and the being of all else, then relation to God is just so far *given with* and *constitutive of* being."[158] Therefore, "This relation to God cannot but accompany each being everywhere and at every moment and indeed from its deepest depths."[159] In other words, the relation implied in creation is "an intrinsic and constitutive relation. . . . As such, this relation is foundational for and recapitulated within all other relations that the creature may undergo."[160] Hence, the relation between the world and God posited by creation can be labeled as the *analogatum princeps* [prime analogate] for worldly relations.[161] As a result, it is impossible to know the world without considering the relation between the world and God.[162] According to Balthasar, "The inner-worldly receives its definitive interpretation in the light of the God-world relation."[163]

It is clear now that the intimate and constitutive relation of a creature with God preserves God's immanence in the world. In "the dualistic conception of the God-world relation" that dominates the scientific consciousness, "the notions of transcendence and immanence . . . are played off against each other as opposites."[164] The Christian doctrine of creation *ex nihilo* helps us to see that divine immanence is not an opposite of divine transcendence, but a consequence of it.[165] If divine transcendence did not

157. Baldner and William Carroll, "Analysis of Aquinas' Writings," 43; Aquinas, *Scriptum Super Libros Sententiarum*, lib. 1, d. 37, q. 1, a.1, co.

158. David L. Schindler, "The Given as Gift," 53. See Pontifical Council of Justice and Peace, *Compendium of Social Doctrine*, n. 109.

159. David L. Schindler, "The Given as Gift," 54.

160. Hanby, *No God, No Science?* 322. This exemplifies the distinction between ontological and temporal origins, and this is why one temporal instant is as good as another for seeing what creation is. Creation can only be seen or thought if being is a question in itself. The incapacity of modern science to understand the question of being has dreadful consequences: the falsification of nature, the elimination of an order of being distinct from time, and the conflation of temporal and ontological origins.

161. See David L. Schindler, "The Given as Gift," 91.

162. Pannenberg, "Theological Questions to Scientists," 66.

163. Balthasar, *Theo-Logic I*, 232.

164. Chapp, *The God of Covenant*, 2.

165. "Genuine transcendence cannot be contrasted with immanence because the very possibility of such a contrast places them within the same order of reality, which makes transcendence self-negating. Genuine transcendence, to the contrary, *implies* immanence" (Hanby, *No God, No Science?* 55). "A transcendence set in opposition to

allow divine immanence, then that divine transcendence would be compromised by the real opposition offered by the world, in the same way that coeval matter would hinder divine transcendence. Balthasar recognized that the "intimacy of God in the creature [immanence] . . . is only made possible by the distinction between God and *esse* [transcendence]."[166] In other words, "It is precisely when the creature feels itself to be separate in being from God that it knows itself to be the most immediate object of God's love and concern; and it is precisely when its essential finitude shows it to be something quite different from God that it knows that, as a real being, it has bestowed upon it that most extravagant gift—participation in the real being of God."[167]

The relation of the creature to God is not opposed to the autonomy of the creature. On the contrary, "The creature's relation to God is the necessary anterior condition for realizing the proper integrity of creaturely identity and power: . . . the former relation, in other words, is directly not inversely related to the latter integrity."[168] As Hanby recognizes, "Natural beings and processes have their own freedom and integrity not in spite but just *because* God is immediately present to the world, indeed closer to it than it is to itself, granting it the *esse* through which it is able to be all that it is."[169] In other words, God's immanence in the creature does not threaten the integrity of the creature but secures it. This is the case because "what God gives to the creature is precisely the creature's *own being* as such. This of course means granting agency and power to the creature in (and for) itself."[170] Therefore, the autonomy of created beings includes autonomous causality. "Since creatures do have their own being, they are able to be true, autonomous causes."[171]

Indeed, creatures are autonomous causes because "the first cause [God], by the pre-eminence of its goodness, gives other beings not only their existence, but also their existence as causes."[172] It is interesting to

immanence, a unity set in opposition to multiplicity is already a transcendent unity that has been brought into a 'real relation' with the world" (ibid., 74).

166. Balthasar, *Glory of the Lord IV*, 403.

167. Balthasar, *Glory of the Lord IV*, 404.

168. David L. Schindler, "Trinity, Creation," 428.

169. Hanby, *No God, No Science?* 323.

170. David L. Schindler, "The Given as Gift," 88.

171. Baldner and William Carroll, "Analysis of Aquinas' Writings," 49; Aquinas, *Scriptum Super Libros Sententiarum*, lib. 2, d. 1, q. 1, a. 4.

172. Aquinas, *De Veritate*, q. 11, a. 1, co. (English translation taken from Aquinas,

note that "a secondary cause is no less genuine a cause because of its dependence upon the primary cause, for the latter's causation is precisely what constitutes the former's causation; the primary cause is a cause of causing."[173] As a cause of causing, the primary cause is not something extrinsic to the creature. Thomas explained that "the operation of the Creator pertains more to what is intimate in a thing than does the operation of any secondary causes." Consequently, the fact "that a creature is the cause of some other creature does not preclude that God operate immediately in all things, insofar as His power is like an intermediary that joins the power of any secondary cause with its effect."[174]

Aquinas also observed that "the causality of the secondary cause is rooted in the causality of the primary cause" because "the power of a creature cannot achieve its effect except by the power of the Creator, from whom is all power, preservation of power, and order [of cause] to effect."[175] Commenting on this passage, Hanby states that "creation, far from being a threat to the integrity of immanent causality, is inherent within and necessary for causality as such."[176] The extrinsic theology inherent in modern science understands creation "as an extrinsic cause modifying the world" and a rival to natural processes because it is unable to see creation "as the precondition of causality" and "as its ontological structure."[177] This is a key point for this book, which I will pick up in the next chapter when I deal with concrete extrinsicist scholars, both scientists and theologians. When they declare "incompatibility between divine omnipotence and creaturely causality," they are declaring their "failure to understand divine transcendence."[178] The distinction between the primary cause and secondary causes is a consequence of divine transcendence. Because extrinsic theology is unable to properly understand divine transcendence, it is unable to understand the distinction between primary and secondary causality.

It is important to note that primary causality does not rival secondary causality because "divine causality and creaturely causality function

Truth, 81).

173. Shanley, "Divine Causation," 108.

174. Aquinas, *Scriptum Super Libros Sententiarum*, lib. 2, d. 1, q. 1, a. 4, co.

175. Aquinas, *Scriptum Super Libros Sententiarum*, lib. 2, d. 1, q. 1, a. 4, co.

176. Hanby, *No God, No Science?* 338.

177. Hanby, *No God, No Science?* 338.

178. William Carroll, "Aquinas on Creation," 87.

at different metaphysical levels."[179] Aquinas said that "one action does not proceed from two agents of the same order. But nothing hinders the same action from proceeding from a primary and a secondary agent."[180] When a concrete effect is attributed to God and to a natural agent, it is erroneous to affirm that the effect "is partly done by God, and partly by the natural agent; rather, it is wholly done by both, according to a different way, just as the same effect is wholly attributed to the instrument and also wholly to the principal agent."[181] Thanks to the different metaphysical levels, we can say that "any created effect comes totally and immediately from God as the transcendent primary cause and totally and immediately from the creature as secondary cause."[182]

Creation and the Trinity

As formerly mentioned, the goal of this chapter is to explain the doctrine of creation in its dual aspect as a doctrine both of God and of the metaphysical constitution of the world. In the following chapter, I will use this doctrine of creation as the foundation for criticizing the extrinsicist theology present in modern cosmology. As I will point out later on, the extrinsicist theology inherent in modern science is ultimately un-trinitarian, at least in its atheistic forms. The mystery of the Trinity is not a factor in what atheistic cosmologists mean by creation, which is an indication that they have not understood what creation is. This is the case because creation can only be understood from a trinitarian perspective. This is the affirmation that I want to defend in this section. As in previous sections, I will use the contributions of Aquinas and the development of Thomistic thought made by Balthasar.

Aquinas defended the necessity of a trinitarian doctrine of God to understand rightly what creation is:

> The knowledge of the divine persons . . . [is] necessary for the right idea of creation. The fact of saying that God made all things by His Word excludes the error of those who say that God produced things by necessity. When we say that in Him there is a procession of love, we show that God produced creatures

179. William Carroll, "Aquinas on Creation," 86.

180. Aquinas, *Summa Theologiae*, I, q. 105, a. 5, ad 2.

181. Aquinas, *Summa Contra Gentiles*, lib. 3, cap. 70, n. 8.

182. Shanley, "Divine Causation," 108.

> not because He needed them, nor because of any other extrinsic reason, but on account of the love of His own goodness.[183]

For the universal doctor, "The affirmation of creation by the Word shows the wisdom of God's creative activity, by excluding the thesis of a necessary emanatism; the affirmation of creation by the Holy Spirit [Love] guarantees for its part the free generosity of divine activity."[184]

More importantly, the central thesis of Aquinas' trinitarian doctrine of creation is the following: "The eternal processions of the persons are the cause and the reason [*causa et ratio*] of the production of creatures."[185] The terms *causa* and *ratio* were completed by Thomas to make his affirmation more precise. He explained "that the procession of the persons is the origin (*origo*) of the procession of creatures [*Super Sent.*, lib. 1, d. 32, q. 1, a. 3], or the principle (*principium*) of creatures [*Super Sent.*, lib. 1, d. 35, *div. text.*]; the procession of creatures has as its exemplar (*exemplatur, exemplata*) the procession of the divine persons [*Super Sent.*, lib. 1, d. 29, q. 1, a. 2, qc. 2; *De Pot.*, q. 10, a. 2, s. c. 2]."[186] If "the Trinitarian processions are the cause (exemplar, efficient, and final) of the procession of creatures, . . . [then] the full and precise understanding of creation . . . requires the knowledge of the procession of the divine persons."[187] In other words, creation is only intelligible from a trinitarian understanding of God. Therefore, the mystery of the Trinity is not an add-on to the doctrine of creation. It is fundamentally necessary for it. This is a remarkable point because, as I have said before, the extrinsicist theology inherent in modern science is ultimately un-trinitarian, at least in its atheistic forms.

For Aquinas, the intra-trinitarian processions are not only the cause of the existence of creatures, but also the cause of their multiplicity. "Every procession and multiplication of creatures is caused by the procession of the distinct divine persons."[188] The diversity within the unity present in the Trinity is the cause for the multiplicity of creation. "One cannot emphasize more forcefully the positive value of the multiplicity of crea-

183. Aquinas, *Summa Theologiae*, I, q. 32, a. 1, ad 3.

184. Emery, "Trinity and Creation," 70–71.

185. Aquinas, *Scriptum Super Libros Sententiarum*, lib. 1, d. 14, q. 1, a. 1, co.; Emery, "Trinity and Creation," 59.

186. Emery, "Trinity and Creation," 59.

187. Emery, "Trinity and Creation," 60.

188. Aquinas, *Scriptum Super Libros Sententiarum*, lib. 1, d. 26, q. 2, a. 2, ad. 2. (English translation taken from Emery, "Trinity and Creation," 72).

tures; . . . [Thomas did] not conceive of plurality as a decline from unity, but to the contrary, as a participation in the fullness of the trinitarian life of God."[189]

Assuming in a critical way the Thomistic tradition, Balthasar also affirmed the difference within the Trinity as the ultimate cause for the goodness of worldly difference: "How could worldly difference in its *maior dissimilitudo* with respect to the divine identity not ultimately be deemed a degradation, rather than something 'very good', if this difference did not have a root in God himself that was compatible with his identity?" To put it another way, "A world marked by difference that springs from a God utterly devoid of it can only be the degraded result of a fall, as every religion that has attempted a speculative penetration of the God-world relation has inevitably concluded."[190] Therefore, only a trinitarian doctrine of God is able to give a positive account of creaturely difference. This affirmation is extremely important for our understanding of creation as the ontological constitution of the world.

As we already know, creation is only intelligible in the light of the mystery of the Trinity. Only a trinitarian understanding of the divine absoluteness can give a positive account of the existence of creation. Only the mystery of the Trinity offers "the 'resolution' to the paradox of creation: how the world can have being 'in its own right', be somehow 'more than God', and be the image of divine goodness and love in its very difference from God, without any of this compromising the transcendent plenitude of the divine being."[191] This is the central problem we are addressing here. In Balthasar's words: "*Where* can there be a place for the world if God is, after all, 'the entire ocean of being' (John Damascene)?"[192] And this is the answer that Balthasar offered: "The infinite distance between the world and God is grounded in the other, prototypical distance between God and God."[193] As Chapp remarks, "We are able to call God 'other' precisely

189. Emery, "Trinity and Creation," 73.

190. Balthasar, *Theo-Logic II*, 184.

191. Hanby, *No God, No Science?* 319.

192. Balthasar, *Theo-Drama II*, 262; Hanby, *No God, No Science?* 311–12. "The [central] question is this. How do we conceive of the superabundant unity of divine being so as not to render the being of the world and its integrity, novelty, and freedom as merely apparent? And conversely, how do we conceive of the integrity, novelty, and freedom of created being in a way that is adequate to their reality and yet does not deny the transcendent absoluteness of divine being?" (ibid.).

193. Balthasar, *Theo-Drama II*, 266.

because of the distance and relationality within God himself. . . . The otherness of creation is grounded within the spaciousness of the Trinitarian relations in such a way that the integrity of the world as existing in its own right is preserved."[194]

Let us now investigate how Balthasar arrived at this idea of the spaciousness of the trinitarian relations. According to the Swiss theologian, the triune God can be characterized as "the absolute freedom of self-possession" that understands "itself, according to its own nature, as limitless self-giving." The identification of absolute self-possession with infinite self-giving is not the result of an external imposition on God's nature. On the contrary, "It *is* the result of its own nature, so much so that, apart from this self-giving, it would not be itself." Indeed, "In generating the Son," the Father "is *always* himself by giving himself. The Son, too, is always himself by allowing himself to be generated and by allowing the Father to do with him as he pleases. The Spirit is always himself by understanding his 'I' as the 'We' of Father and Son, by being 'expropriated' for the sake of what is most proper to them."[195] The absolute freedom of the divine persons implies that, "in what takes place between the divine 'hypostases,' there must be *areas of infinite freedom* that are *already there* and do not allow everything to be compressed into an airless unity and identity." The infinite intimacy between divine persons does not annul the distinction between them. "Something like infinite 'duration' and infinite 'space' must be attributed to the acts of reciprocal love so that the life of the *communio*, of fellowship, can develop."[196]

The spaciousness between divine persons provides "room for the world by incorporating it into the intra-divine relations in a manner which does not simply divinize the world in a univocal sense: i.e. the world does not simply blend into God and become moments within the Trinitarian relations."[197] This is the case because, as Balthasar said, "God himself is always greater than himself on the basis of his triune freedom. Only in this way can the creature endure being totally and utterly naked before God." Therefore, "Finite freedom can really fulfill itself in infinite freedom and in no other way. If *letting-be* belongs to the nature of infinite freedom . . . there is no danger of finite freedom, which cannot fulfill itself

194. Chapp, *The God of Covenant*, 167.
195. Balthasar, *Theo-Drama II*, 256.
196. Balthasar, *Theo-Drama II*, 257.
197. Chapp, *The God of Covenant*, 166.

on its own account . . . , becoming alienated from itself in the realm of the Infinite."[198] It is important to note here that "the ultimate foundation for such a taking up of the world into God without becoming ontologically confused with God is the hypostatic union of the divine and human natures in Christ."[199]

The inclusion of the finite world into the triune God should not be conceived "in terms of a contracting of God in order to create a space for the finite within God."[200] Each divine person does not need the other two to retreat in order to be himself; each divine hypostasis lets the other two be. "No one hypostasis wishes to be the other two. This is not a retreat or resignation: it is the positive form of infinite love. For that reason, God himself does not need to retreat either; he does not need to 'close in on himself,' he needs no 'kenosis' when causing the world to exist within himself."[201]

The finite world can be included in the Trinity because of the coincidence of unity and difference in the Trinity. The reconciliation of unity and difference in the triune God "is effected through the identification of the divine essence with love, a claim which presupposes that difference is a necessary ingredient of love." Certainly, "For the veracity of love to be preserved, a certain irreducible difference between the lover and beloved must be sustained even in their unity, indeed as the form and condition of their unity, lest ecstasy be replaced with absorption and love for the other becomes merely self-love." Therefore, "The infinity, indeed the infinite difference, of each of the Trinitarian *personae* is not antithetical to the unity and simplicity of love but it is the form and condition of this unity."[202]

Throughout this section, we have seen that the understanding of God as Trinity enables us to give a positive account of the world. Thanks to the trinitarian understanding of God, "finitude must not be viewed as some kind of a declension from the absolute One. . . . Finitude . . .

198. Balthasar, *Theo-Drama II*, 259.

199. Chapp, *The God of Covenant*, 169.

200. Chapp, *The God of Covenant*, 166.

201. Balthasar, *Theo-Drama II*, 262. Thanks to the intratrinitarian relations, where unity and difference coincide, "God does not need the world to confirm him as God or to provide him with a series of stages to go through and so perfect himself; indeed, he does not even need the world to reveal to himself the possibilities of his omnipotence" (ibid., 261).

202. Hanby, *No God, No Science?* 318.

should be viewed rather as the positive expression of the divine image in a worldly modality, i.e. as an analogy for various positive perfections within God."[203] Therefore, worldly realities are positive realities because they are rooted in the Trinity. Most notably, "The temporal nature of creation, with its dynamic of becoming, development and change, points positively to something analogous within the divine life, and not to the realm of *vanitas* that will pass away once the world returns to its divine source."[204]

Because cosmologists misunderstand the concept of time when dealing with creation, I will devote the last part of this section to the topic of time from a trinitarian perspective. This will be helpful for the next section. According to Balthasar, "'The divine life,' precisely because it is 'the fullness of life . . . [is] perfect peace.' Yet this peace, or rest, is not inert, but 'eternal movement,' since the divine processions that give rise to the fellowship of the Persons are not subject to temporal limitation but are eternally operative."[205] Therefore, "What happens in the Trinity is . . . far more than a motionless order or sequence, for expressions such as 'beget,' 'give birth,' 'proceed' and 'breed forth' refer to eternal acts in which God genuinely 'takes place.'" We find then in the Trinity the unity of "two apparently contradictory concepts . . . : eternal or absolute Being—and 'happening.'" Balthasar carefully noted that the divine *happening* "is not a becoming in the earthly sense: it is the coming-to-be, not of something that once was not . . . , but, evidently, of something that grounds the idea, the inner possibility and reality of becoming. All earthly becoming is a reflection of the eternal 'happening' in God, which . . . is per se identical with the eternal Being or essence."[206]

The eternal *happening* in God enables us to talk about time, in an analogous way, in the Trinity. Indeed, "Life within God is not eternally the same, in a sense which would imply a kind of everlasting boredom. Rather, . . . trinitarian life is a 'communion of surprise' (in the sense of an infinite ever-flowing fulfillment . . .)."[207] The liveliness and ever-greater fulfillment of the trinitarian life allows us to think about "eternal *being* in

203. Chapp, *The God of Covenant*, 187.

204. Chapp, *The God of Covenant*, 187.

205. Balthasar, *Theo-Drama V*, 77–78. The inside quotation is from Speyr, *The Word Becomes Flesh*, 42–43.

206. Balthasar, *Theo-Drama V*, 67.

207. David L. Schindler, "Time in Eternity," 226. Schindler refers here to Balthasar, *Theo-Drama V*, 79n54.

terms of eternal *event*," and not in terms of "mere *nunc stans*."[208] As David L. Schindler asserts, "What exists in God is not the absence of time—and all its concomitant attributes—but the original image . . . of time."[209] The eternity of God is not the negation of time but its primal idea.[210] There cannot be antagonism between time and eternity. "Time is not the antithesis of eternity but is its moving (and thus analogous) image, such that what is eternally true does not preclude temporal 'development.'"[211]

Balthasar recognized that "'there is a deep analogy' between time and eternity, so eternity can always be inside time, just as time can participate in eternity."[212] The interrelation between time and eternity finds its paradigm in the Incarnation of the Son because "He is the very presence of eternity in time, in the very modality of time."[213] In this regard, David L. Schindler says that "the mission of the Son in his Incarnation is a continuation of the Son's eternal procession from the Father. Thus the Son, in taking on flesh and temporality, does not leave eternity behind. On the contrary, Jesus' every moment, precisely *in* time, reveals eternity."[214] There is no opposition between time and eternity in Jesus. "The deepest meaning of temporality is found in relation to eternity, in the relation of love which is from and for the Father: because *that is what Jesus is*."[215]

Only the Christian revelation of God as a community of persons can "ground the full ontological importance of time as more than one damn thing following another."[216] Only when "we see eternal *being* in terms of eternal *event*," are we able to value "world-time (in all transience) [as] exciting and delightful."[217] This positive valuation of time is a consequence of the doctrine of the Trinity. The trinitarian understanding of God helps us to value not only time as something positive but also

208. Balthasar, *Theo-Drama V*, 91.

209. David L. Schindler, "Time in Eternity," 227.

210. Balthasar, *Theo-Drama V*, 91.

211. Hanby, *No God, No Science?* 368n33.

212. Balthasar, *Theo-Drama V*, 101. The inside quotation is from Speyr, *Gates of Eternal Life*, 107.

213. Chapp, *The God of Covenant*, 198. See the characterization of Christ as the concrete universal in ibid., 168–73.

214. David L. Schindler, "Time in Eternity," 232. Schindler refers here to Balthasar, *Homo Creatus Est*, 44.

215. David L. Schindler, "Time in Eternity," 232.

216. Chapp, *The God of Covenant*, 197.

217. Balthasar, *Theo-Drama V*, 91.

other expressions of worldly finitude, such as differentiation and motion. Creaturely finitude is more than a mere negation of God because it has an analogical image in the life of the Trinity. Therefore, the doctrine of the Trinity helps us to value creation in its own finitude as something positive. The doctrine of the Trinity speaks not only about the inner life of God but also about the ontological constitution of the world. As we have seen, creation can be something other than God that is not simply a subtraction from God.

In this section, I have defended that creation can be properly understood only from a trinitarian perspective. Because modern scientists do not apprehend what creation truly is, they are unable to have an adequate image of God; what they ultimately have is a falsified and un-trinitarian concept of God. This deficient image of God will be obvious when I deal with cosmologists in the third chapter.

Misconceptions about Creation

We have seen in this chapter that the doctrine of creation is fundamentally a doctrine of God. The doctrine of creation enables us to see the absolute transcendence of God who, consequently, is intimately present in every creature through the gift of being (*esse*). Precisely because it is a doctrine of God, the doctrine of creation is, at the same time, a doctrine about the world. More precisely, it speaks about the ontological constitution of the world on a different plane from cosmology or the other natural sciences. Creation, in its active sense, is the divine essence along with a rational relation. In its passive sense, creation is the world itself with a real relation to God. As Hanby recognizes, "Creation is thus not an event within the world, but the event *of* the world itself: the novel appearance . . . of a gratuitous 'surplus' of being that is somehow not God." Therefore, "To 'see' creation . . . is not to isolate empirically or experimentally some qualification of the world. It is to see the world itself more deeply and comprehensively."[218] This is a very important aspect of the doctrine of creation which scientists do not grasp. Indeed, they apprehend creation as a natural event *within* the world, in competition with other natural events. The failure to understand creation is concomitant with the failure to grasp the distinction between temporal and ontological origins. The conflation of both origins is something characteristic of modern science.

218. Hanby, *No God, No Science?* 323.

Because the purpose of this chapter is to explain the meaning of creation and because I am going to deal with scientists in the following chapter, it is appropriate to finish this one with this section devoted to disentangling the meaning of creation from the misconceptions of scientists.

The first thing to notice is that creation is not a change. According to Aquinas, "Change means that the same something should be different now from what it was previously."[219] Therefore, changes are "'from something' to 'something' and therefore presuppose being."[220] But creation "presupposes nothing in the thing which is said to be created."[221] In fact, creation "is responsible for the total being (*totus esse*) of a thing."[222] Thus, creation is not a change because "the whole substance of a thing is produced."[223]

Regarding causality, creation differs from changes because in changes "the causality of the [agent] . . . does not extend to everything which is found in the thing, but only to the form, which is brought from potency into actuality. The causality of the Creator, however, extends to everything that is in the thing."[224] The causality of the creator is what we previously called primary causality. The causality of worldly processes, or changes, is what we called secondary causality. Primary causality does not rival secondary causality, but it is its condition of possibility. In other words, "God's agency to the creature does not negate but rather constitutes the creature's own agency as its own."[225] The act of creation, as primary causation, is not an alternative process in competition with the worldly processes described by natural sciences. As Hanby states, "The 'action' of creating is intrinsic to immanent processes and their effects."[226]

The act of creation and natural processes should not be considered as mutually exclusive, because primary and secondary causation are not mutually exclusive. In principle, the doctrine of creation and scientific explanations of the world should not exclude each other, because they

---

219. Aquinas, *Summa Theologiae*, I, q. 45, a. 2, ad 2.

220. Hanby, *No God, No Science?* 322.

221. Aquinas, *Scriptum Super Libros Sententiarum*, lib. 2, d. 1, q. 1, a. 2, co.

222. Hanby, *No God, No Science?* 322.

223. Aquinas, *Summa Theologiae*, I, q. 45, a. 2, ad 2.

224. Aquinas, *Scriptum Super Libros Sententiarum*, lib. 2, d. 1, q. 1, a. 2, co.

225. Hanby, *No God, No Science?* 323.

226. Hanby, "Creation without Creationism," 687; Aquinas, *Summa Theologiae*, I, q. 8, a. 1, co.

belong to different orders of being and explanation.[227] However, modern science confuses those orders and so scientific claims are bound up with a theology and a metaphysics that are in conflict with an adequate understanding of God and creation. The doctrine of creation should not be considered as an alternative to scientific explanation, because "the natural sciences have as their subject the world of changing things, and creation is not a change."[228] Therefore, it is a mistake to think that a scientific theory can refute the doctrine of creation. This is the case because "what creation accounts for is not a process at all, but a metaphysical dependence in the order of being."[229] The previous mistake is a common one among atheistic scientists who attempt to negate the existence of God by avoiding the initial singularity of the Big Bang model. These scientists interpret the initial singularity as the beginning of the universe and the moment of divine creation, and they think that, once the initial singularity is absent from the scientific explanation of the world, divine intervention is superfluous. The problem here, as Hanby explains, is the understanding of the "*act* of creation as a kind of fabrication in competition with natural processes and forces and the [understanding of the] doctrine of creation, now reduced to a question of *temporal* origins, as an explanation belonging to the same order as those of the natural sciences and in competition with them."[230] Scientists reduce the doctrine of creation to a question of temporal origins because they assume, at least implicitly, the collapse of the order of being to the order of process and history inherent in modern science.[231]

Because of the reduction of the order of being to the order of history, it is common among scientists to understand creation as a historical event that takes place in time. However, creation cannot be a historical event because it is the positive ground of every process at every moment. As Aquinas said, "Succession characterizes motion. But creation is not a motion, nor the term of a motion, as a change is; hence, there is no succession in it."[232] The act of creation does not take place in time because creation is successionless and because there is no time before creation.

227. Hanby, *No God, No Science?* 323.

228. William Carroll, "Two Creators or One?" 132.

229. William Carroll, "Big Bang Cosmology," 70.

230. Hanby, *No God, No Science?* 321.

231. Hanby, *No God, No Science?* 140n69. See Jonas, "Philosophical Aspects of Darwinism," 40.

232. Aquinas, *Summa Contra Gentiles*, lib. 2, cap. 19, n. 1.

Time itself is a creature. In this regard, Augustine said that "the world was made, not in time [*in tempore*], but simultaneously with time [*cum tempore*]. . . . Simultaneously with time the world was made."[233] Aquinas insisted on this, too: "Things are said to be created in the beginning of time, not as if the beginning of time were a measure of creation, but because together with time [*cum tempore*] heaven and earth were created."[234] And he added that "before the beginning of the world there was no time."[235]

As noticed before, scientists reduce creation to a mere question of temporal origins. Cosmologists think that creation answers "the question of *how* the world came to be."[236] However, "The doctrine of creation does not . . . seek to explain *how* the world came to be in any scientific sense of the word 'how.' Rather, it tells us what the world *is*. The question of creation is therefore a question of *ontological* rather than temporal origins."[237] Explaining the meaning of creation, Aquinas remarked that "non-being is prior to being in the thing which is said to be created. This is not a priority of time or of duration, such that what did not exist before does exist later, but a priority of nature, so that, if the created thing is left to itself, it would not exist, because it only has its being from the causality of the higher cause."[238] In other words, "The creature is naturally non-being rather than being, which means that the creature is completely dependent, throughout its entire duration, upon the constant causality of the Creator." The dependence of the creature "upon the cause of its being is precisely the same at the beginning of the creature's duration as it is all throughout its duration."[239] Therefore, "Creation is not merely some distant event; it is the on-going, complete causing of the existence of whatever is."[240] The on-going relation of metaphysical dependence of the creature on God is then more important than its temporal beginning. To be sure, the intent is not to deny creation *ab initio temporis* "but to insist that time itself is a creature and that temporal origins take their meaning from this more fundamental ontological origin."[241] In other words, a

233. Augustine, *The City of God* (2013), 315 (XI, 6).

234. Aquinas, *Summa Theologiae*, I, q. 46, a. 3, ad 1.

235. Aquinas, *De Potentia Dei*, q. 3, a. 2, co.

236. Hanby, *No God, No Science?* 5.

237. Hanby, *No God, No Science?* 324; See Ratzinger, *In the Beginning*, 50.

238. Aquinas, *Scriptum Super Libros Sententiarum*, lib. 2, d. 1, q. 1, a. 2, co.

239. Baldner and William Carroll, "Analysis of Aquinas' Writings," 42.

240. Baldner and William Carroll, "Analysis of Aquinas' Writings," 43.

241. Hanby, *No God, No Science?* 331n64. The affirmation of creation *ab initio*

temporal beginning is subordinate to the more fundamental distinction between being and non-being. This is the case because the question of time is subordinate to the question of being.

As we know, the question of creation is not a question of the temporal origin of the universe but "a question of the ontological structure of the world not just simply in the so-called Planck Time, but at every moment of its existence."[242] Simon Oliver clarifies that "creation *ex nihilo*—the doctrine that creation, at every moment is of nothing—as such privileges no *particular* temporal instant as revealing more acutely the nature of the cosmos as suspended over the *nihil*."[243] In a certain sense, we can say that creation transcends time, not because creation is outside of the limits of rectilinear time, but because creation, in its actuality, embraces all temporal moments. "Our normal way of thinking that limits physical being to the flux of time" is erroneous. Time should be seen "as belonging to things, as unfolding from above in reference to what transcends things. The physical world does exist in time, but not reductively so: all real beings 'stick out' ec-statically into the eternity of God who made them from nothing and 'continues' so to make them."[244] In this way, every created being is somehow outside of time yet in time.[245] This is only possible because, as we have seen, eternity is the primal idea of time.

---

temporis was defined in Lateran Council IV in 1215: "Firmly we believe and we confess simply that the true God is one alone, eternal, immense, and unchangeable, incomprehensible, omnipotent and ineffable, *Father and Son and Holy Spirit . . .* one beginning of all, creator of all visible and invisible things, of the spiritual and of the corporal; who by His own omnipotent power at once from the beginning of time [*ab initio temporis*] created each creature from nothing, spiritual, and corporal, namely, angelic and mundane, and finally the human, constituted as it were, alike of the spirit and the body" (Denzinger, *Sources of Catholic Dogma*, n. 428). Later on, pope John XXII condemned in 1329 as an error that "the world existed from eternity" (ibid., n. 503). Finally, in 1870 Vatican Council I corroborated the teaching of Lateran Council IV regarding the beginning of time (ibid., n. 1783).

242. Hanby, *No God, No Science?* 324. "The origin, where t = 0, represents the Big Bang, and the next landmark, just to the right of the left-hand edge, is the Planck time, 5.391×10^{-44} seconds after the Big Bang. The conventional assumption . . . is that our current physics fails us before the Planck time . . . with the result that the interval between the Big Bang and the Planck time remains shrouded in mystery" (Lockwood, *The Labyrinth of Time*, 347).

243. Oliver, "Physics, Creation and Trinity," 191.

244. D. C. Schindler, "Historical Intelligibility," 42.

245. "*Insofar as something is whole, and to that extent it represents something essentially greater than and irreducible to its parts, that thing transcends time.* It is important to see the implication: it is not simply a *part* of a substance—for example, the abstract

The previous insights about time are missed by modern scientists, who understand time mechanistically as "a linear series of 'nows' extrinsic and contiguous to each other and following densely upon one another in close succession."[246] As Hanby advocates, time should be understood as a kind of actuality, which is an Aristotelian understanding of time.[247] Only if we affirm time as "a 'now,' an actuality that acts as a boundary dividing and uniting the nonexistent past and the nonexistent future," can we affirm in every being "a unity that transcends its point identity at any given instant," and, therefore, also affirm that "each thing is 'eternal,' or at least 'supratemporal,' insofar as it is at all."[248] Note that "'eternal' does not here mean 'lasting for a long time,' but indivisibly actual."[249] A thing participates in eternity by the mere act of existing. This is so because existence is a participation in the actuality of being that is ultimately from God. The now of time is a kind of participation in the fullness of actuality that is being.

Hanby remarks that "the indivisible transcendence of being is not juxtaposed to history as stasis to movement; rather, it is inherent in the movement of history as its very (albeit participated) actuality. Being and history are thus neither identical nor antithetical."[250] However, modern science implicitly identifies being with history.[251] As a result, modern cosmology is unable to discern that creation and the temporal origin of the universe belong to different levels, as indicated previously. The choice of atheistic cosmologists "between a divine intention for the world and the world's unfolding in its proper freedom . . . is a false dilemma rooted

---

form or the 'ideal' reality of the thing—that transcends time, but that each individual substance must transcend time precisely to the extent that the substance represents an irreducible unity. This does not mean the thing does not exist in time, but only that its temporal reality is not the whole of its reality" (D. C. Schindler, "Historical Intelligibility," 38–39).

246. Hanby, *No God, No Science?* 197.

247. See Hanby, *No God, No Science?* 277–79 and 339; See Aristotle, *Physics*, V, 11, 220a5–26; See Koninck, *The Hollow Universe*, 64–69.

248. Hanby, *No God, No Science?* 339. See D. C. Schindler, "Historical Intelligibility," 15–44.

249. Hanby, *No God, No Science?* 365n14.

250. Hanby, *No God, No Science?* 346.

251. Even in tacitly reducing being to history, modern science continues to rely (on both the subject and object side) on the self-transcending unity and interiority conferred on things by form and *esse*.

in defective notions of God, creation, and causality."[252] In fact, creation is the necessary precondition for the temporal origin of the universe, the cosmic evolution, "and indeed for history as such, because it is the precondition for just that novelty and difference as well as the supra temporal existence necessary for there *to be* history."[253]

In this section I have dealt with scientific misconceptions about creation. I have defended the claim that creation is neither a change nor an event in time. This is part of a chapter that has been dedicated to offering a coherent understanding of creation, both from the theological and metaphysical points of view. The doctrine of creation, as a doctrine of God and of the metaphysical constitution of the world, will be helpful in the upcoming chapter to my criticism of the extrinsic theology presupposed by modern cosmology.

252. Hanby, *No God, No Science?* 345.
253. Hanby, *No God, No Science?* 345–46.

3

The Theological Extrinsicism
of Modern Cosmology

Introduction

IN THE PREVIOUS CHAPTER, I offered a plausible understanding of creation, both from the theological and metaphysical points of view. I explained that the doctrine of creation *ex nihilo* is first and foremost a doctrine of God. As such, the doctrine of creation *ex nihilo* primarily expresses the absoluteness of God as first principle. The lack of compulsion for God in the act of creation is an immediate consequence of the fullness of the divine being.[1] Remember that by lack of compulsion for God I mean that there is nothing, internal or external, that forces God to create, thus taking away God's freedom. As previously mentioned, divine freedom is not independent from God's nature. In fact, divine freedom is conditioned by the goodness, beauty and truth of God's own nature as trinitarian love. Consequently, the affirmation that divine freedom is absent of presuppositions is incorrect. That kind of freedom would be voluntaristic and arbitrary. As explained earlier in the second chapter, the doctrine

---

1. I noted in the second chapter that, even though God's being and God's freedom must be ontologically convertible, the question of the absolute aseity of God is logically first. Making the absoluteness of divine freedom the central issue at stake in creation would be divine voluntarism.

of creation preserves God's transcendent otherness from the world. The being of God and the being of the world are completely different. They are not different species of the same genus.[2] The being of God is the *ipsum esse subsistens* and the being of the world (*esse commune*) is "the non-subsistent fullness and perfection of all reality. . . . So God can no longer in any way be regarded as the being of things." Therefore, in a radical manner, "God is placed over and above all cosmic being, above everything that can be calculated or attained within the structures, real or ideal, of the cosmos: he is indeed 'the Wholly Other.'"[3] The radical transcendence of God is the necessary condition for the intimate divine presence in every creature, through the gift of being (*esse*).

As is already known, the doctrine of creation not only expresses an image of God but also an image of nature. The doctrine of creation tells us not only who God is but also what the world is. In other words, the doctrine of creation is simultaneously a theological doctrine of God and a metaphysical doctrine of the constitution of the world. These two doctrines, theological and metaphysical, are inseparable because of who God is and what being is, which is the ground of the relation between theology and metaphysics as forms of thought. As a metaphysical doctrine of the world, the doctrine of creation allows us to understand each creature in both its contingency and radical peculiarity. We have seen that each being is unique, irreplaceable, a bottomless mystery that communicates itself by the mere act of existing, yet cannot be exhausted by our apprehension. The peculiarity of every particular thing cannot be separated from its unity with the rest of things, because all of them share the same *esse commune*. Paradoxically, the act of being of every thing is what makes it peculiar and, at the same time, universal (and therefore intelligible). Both important aspects of each creature, bottomless mystery and intelligibility, are expressed in the concept of form. "As the visible expression of an

2. "We cannot lump together in one genus God and everything else, as if the word 'being' applied to them all in precisely the same sense, and then pick out God as the supreme one. For if God is the Supreme Being, in the sense in which Christian theology uses the term, 'being' as applied to him is not just one more instance of what 'being' means when applied to anything else. So far from being just one item, albeit the supreme one, in a class of beings, he is the source from which their being is derived; he is not in their class but above it. . . . In the technical term, when we apply to God a term which is normally used of other beings, we are using it not univocally but analogically; for he is not just one member of a class with them, but their ground and archetype" (Mascall, *He Who Is*, 9).

3. Balthasar, *Glory of the Lord IV*, 393–94.

infinite interior depth, form is simultaneously a principle of intelligibility, identity, *and* mystery at once."[4]

The doctrine of creation *ex nihilo* properly expresses what the act of creation is. Certainly, it is neither a "process of immanent manufacture" nor a "mechanical explanation seeking to account for the 'how' of the world." As we saw, creation is the "gratuitous gift of being that calls forth its own recipient."[5] Creation is about the unasked-for giving of being to what was nothing, i.e., the giving of the world to itself. To create is to make something from nothing; it is the passage from non-being to being.

The rich and profound understanding of both God and the world provided by the doctrine of creation is the counterpoint necessary to criticize the extrinsicist theology inherent in modern cosmology, which is the main goal of this book. We already know that extrinsicism suffers from falsified and reduced images of God and creation. For that reason, extrinsicism never ascends to a real discussion of God and creation. Because modern science is extrinsicist, it suffers in its understanding of the world and in its self-understanding of its own nature and limits. This is why modern science ultimately has a real unreasonable dimension, as we will see in this chapter.

Modern cosmology, as a branch of modern science, adopts its faulty presuppositions: the epistemological superiority of the scientific method, the neutrality of science, and the extrinsic relationship between science and metaphysics. These presuppositions are evident in the very differentiation between physical and metaphysical cosmology offered by scientists. On the one hand, physical cosmology studies "the Universe through scientific calculation, observation, and experiment."[6] On the other hand,

> Metaphysical cosmology describes the philosophical study of cosmology. It addresses questions about the Universe which are beyond the scope of science, and makes conjectures which are not (yet) observationally testable. For example, what caused the big bang? Is there a creator? What, if any, is the "purpose" of the Universe? Is our Universe just one of a large number, making up a multiverse? As our scientific understanding of the Universe increases, some metaphysical topics may enter the realm of physical cosmology. As an example, prior to the 20th century,

4. Hanby, *No God, No Science?* 385.

5. Hanby, *No God, No Science?* 284.

6. Liddle and Loveday, *Oxford Companion to Cosmology*, 82.

the existence of separate "island universes" was a matter of conjecture. We now have sound scientific evidence for the existence of other galaxies. We may, in the future, gain a scientific understanding as to the origin of the big bang.[7]

Notice how metaphysics is placed outside the scientific realm. Since truth is only obtained through "scientific calculation, observation, and experiment," metaphysics can only make "conjectures."[8] These conjectures can only be made when there is no possibility of scientific calculation, observation, and experimentation. As the scientific method expands its realm of application to new areas of reality, which were previously assigned to metaphysical conjectures, metaphysics has had to retreat to a smaller area. For scientists, science is the real metaphysics, the first science, and metaphysics is relegated to the outskirts of truth. This deficient metaphysics goes hand in hand with an extrinsic theology, in which God is a god of the gaps, as I will show in this chapter.

Modern cosmology is a relatively new branch of physics, which started in the beginning of the twentieth century with Einstein's theory of general relativity and the discovery of the expansion of the universe by Edwin Hubble. Modern cosmology deals with questions directly related to the temporal origin of the universe, questions that cosmologists presume to be very pertinent to metaphysics and theology. This is the case because of the positivism inherent in modern science. Positivism "declares the question of being meaningless,"[9] and "takes for granted the brute facticity of being."[10] As a consequence, there is eventually a conflation of ontological and temporal origins. Notice that, according to the extrinsicist nomenclature of modern science, the questions of modern cosmology are in the borderline between science and theology and metaphysics. This fact provides an excellent opportunity for scientists to express their metaphysical and theological assumptions, especially when they write popular scientific books and articles. Some of the scientists even venture to speak openly about God and his involvement in the universe. I will take advantage of these popular science publications about cosmology to uncover and criticize the extrinsicist theology implicit in them.

7. Liddle and Loveday, *Oxford Companion to Cosmology*, 82.

8. Liddle and Loveday, *Oxford Companion to Cosmology*, 82.

9. Hanby, *No God, No Science?* 382.

10. Hanby, *No God, No Science?* 221.

The question of the beginning of the universe is possibly the most important task of modern cosmology, and it is of crucial importance in our critique of theological extrinsicism. The experimental confirmation of the expansion of the universe in 1929 by Hubble made astronomers think about a beginning of the expanding universe, when all the universe was concentrated in a single point of infinite density and temperature.[11] The beginning of the expansion, the moment of the Big Bang, was a mathematical singularity in space-time. In other words, the laws of gravitation broke at the initial singularity. There was no way to know what happened at the very beginning. To those holding extrinsicist theological assumptions, both theologians and scientists, the fact of a beginning of the universe that could not be described by the known laws of physics pointed to divine intervention in creation. As the cosmologist Alexander Vilenkin remarks, "The beginning of the universe looked too much like a divine intervention; there seemed to be no possibility to describe it scientifically. This was one thing scientists and theologians seemed to agree upon."[12]

The existence of a beginning in the Big Bang theory has been warmly welcomed by extrinsicist theologians and scientists as an opportunity to provide scientific proof for the existence of God. Conversely, the beginning of the universe, with its initial singularity, predicted by the Big Bang theory, is something rejected by atheistic cosmologists in order to deny the existence of God. It is my contention that both theologians and cosmologists share the same extrinsicist theology, in which God's transcendence is lost and, therefore, he is reduced to an object within a more comprehensive order of being that is taken for granted but never thought through or explicated by these thinkers. God belongs then to the same order as creatures. God ceases being the *ipsum esse subsistens* to become an object, albeit an extremely important one, participating in *esse commune*. This extrinsic God is implicitly locked into an antagonistic relation with nature because those thinkers consider that a divine intervention would negate the integrity of nature qua nature. Therefore, God is not allowed to take part in the meaning of nature. God makes no difference to what remains an essentially mechanistic understanding of nature. Because being is taken for granted, because being is not a question for those extrinsicist thinkers, they do not properly understand creation as a question of being and nothing. For them, creation is a natural event taking

11. Using Einstein's theory of gravitation, the expanding universe had been theoretically predicted by Lemaître in 1927.

12. Vilenkin, *Many Worlds in One*, 177.

place within the world, in competition with other natural events. When extrinsicist thinkers, both scientists and theologians, deny or affirm God and creation, they are rejecting or denying the same defective and extrinsic ideas of God and creation, and they do not completely engage the substance of the issues they consider. In the first part of this chapter, I will criticize the theological extrinsicism present in those using the beginning of the universe as evidence for the existence of God and in those atheistic cosmologists who reject the initial singularity of the beginning in order to reject the existence of God. I will show that, although the former and the latter disagree about the existence of God, they agree in their extrinsicist theological presuppositions.

Apart from the beginning of the universe, there is another cosmological issue relevant to our endeavor to criticize theological extrinsicism. This is the question of the anthropic principle. This principle states that the physical constants[13] of the universe have been finely tuned for the emergence of humankind.[14] Evidently, the order that we find in creation is not a negligible fact. After all, since there is no being without order, the presence of order in creation can be an indication of divine design.[15] In

13. Examples of physical constants are the speed of light in vacuum, the electric charge of the electron, and the gravitational constant.

14. This is in fact the so-called *strong* anthropic principle. It is called so in order to distinguish it from the *weak* anthropic principle. In accordance with the weak anthropic principle, "the observed values of all physical and cosmological quantities are not equally probable but they take on values restricted by the requirement that there exist sites where carbon-based life can evolve and by the requirement that the Universe be old enough for it to have already done so" (Barrow and Tipler, *The Anthropic Cosmological Principle*, 16). John Barrow and Frank Tipler stress that the weak anthropic principle "is in no way either speculative or controversial. It expresses only the fact that those properties of the Universe we are able to discern are self-selected by the fact that they must be consistent with our own evolution and present existence" (ibid.). The same physicists phrase the strong anthropic principle in this way: "The Universe must have those properties which allow life to develop within it at some stage in its history" (ibid., 21). The strong anthropic principle "is open to the criticism of being unscientific, as it is not falsifiable. Ordinarily the strong anthropic principle is avoided by cosmologists" (Liddle and Loveday, *Oxford Companion to Cosmology*, 17).

15. "For all men who were ignorant of God were foolish by nature; and they were unable from the good things that are seen to know him who exists, nor did they recognize the craftsman while paying heed to his works" (Wis 13:1 RSV-CE); "For from the greatness and beauty of created things comes a corresponding perception of their Creator" (Wis 13:5 RSV-CE); "For as they live among his works they keep searching, and they trust in what they see, because the things that are seen are beautiful. Yet again, not even they are to be excused; for if they had the power to know so much that they could investigate the world, how did they fail to find sooner the Lord of these

fact, "the Christian theologian has reason to speak by way of analogy of the Trinitarian God as an artificer and creatures as divine artifacts."[16] The Sacred Scriptures and patristic sources support this analogy.[17] Aquinas also approved it.[18] Nevertheless, God is not an artificer or designer in the identical way that humans are.[19] In this regard, Simon Gaine asserts that "in contrast to human artificers, who do their making out of pre-existing material, God creates the whole being of something out of nothing, with nothing else presupposed."[20] Moreover, Velde defends that when "a human artificer produces a thing, the exercise of his skill requires a tool of a nature external to himself. God, by contrast, exercises his skill in virtue

---

things?" (Wis 13:7–9 RSV-CE).

16. Gaine, "God Is an Artificer," 495.

17. Gaine, "God Is an Artificer," 496–97. "The Letter to the Hebrews 11:10 names God as a 'τεχνίτης'—in this case, the artificer of the city for which Abraham hoped. But God is portrayed in the Bible not only as eschatological artificer, but as the protological artificer of creation, for example, in the opening chapters of Genesis, where in 2:7 God forms a man of dust from the ground, and so on. Scripture, moreover, speaks not only of God creating by his word—John 1:3 says that through the Word was everything made that was made—but speaks also in this connection of divine wisdom. 'By wisdom the LORD founded the earth,' says Proverbs 3:19. Then in 8:30, 'Wisdom' is presented as a figure alongside God at the creation, putting things together, harmonizing them, so to speak. Then in the Wisdom of Solomon 7:22, Wisdom is named a 'τεχνίτης,' where the author confesses: 'Wisdom, the artificer of all things, taught me.' And in 8:5–6, we find: 'What is richer than Wisdom who effects all things? And if understanding is effective, who more than she is artificer of what exists?'" (ibid., 496).

18. These are some examples: "God, Who is the first principle of all things, may be compared to things created as the architect is to things designed [ut artifex ad artificiata]" (Aquinas, Summa Theologiae, I, q. 27, a. 1, ad 3); "For the knowledge of God is to all creatures what the knowledge of the artificer is to things made by his art [sicut scientia artificis se habet ad artificiata]" (ibid., I, q. 14, a. 8, co.); "God is the cause of things by His intellect and will, just as the craftsman is cause of the things made by his craft [sicut artifex rerum artificiatarum]" (ibid., I, q. 45, a. 6, co.). Furthermore, Aquinas understood creation as divine art: "Nature is nothing but a certain kind of art, i.e., the divine art [natura nihil est aliud quam ratio cuiusdam artis, scilicet divinae], impressed upon things, by which these things are moved to a determinate end" (Aquinas, Commentary on Aristotle's Physics, 134 (lib. 2, l. 14, n. 8)).

19. Gaine, "God Is an Artificer," 499. For a comprehensive study of Aquinas on the differences between divine and human art, see Kovach, "Divine Art," 665–70, and Doolan, Aquinas on Divine Ideas, 223–28.

20. Gaine, "God Is an Artificer," 500. "As a created workman [artifex creatus] makes a thing out of matter, so God makes things out of nothing . . . , not as if this nothing were a part of the substance of the thing made, but because the whole substance of a thing is produced by Him without anything else whatever presupposed" (Aquinas, Summa Theologiae, I, q. 41, a. 3, co.).

of his own nature. God's *art* as well as his nature are both involved in his creative action."[21] As Gaine points out, "Acknowledging God as a divine artificer need not mean confusing natural objects with human artifacts. Rather, as extrinsic teleology in human artifacts can lead us to their human artificers, so intrinsic teleology in divine artifacts can lead us to the divine artificer."[22] Unfortunately, both supporters and opponents of fine-tuning identify creation (natural objects) with design (human artifacts). That identification entails a conception of God as divine designer that suffers from an extrinsic theology. On the one hand, the fine-tuning is taken by extrinsicist theologians and scientists as evidence for the existence of a divine designer. On the other hand, atheistic cosmologists, having in mind that divine designer, strive to offer an alternative to him from the scientific point of view. Once more, both defenders of the existence of God and opponents share the same extrinsicist theology. They are like two sides of the same coin. In the second part of this chapter, I will deal with this issue of the finely tuned universe as a way to criticize the theological extrinsicism present in those theologians and scientists defending the argument from design and in those atheistic cosmologists offering a scientific alternative to the anthropic principle.

This chapter, then, will treat two main cosmological issues, which are the beginning of the universe and the finely tuned universe. The extrinsic image of God will be evident when I discuss the contributions of those dealing with these two main cosmological issues, either to defend the existence of God or to deny it. The atheistic cosmologist Sean Carroll identifies our two main cosmological issues as the two main cosmological topics offering an opportunity to give scientific evidence for the existence of God. Let us briefly review his reasoning. Carroll explains that there are two possible situations that could offer scientific evidence of divine action in our world. The first situation happens when "there is something inherently missing in a materialist description of nature." Carroll describes the God behind this line of reasoning as a "God of the

---

21. Velde, *Participation and Substantiality*, 103–4. "Accordingly the forms of things are in God in both ways. Because while his action in reference to things is from his intellect, it is not without the action of nature. But whereas here below the craftsman's art [*artificibus ars*] acts by virtue of an extraneous nature which it employs as an instrument, as a brick maker uses fire to bake his bricks: on the other hand God's art [*ars divina*] employs no extraneous nature in its action, but produces its effect by virtue of his own nature" (Aquinas, *De Potentia Dei*, q. 7, a. 1, ad 8).

22. Gaine, "God Is an Artificer," 500.

gaps."[23] The initial conditions at the Big Bang "are by no means generic; the curvature of space (as opposed to that of spacetime) was extremely close to zero, and widely separated parts of the universe were expanding at nearly identical rates."[24] Carroll frankly accepts the inability of modern cosmology to explain the Big Bang.[25] The second possible situation that could give scientific evidence of divine action in the universe would occur "if, upon constructing various models for the universe, we found that the God hypothesis accounted most economically for some of the features we found in observed phenomena."[26] Cosmology offers an excellent example for this second situation with the argument from design, which seeks to establish scientifically "that certain aspects of the universe . . . [are] designed rather than assembled by chance."[27] According to Sean Carroll, then, there are two major concepts in cosmology that can provide evidence for God: the initial singularity of the Big Bang and the finely tuned universe. As indicated previously, the very act of conceiving a scientific proof for the existence of God determines the understanding of God. The image of God inherent in the cosmological proofs of God's existence is an extrinsic one, as I will show.

Finally, for the agnostic astronomer Robert Jastrow, our two main cosmological topics were the ones with the most theological significance. When Jastrow was asked to identify "results in science that have a bearing on the religious view of reality," he gave a twofold answer: "The evidence for the abrupt birth of the Universe," and the fact that "the smallest change in any of the circumstances of the natural world, such as the relative strengths of the forces of nature, or the properties of the elementary particles, would have led to a Universe in which there could be no life and no man."[28] Now that I have established the theological significance of our two main cosmological topics, I will begin with the first one.

23. Sean Carroll, "Why Cosmologists Are Atheists," 628. Note that the "God of the gaps" is itself necessitated by a reductive understanding of nature, which is characterized by vast gaps in its description of reality.

24. Sean Carroll, "Why Cosmologists Are Atheists," 629.

25. Sean Carroll, "Why Cosmologists Are Atheists," 629.

26. Sean Carroll, "Why Cosmologists Are Atheists," 631.

27. Sean Carroll, "Why Cosmologists Are Atheists," 628.

28. Jastrow, "The Astronomer and God," 21.

The Beginning of the Universe as Scientific
Evidence for the Existence of God

One of the most remarkable supporters of the beginning of the universe as evidence for the existence of God is the philosophical theologian William L. Craig. His most relevant contributions to our topic are his discussions of the *kalam* cosmological argument.[29] In general, the cosmological argument indicates "a family of arguments which seeks to demonstrate the existence of a *sufficient reason* or *first cause* of the existence of the cosmos." This family of arguments "can be grouped into three basic types: the *kalam* cosmological argument for a First Cause of the beginning of the universe, the Thomist cosmological argument for a sustaining Ground of Being of the world, and the Leibnizian cosmological argument for a Sufficient Reason why something exists rather than nothing." The *kalam* cosmological argument "aims to show that the universe had a beginning at some moment in the finite past and, since something cannot come out of nothing, must therefore have a transcendent cause, which brought the universe into being."[30] Craig states the *kalam* cosmological argument in this syllogistic way:

29. "In light of the central role played by this form of the cosmological argument [impossibility of an infinite temporal regress of events] in medieval Islamic theology, as well as the substantive contribution to its development by its medieval Muslim proponents, we use the word '*kalam*' to denominate this version of the argument. The Arabic word for speech, *kalam* was used by Muslim thinkers to denote a statement of theological doctrine and eventually of any intellectual position or an argument supporting such a position. . . . Ultimately, *kalam* became the name of the whole movement within Muslim thought that might best be described as Islamic scholasticism" (Craig and Sinclair, "The *Kalam* Cosmological Argument," 101–2).

30. Craig, "The Cosmological Argument," 112. I will later explore further the distinctions between the *kalam* and Thomist cosmological arguments, emphasizing their respective metaphysical assumptions. For the sake of completion, I present here the Leibnizian cosmological argument: "The German polymath Gottfried Wilhelm Leibniz, for whom the third form of the argument is named, sought to develop a version of the cosmological argument from contingency without the Aristotelian metaphysical underpinnings of the Thomist argument. 'The first question which should rightly be asked,' he wrote, 'is this: why is there something rather than nothing?' [Leibniz, *Leibniz: Selections*, 527]. Leibniz meant this question to be truly universal, not merely to apply to finite things. On the basis of his Principle of Sufficient Reason, that 'no fact can be real or existent, no statement true, unless there be a sufficient reason why it is so and not otherwise' [ibid., 539], Leibniz held that this question must have an answer. It will not do to say that the universe (or even God) just exists as a brute fact. There must be an explanation [of] why it exists. He went on to argue that the Sufficient Reason cannot be found in any individual thing in the universe, nor in the collection

1.0. Everything that begins to exist has a cause.

2.0. The universe began to exist.

3.0. Therefore, the universe has a cause.[31]

The philosophical theologian argues that "classical proponents of the [*kalam*] argument sought to demonstrate that the universe began to exist on the basis of philosophical arguments against the existence of an infinite, temporal regress of past events."[32] He goes on, affirming that "contemporary interest in the argument arises largely out of the startling empirical evidence of astrophysical cosmology for a beginning of space and time."[33] Craig firmly believes that astronomy and astrophysics have provided "provocative empirical evidence that the universe is not past eternal."[34] He thinks that physical evidence for a beginning of the universe is provided by two main facts: the expansion of the universe and the second law of thermodynamics.[35] Regarding the expansion of the universe, Craig argues that "the standard (Friedman-LeMaître-Robertson-Walker) Big Bang cosmogonic model implies that the universe is not infinite in

---

of such things which comprise the universe, nor in earlier states of the universe, even if these regress infinitely. Therefore, there must exist an ultra-mundane being which is metaphysically necessary in its existence, that is to say, its non-existence is impossible. It is the Sufficient Reason for its own existence as well as for the existence of every contingent thing" (Craig, "The Cosmological Argument," 113–14).

31. Craig and Sinclair, "The *Kalam* Cosmological Argument," 102. I will explain later on the idea of beginning that is behind Craig's *kalam* cosmological argument.

32. Craig, "The Cosmological Argument," 112. "One of the traditional arguments for the finitude of the past is based upon the impossibility of the existence of an actual infinite. It may be formulated as follows: 2.11. An actual infinite cannot exist. 2.12. An infinite temporal regress of events is an actual infinite. 2.13. Therefore, an infinite temporal regress of events cannot exist" (Craig and Sinclair, "The *Kalam* Cosmological Argument," 103). "A second philosophical argument in support of the premise that the universe began to exist [is] . . . the argument from the impossibility of the formation of an actual infinite by successive addition. The argument may be simply formulated as follows: 2.21. A collection formed by successive addition cannot be an actual infinite. 2.22. The temporal series of events is a collection formed by successive addition. 2.23. Therefore, the temporal series of events cannot be an actual infinite" (ibid., 117).

33. Craig, "The Cosmological Argument," 112–13. "Today the controlling paradigm of cosmology is the Standard Big Bang Model, according to which the space-time universe originated *ex nihilo* about 15 billion years ago. Such an origin *ex nihilo* seems to many to cry out for a transcendent cause" (ibid., 113).

34. Craig and Sinclair, "The *Kalam* Cosmological Argument," 125.

35. Sean Carroll and Craig, "God and Cosmology," 23. This book section reproduces the debate between Craig and Sean Carroll, held in February 2014 in the Greer-Heard Point-Counterpoint Forum in Faith and Culture.

the past but had an absolute beginning a finite time ago."[36] Although the standard model has been modified and other cosmological options have been proposed, Craig defends that the singularity theorems presented by Vilenkin and other scientists make it impossible for tenable cosmological models to avoid a beginning.[37] Concerning the second law of thermodynamics, Craig argues that if the universe were to have existed forever, it would have reached the state of thermodynamic heat death, a state from which there is no available energy.[38] Obviously, there is available energy in our universe and, therefore, the universe has not existed forever.[39] In the end, this is Craig's conclusion:

> Thus, we have good evidence both from the expansion of the universe and from the second law of thermodynamics that the universe is not past eternal, but had a temporal beginning. So, the second premise of the *Kalām* Cosmological Argument receives significant confirmation from the evidence of contemporary cosmology. We have, then, a good argument for a transcendent cause of the universe.[40]

Craig is the main promoter of the *kalam* cosmological argument, and he has been defending it for decades.[41] The Jesuit Robert J. Spitzer is another defender of the *kalam* cosmological argument, whose main contribution to this subject is his book *New Proofs for the Existence of God: Contributions of Contemporary Physics and Philosophy*.[42] In this book,

36. Sean Carroll and Craig, "God and Cosmology," 24–25.

37. Sean Carroll and Craig, "God and Cosmology," 25. "A series of remarkable singularity theorems has increasingly tightened the loop around empirically tenable cosmogonic models by showing that under more and more generalized conditions, a beginning is inevitable. In 2003 Arvind Borde, Alan Guth, and Alexander Vilenkin were able to show that any universe which is, on average, in a state of cosmic expansion throughout its history cannot be infinite in the past, but must have a beginning. In 2012 Vilenkin showed that cosmogonic models which do not fall under this condition . . . fail on other grounds to avert the beginning of the universe" (ibid.). Craig refers here to Borde et al., "Inflationary Spacetimes," and to Mithani and Vilenkin, "Did the Universe?"

38. Sean Carroll and Craig, "God and Cosmology," 29.

39. Copan and Craig, *Creation out of Nothing*, 241.

40. Sean Carroll and Craig, "God and Cosmology," 31–32.

41. Craig has more than thirty publications (books and articles) about the *kalam* cosmological argument. For a detailed list of publications see https://www.reasonable-faith.org/william-lane-craig/. Among his publications, his foundational work is Craig, *The Kalām Cosmological Argument*.

42. This book received the 2011 Catholic Press Association Book Award in the

"Spitzer claims that modern physics reinforces the mediaeval Kalam cosmological argument and shows us that the past time of the universe is finite."[43] This is the Jesuit's proposal for the *kalam* cosmological argument:

> (1) If there is a reasonable likelihood of a beginning of the universe (prior to which there was no physical reality whatsoever), and (2) if it is a priori true that "from nothing, only nothing comes," then it is reasonably likely that the universe came from *something* which is *not* physical reality. This is commonly referred to as "transcendent cause of the universe (physical reality)" or "a creator of the universe."[44]

Spitzer explains that there are two types of arguments that suggest a beginning of the universe: "(a) Arguments about the possible geometrics of space-time and (b) arguments based on the Second Law of Thermodynamics."[45] These two arguments are basically the same as the two proposed by Craig.[46] After discussing the arguments, Spitzer concludes that "the preponderance of cosmological evidence favors a beginning of the universe (prior to which there was no physical reality whatsoever). This beginning of physical reality marks the point at which our universe came into existence. There are currently no truly satisfactory alternatives to this beginning of physical reality."[47]

Theologians are not the only ones who defend the beginning of the universe as scientific evidence for the act of creation and the existence of a creator. Some astronomers support the same ideas. For instance, Jastrow, the founder of NASA's Goddard Institute for Space Studies, thought that "the idea of a big bang . . . suggested a beginning and a creation, and a creation suggested a Creator."[48] This scientist also affirmed that "astrono-

---

topic of Faith and Science.

43. William Carroll, "Aquinas and Contemporary Cosmology," 11.

44. Spitzer, *New Proofs*, 45. Spitzer gives another formulation of the same *kalam* cosmological argument: "1) Any universe must have a beginning . . . 2) Any universe could not have caused itself to exist . . . 3) Something transcending every universe must cause that universe to exist" (ibid., 211). According to the Jesuit, "The above three deductions are a restatement of what William Lane Craig terms the Kalam argument" (ibid., 211n38). As I previously said when talking about Craig, I will explain later on the idea of beginning which is behind Spitzer's *kalam* cosmological argument.

45. Spitzer, *New Proofs*, 22.

46. Spitzer, *New Proofs*, 24–43. See William Carroll, "Aquinas and Contemporary Cosmology," 11.

47. Spitzer, *New Proofs*, 43.

48. Heeren and Jastrow, *Evidence for God?*

mers now find they have painted themselves into a corner because they have proven, by their own methods, that the world began abruptly in an act of creation to which you can trace the seeds of every star, every planet, every living thing in this cosmos and on the earth."[49]

Up to this point, I have described how both theologians and scientists use the beginning of the universe as scientific evidence for the existence of a creation and, accordingly, of a creator. This is the kernel of the *kalam* cosmological argument. As indicated previously, this argument is a particular kind of cosmological argument. In order to get a better idea of what this argument entails, I will contrast it with the Thomist cosmological argument.[50] Craig notices that "Thomas Aquinas' formulation of an argument from contingency for the existence of God . . . is a

---

49. Durbin and Jastrow, "A Scientist Caught," 15.

50. According to Craig, "Of the Five Ways [*Summa Theologiae*, I, q. 2, a. 3] only the first three are cosmological arguments. In each of the first three proofs Aquinas reasons from a particular datum of experience in general—change, causation, contingent beings—to an ultimate Being which is the cause of these in the world. . . . Each of these three ways is an *a posteriori* argument" (Craig, *Cosmological Argument from Plato*, 160). When Craig refers to the Thomist cosmological argument (in singular), he refers most particularly to the third way (the way of contingency). See Craig, "The Cosmological Argument," 113 and Craig, *A Rabbi Looks*. It is very interesting to note that Craig rejects a metaphysical interpretation of the Thomist cosmological argument and defends a mere physical understanding. "Therefore, the most probable interpretation of the first way would appear to be that Aquinas has followed Aristotle, just as he says, in expounding a physical proof from motion for an unmoved first mover" (Craig, *Cosmological Argument from Plato*, 172). "It has been argued that the third way, like the first, really has a 'metaphysical' starting point instead of a merely physical one, that is to say, it considers beings whose essence does not involve their existence. But such an interpretation ignores the second half of the third way as well as the historical ties to earlier Arabic and Jewish versions. It is generally recognized today that the first part of the third way begins by considering possibility and necessity in purely physical terms" (ibid., 183). In the end, the philosophical theologian rejects the Thomist argument because of his problems with the understanding of contingency: "The difficulty with appeal to the Thomist argument, however, is that it is very difficult to show that things are, in fact, contingent in the special sense required by the argument. Certainly things are naturally contingent in that their continued existence is dependent upon a myriad of factors including particle masses and fundamental forces, temperature, pressure, entropy level, and so forth, but this natural contingency does not suffice to establish things' metaphysical contingency in the sense that being must continually be added to their essences lest they be spontaneously annihilated. Indeed, if Thomas's argument does ultimately lead to an absolutely simple being whose essence is existence, then one might well be led to deny that beings are metaphysically composed of essence and existence if the idea of such an absolutely simple being proves to be unintelligible" (Craig, "The Cosmological Argument," 116).

quite distinct argument from the *kalam* argument." The latter argument assumes "the sort of temporally ordered causal series like the chicken and the egg," and defends the existence of a first cause in a chronological sense. In contrast, the Thomist argument talks "about a very particular kind of causal series, one in which the causes and effects are not linearly ordered in time, but they are hierarchically ordered at one moment of time. And so the cause that is first is not chronologically first, it's first in the sense of rank, like the general is first in the chain of command, say, but he's not temporally first."[51] Certainly, this points back to the distinction between temporal and ontological origins. This distinction, and the priority of ontological origin to temporal origin, transforms the meaning of temporal origin, making time not simply a linear series of instants but a participation in the actuality of eternity, as I suggested in the second chapter. According to Aquinas,

> The most efficacious way to prove that God exists is on the supposition that the world is eternal. Granted this supposition, that God exists is less manifest. For, if the world and motion have a first beginning, some cause must clearly be posited to account for this origin of the world and of motion. That which comes to be anew must take its origin from some innovating cause; since nothing brings itself from potency to act, or from non-being to being.[52]

Therefore, "Aquinas didn't disagree that if the universe began to exist then there had to be a transcendent creator. . . . The problem was for Aquinas he didn't think you could show with absolute certainty . . . that the universe began to exist."[53] Since Thomas "did not regard the *kalam* arguments for the past's finitude as demonstrative, he argued for God's existence on the more difficult assumption of the eternity of the world." In other words, Aquinas did not presuppose a beginning of the universe. However, he did presuppose that "every existing finite thing is composed of essence and existence and is therefore radically contingent." Aquinas defended that "essence is in potentiality to the act of being, and therefore

---

51. Craig, *A Rabbi Looks.* "Sometimes it's helpful to think of these causes arranged vertically as opposed to horizontally. If you think of the temporal causal series as arranged horizontally, what Aquinas is thinking about is a causal series that is arranged vertically and gets back to a first mover in the sense of an ultimate, highest, top causal source of the effects that you observe" (ibid.).

52. Aquinas, *Summa Contra Gentiles*, lib. 1, cap. 13, n. 30.

53. Craig, *A Rabbi Looks.*

without the bestowal of being the essence would not be exemplified. For the same reason no substance can actualize itself; for in order to bestow being upon itself it would have to be already actual. A pure potentiality cannot actualize itself but requires some external cause." For Thomas, "There can be no intermediate causes of being at all, . . . [for] any finite substance is sustained in existence immediately by the Ground of Being." This Being "requires no sustaining cause" because his essence is his existence. "In a sense, this being has no essence; rather it is the pure act of being, unconstrained by any essence. It is, as Thomas says, *ipsum esse subsistens*, the act of being itself subsisting. Thomas identifies this being with the God whose name was revealed to Moses as 'I am' (Exod. 3.15)."[54] We see, then, that the Thomist cosmological argument does not depend upon whether the universe has a beginning *ab initio temporis* or not. In contrast, the *kalam* cosmological argument is based on the beginning of the universe. The difference between the Thomist and the *kalam* arguments points to a profound difference in what each takes creation to be.

It is necessary to notice that the Thomist argument cannot be understood as freestanding or self-evident. The argument obviously presupposes Thomist metaphysics, such as the conception of being as act, the real distinction, and the contingency of the universe as an admixture of potency and act.

> From the outset . . . Thomas sees the world in a cause/effects perspective. More properly, perhaps, he is relying, tacitly, on the doctrine that the world is created. The demonstrations that "God exists" which he will offer are articulations of the already accepted presupposition that the world has a creator—not arguments that start from features of a world that are not yet identified as "effects."[55]

As opposed to the positivism of the *kalam* argument,[56] "Thomas's 'theistic proofs' do not begin from a world which 'just is' and from which we have to deduce its 'cause'. On the contrary, the idea of 'just being' would have been unintelligible to him."[57] The Thomist argument does not intend to "convince hypothetical open-minded atheists" of the existence of

---

54. Craig, "The Cosmological Argument," 113.

55. Kerr, *After Aquinas*, 59.

56. The positivism of the *kalam* cosmological argument will be discussed later on.

57. Kerr, *After Aquinas*, 68. Kerr is commenting on McDermott, "Introduction," xxiii.

God, as the *kalam* argument does, "so much as to deepen and enhance the mystery of the hidden God. From the start, the 'theistic proofs' are the first lesson in Thomas's negative theology. Far from being an exercise in rationalistic apologetics, the purpose of arguing for God's existence is to protect God's transcendence."[58]

Craig, currently the most ardent defender of the *kalam* cosmological argument, is a rationalistic apologist. He adopts the positivistic mindset of modern science, and thus he rejects the analogical understanding of being. As a positivist, he defends that "there is a univocal concept of being which applies to both God and creatures." Therefore, as Craig states, "When we say that God is or exists, we are using the term in the same sense in which we say that a man is or exists." It comes as no surprise that Craig qualifies the Thomistic claim that "we can speak of God only in analogical terms" as "most disturbing." Even more, the philosophical theologian thinks that "without univocity of meaning, we are left with agnosticism about the nature of God, able to say only what God is not, not what He is."[59] From his positivistic perspective, Craig is only able to interpret Aquinas' negative theology as agnosticism.

After contrasting the *kalam* cosmological argument and the Thomist one, it is time now to explore the key terms in the *kalam* cosmological argument. The key terms are *beginning, cause,* and *creation.* The exploration of these key terms will help us to expose the extrinsic presuppositions behind those terms. Let us begin with the idea of *beginning.* Remember that the first premise of the *kalam* cosmological argument, according to Craig, is this: "Everything that begins to exist has a cause."[60] The philosophical theologian specifies the expression "begin to exist" in this manner:

> In affirming that the universe began to exist, the proponents of the *kalam* cosmological argument understand "begin to exist" in the following way, where "x" ranges over any entity and "t" ranges over times, whether instants or moments:
> A. x begins to exist at t iff x comes into being at t.
> B. x comes into being at t iff (i) x exists at t, and the actual world includes no state of affairs in which x exists timelessly, (ii) t is either the first time at which x exists or is separated from any $t' < t$ at which x existed by an interval

58. Kerr, *After Aquinas,* 58.

59. Craig, "Is God a Being?"

60. Craig and Sinclair, "The *Kalam* Cosmological Argument," 102.

during which x does not exist, and (iii) and x's existing at t is a tensed fact.[61]

As we can see, Craig understands beginning in a *temporal* sense. The philosophical theologian recognizes that his "explication of 'x begins to exist at t' leaves it an open question whether there are times prior to t or not."[62] When Craig affirms in the second premise of the *kalam* cosmological argument that "the universe began to exist,"[63] he has in mind a temporal beginning of the universe at $t = 0$. From the scientific point of view, Craig equates the universe having a beginning with the universe being not past eternal.[64] The Jesuit Spitzer also understands the beginning of the universe in a temporal sense. For him, the affirmation that the universe has a beginning is the same as the assertion that time has a beginning.[65] The close association between beginning and time has direct consequences for their understanding of creation, as I will show in a moment.

But first, let us consider the idea of *causation* assumed by the adherents of the *kalam* cosmological argument. Craig declares that "the univocal concept of 'cause'" that he employs in his argumentation "is the concept of efficient causality, that is to say, something which produces or brings into being its effects. Whether such production involves transformation of previously existing materials or creation *ex nihilo* is completely incidental."[66] The fact that Craig considers cause exclusively as efficient cause is a clear indication of his adherence to the presuppositions of modern science. Remember that, in modern science, "efficient causes are taken to be the only real forms of causation and any appeal to metaphysical notions of final or formal causation are taken to be philosophically illegitimate attempts to reintroduce supernaturalism through the back door."[67] The alleged elimination of "metaphysical" causation (final and formal) entails a new understanding of efficient causality. This causality "was no longer understood to be the communication of act in the constitution of a being, and came to be understood, rather, as the initiation of

61. Craig, "J. Howard Sobel," 582. "Iff" is an abbreviation for "if and only if."

62. Craig, "Graham Oppy," 327.

63. Craig and Sinclair, "The *Kalam* Cosmological Argument," 102.

64. Craig and Sinclair, "The *Kalam* Cosmological Argument," 125.

65. Spitzer, *New Proofs*, 22.

66. Craig, "The Origin and Creation," 234–35.

67. Chapp, *The God of Covenant*, 1.

a displacement by impulse."[68] Efficient causality came to mean "an active force or impulse that initiated change by transfer of energy to another, resulting in a displacement of particles in a new configuration and with an accelerated or decelerated rate of motion among the particles."[69] Although modern science has tried to eliminate the Aristotelian fourfold causality, this is impossible to do. As D. C. Schindler remarks, Aristotle's causes cannot be rejected, but only transformed: "The essence of the scientific revolution, viewed specifically in relation to the issue of causality, is not that it retains only some of Aristotle's causes and rejects others, but that it retains *all* of them in some sense even while it radically transforms the meaning of each. . . . This transformation is not arbitrary, but itself reflects a change in the understanding of being."[70] As we saw in the first chapter, being is reduced "from actuality to pure facticity."[71]

Spitzer is very cautious in his definition of causality because he does not want to "limit the notion [of causality] to a particular kind of physics (such as Newtonian physics)." The Jesuit wants to apply the concept of causality "to every known intelligible structure (from quantum theory to inflationary cosmology and beyond)." Following the philosopher and theologian Bernard J. F. Lonergan, Spitzer describes causality as "a fulfillment of a conditioned reality's conditions."[72] He opines that "dependence on conditions is all that needs to be known in order for the proof [the *kalam* cosmological argument] to function. The *kind* of condition is absolutely irrelevant to the *functioning* of the proof."[73] He also thinks that, despite the fact that "philosophers and scientists can keep changing

68. Schmitz, *The Gift*, 122.

69. Schmitz, *The Texture of Being*, 34.

70. D. C. Schindler, "Historical Intelligibility," 23.

71. Hanby, *No God, No Science?* 250.

72. Spitzer, *New Proofs*, 154. See also chapter 4 of the referred book. In his definition of causality, Spitzer asserts that "recourse was made to three categories which could adequately cover the entire range of action, interaction, interrelationship, and energy emission in the General Theory of Relativity, Quantum Theory, quantum cosmology, string theory, etc.—namely, 'conditioned realities' (realities which depend on the fulfillment of conditions of any kind for their existence) and 'conditions' (any reality upon which a conditioned reality depends for its existence) and 'unconditioned reality' (a reality which does not depend on conditions of any kind for its existence). Conditioned realities and conditions can include space-time manifolds, electromagnetic fields, quantum fields, plasma fields, positions in the space-time manifold, structures of complexes, magnetic monopoles—literally any reality which is not unconditioned" (ibid., 223).

73. Spitzer, *New Proofs*, 223.

and expanding their views of causation," the validity or intelligibility of the *kalam* cosmological argument is not affected. For Spitzer, his definition of causality embraces "all particular manifestations of causality that science may adduce both now and in the future."[74] Notice how closely bound Spitzer's definition of causality is to science, and more specifically to physics. There is no surprise when the Jesuit uses the terms *force* and *power* in close connection with, or even as synonyms of, the term *cause*.[75] In the context of the act of creation, the astronomer Jastrow equates causality with forces.[76] Indeed, causation is understood in modern science in terms of force and power: "Causality itself ceases to be a matter of communication of form between cause and effect, as it had been for Plato and Aristotle, and becomes instead a production of 'power,' which reveals nothing of the nature of its source."[77] Again, this transformation reflects a change in the understanding of being from act to brute fact.

Now that I have explored the understanding of *beginning* and *cause* for the advocates of the *kalam* cosmological argument, I can deal with their conception of *creation*. Because they harbor a mechanistic ontology in which being is taken for granted, they can understand creation only as a mechanical event, as they communicate in their writings.[78] Creation is also explained as a temporal beginning. They can understand creation only in a temporal sense because they understand beginning in a temporal sense. For Spitzer, creation is "a [temporal] beginning . . . prior to which there is no time."[79] Craig's linkage of creation and time is very significant:

74. Spitzer, *New Proofs*, 224.

75. "Transcendent, creative *power*" (Spitzer, *New Proofs*, 1); "A *causative power* transcending universal space and time" (ibid, 3); "A creative *power* transcending universal space-time asymmetry" (ibid., 105); "Creative *power*" (ibid., 107); "A *causative force* outside of universal space-time asymmetry" (ibid., 215); "A transcendent *powerful* creative *force*" (Spitzer, "Cosmology.") All emphases are mine.

76. "Astronomers now find they have painted themselves into a corner because they have proven, by their own methods, that the world began abruptly in an act of creation to which you can trace the seeds of every star, every planet, every living thing in this cosmos and on the earth. And they have found that *all this happened as a product of forces* they cannot hope to discover" (Durbin and Jastrow, "A Scientist Caught," 15; emphasis mine).

77. Hanby, *No God, No Science?* 110. See D. C. Schindler "Historical Intelligibility." See also Dodds, *Unlocking Divine Action*, 50.

78. See Craig and Sinclair, "The *Kalam* Cosmological Argument," 175–76, 193–94, and 196; Spitzer, *New Proofs*, 4, 14, 57–59, and 215; and Durbin and Jastrow, "A Scientist Caught," 15 and 18.

79. Spitzer, *New Proofs*, 5. Moreover, Spitzer declares that "'creation' means the

"A temporal beginning is a vital element of the doctrine of creation." He defends explicitly that "it is clear that the biblical authors' notion of creation is not some metaphysical doctrine of ontological dependence, but involves the idea of a temporal origin of that which is created."[80] As we saw in the second chapter, creation is the passage from non-being to being. As outlined in that chapter, "*Creatio ex nihilo* is not primarily an answer to the question of temporal origin. . . . *Creatio ex nihilo* is, instead, about the ultimate ontological origin of reality—most fundamentally it describes in a very bald and unadorned way the *ultimate dependence* of everything on the Creator." Therefore, *creatio ex nihilo* "is not about a creation event, but about a *relationship* which everything that exists has with the Creator. So *creatio ex nihilo* is also *creatio continua*, continuing creation."[81] Because Craig understands creation as "an absolute [temporal] beginning of existence, [and] not [as] a transition . . . from nonbeing into being,"[82] he concludes that "the doctrine of *creatio continuans* implies that at each instant God creates a brand new individual, numerically distinct from its chronological predecessor." This is nothing else but occasionalism, "according to which no persisting individuals exist, so that personal agency and identity over time are precluded." Craig has no other option than to remove the idea of continuing creation from creation itself. For him, "It is therefore preferable to take 'continuing creation' as but

---

ultimate fulfillment of a conditioned reality's conditions. The word 'ultimate' is used here to differentiate creation from a 'proximate cause' (a proximate fulfillment of conditions). For example, the existence and proper structure of a cat's cells is a proximate fulfillment of the cat's conditions. Alternatively, 'creation' refers to the ultimate fulfillment of the cat's conditions by the one unconditioned Reality itself" (ibid., 140). Note that Spitzer does not see any contradiction between the creation event and conservation. He thinks that his definition of creation "simply includes the possibility of the Creator (the source, power, or activity of the ultimate fulfillment of conditions) continuously fulfilling conditions ultimately, and, as it were, 'holding or conserving' conditioned realities in being" (ibid., 142). Afterward, we will see Craig's opinion about the same topic of creation and conservation.

80. Craig, "Creation and Conservation," 180–81. For the philosophical theologian, creation is a process of "efficient causation in the absence of material causation" (Craig and Sinclair, "The *Kalam* Cosmological Argument," 140n38). Notice here again the emphasis on efficient causation. It is ironic that Craig's biblicism, without the mediation of a proper metaphysics of creation to help in its interpretation, leaves him with an account of creation that concedes the world to the mechanistic reductionism of science.

81. Stoeger, "The Big Bang," 172.

82. Moreland and Craig, *Philosophical Foundations*, 556.

a manner of speaking and to distinguish creation from conservation."[83] In other words, conservation is not considered, properly speaking, as a species of creation.[84] Again, this is a consequence of considering creation as a temporal event. The reduction of creation to a temporal beginning is itself the result of the metaphysical reduction of being to facticity. Because Craig has an inadequate doctrine of God and no metaphysics of participation, creation is ultimately reduced to temporal origin and continuing creation—i.e., participation—disappears. As a result, affirming creation on Craig's terms would teach us nothing about nature beyond what we learn from the physical sciences.

Obviously, the promoters of the *kalam* cosmological argument do not understand creation properly, because they reduce creation to a mere question of temporal origins. They think that creation answers "the question of *how* the world came to be."[85] However, "The doctrine of creation does not . . . seek to explain *how* the world came to be in any scientific sense of the word 'how.' Rather, it tells us what the world *is*. The question of creation is therefore a question of *ontological* rather than temporal origins,"[86] as I remarked in the second chapter. Only when the importance of ontological origin over temporal origin is taken into account is creation properly understood, and can a scientist thus obtain a more comprehensive sense of what nature itself is. Regarding the ontological priority, Thomas Aquinas stated that "non-being is prior to being in the thing which is said to be created. This is not a priority of time or of duration, such that what did not exist before does exist later, but a priority of nature, so that, if the created thing is left to itself, it would not exist, because it only has its being from the causality of the higher cause."[87] In other words, "The creature is completely dependent, throughout its entire duration, upon the constant causality of the Creator." The dependence of the creature "upon the cause of its being is precisely the same at the beginning of the creature's duration as it is all throughout its duration."[88] Therefore, "Creation is not merely some distant event; it is the on-going, complete causing of the existence of whatever is."[89] The on-going rela-

---

83. Moreland and Craig, *Philosophical Foundations*, 555.

84. Craig, "Creation and Conservation," 180.

85. Hanby, *No God, No Science?* 5.

86. Hanby, *No God, No Science?* 324; See Joseph Ratzinger, *In the Beginning*, 50.

87. Aquinas, *Scriptum Super Libros Sententiarum*, lib. 2, d. 1, q. 1, a. 2, co.

88. Baldner and William Carroll, "Analysis of Aquinas' Writings," 42.

89. Baldner and William Carroll, "Analysis of Aquinas' Writings," 43.

tion of metaphysical dependence of the creature upon God is, then, more fundamental than its temporal beginning. As explained in the second chapter, a temporal beginning is subordinate to the more fundamental distinction between being and non-being. This is the case because the question of time is subordinate to the question of being.[90] In fact, creation is the necessary precondition for the temporal origin of the universe, in particular, and for history, in general.[91] Nevertheless, modern cosmology is unable to discern that creation and the temporal origin of the universe belong on different levels, because modern science identifies being with history, as indicated in the second chapter. As a consequence, modern cosmology suffers in its comprehension of the world.

Creation is not a mechanical event that took place at the beginning of time. However, the supporters of the *kalam* cosmological argument understand creation as an event because they assume the mechanical understanding of nature inherent in modern science, based on a positivistic conception of being. These supporters understand the Big Bang as the creation event. For Craig, "The standard Big Bang model . . . describes a universe which is not eternal in the past, but which came into being a finite time ago. Moreover—and this deserves underscoring—the origin it posits is an absolute origin *ex nihilo*. For not only all matter and energy, but space and time themselves come into being at the initial cosmological singularity."[92] Therefore, "The big bang does plausibly represent the creation event."[93] For Spitzer, "The preponderance of cosmological evidence favors a beginning of the universe (prior to which there was no physical reality whatsoever). This beginning of physical reality marks the point at which our universe came into existence."[94] Regarding scientists, it is fitting here to restate Jastrow's words: "Astronomers now find they have painted themselves into a corner because they have proven, by their own methods, that the world began abruptly in an act of creation to which

90. The differentiation between ontological and temporal beginning does not aim to deny creation *ab initio temporis* or even to reduce it to a mere fideistic question. The differentiation intends to clarify that ontological origin is a notion more basic than temporal origin, and also that the distinction between being and non-being dictates the meaning of time and temporal origin. Certainly, the meaning of time cannot be determined without metaphysics, and there is always a metaphysics already at work in any conception of time.

91. Hanby, *No God, No Science?* 345.

92. Craig, "Ultimate Question of Origins," 725.

93. Copan and Craig, *Creation out of Nothing*, 18.

94. Spitzer, *New Proofs*, 43.

you can trace the seeds of every star, every planet, every living thing in this cosmos and on the earth."[95] In summary, the advocates of the *kalam* cosmological argument interpret the singularity of the Big Bang model as the absolute temporal beginning of the universe and the creation event.

The Jesuit and astrophysicist William Stoeger appropriately pointed out that "the origins with which science can deal are always what we might call 'relative origins,' which are indeed very important. . . . But they are not absolute, or ultimate, origins. This is because . . . the natural sciences must always presuppose the existence of something to study and an order or regularity which characterizes the behavior of that something."[96] Therefore, "Cosmology and the other sciences cannot disclose . . . [the creation event] simply because they are incapable of transcending the barrier between absolute nothingness and something, between absolute chaos and order." Modern sciences, and especially cosmology, "do not have access to what is 'before' existence and 'before' order, simply because they have presupposed both basic existence and basic order and have not questioned the ground of either."[97] Creation provides an explanation of the "ultimate ground of existence and order in the universe—and for reality as a whole."[98] The theologian William Carroll properly defends that "creation concerns first of all the origin of the universe, not its temporal beginning." The origin of the universe "affirms the complete, continuing dependence of all that is on God as cause. Whatever is created has its origin in God."[99]

The validity of the *kalam* cosmological argument can be called into question by the fact that it is based on an absolute temporal beginning of the universe. As indicated previously, modern science can only deal with a relative beginning of the universe because science always presupposes being. Nevertheless, I do not want to focus on this point. My emphasis is on the fact that the *kalam* cosmological argument does not really understand what creation is. Creation is not the first mechanical event in a long succession of mechanical events because, as stated above, creation is primarily a question of ontological origin rather than temporal origin. Nor is creation a change, for change presupposes being, and in creation

95. Durbin and Jastrow, "A Scientist Caught," 15.
96. Stoeger, "Origin of the Universe," 263.
97. Stoeger, "Origin of the Universe," 264.
98. Stoeger, "The Big Bang," 171.
99. William Carroll, "Aquinas and Contemporary Cosmology," 16.

the whole being is produced. Creation is truly the ultimate dependence of everything that exists upon God. Indeed, creation is the upholding of the being of every creature over non-being.[100] The adherents of the *kalam* cosmological argument do not consider the question of creation as a question of being and nothing because they take being for granted, and thus they do not properly consider being at all. In conclusion, the *kalam* cosmological argument does not prove creation, because what the argument claims to prove is *not what creation properly is*.

In the second chapter I explained that the doctrine of creation is a theological doctrine. Creation, as the on-going relation of metaphysical dependence of the being of every creature upon God, is inexorably related to God. Therefore, the defenders of the *kalam* cosmological argument cannot properly grasp the idea of a creator God because they do not properly grasp the idea of creation. When creation is understood as the first mechanical event in a long succession of mechanical events, the world is conceived as a mechanism, and God is also understood as the "first efficient cause in a temporal sequence of efficient causes."[101] Because "the whole notion of causation has been leveled-out to a single notion of efficient agency, the first efficient cause cannot help but appear as a finite part of the cosmos."[102] In the end, God is reduced to an object within a more comprehensive order of being that is taken for granted but never thought through or explicated by the supporters of the *kalam* cosmological argument. These scholars are trying to offer scientific proof for God's existence. However, what they are affirming is not the Christian God, but an extrinsic one.

Craig identifies the creator with "an 'external cause' of the beginning of the universe."[103] In like manner, Spitzer couples the "creator of the universe" with "a transcendent cause of the universe (physical reality),"[104]

---

100. "Creation *ex nihilo*—the doctrine that creation, at every moment, is of nothing—as such privileges no particular temporal instant as revealing more acutely the nature of the cosmos as suspended over the *nihil*" (Oliver, "Trinity, Motion and Creation," 142); "When people speak of God as creator, they often entertain absurd imagery. They connect creation with initiation, whereas it truly has no more to do with the first than with any later moment" (Dummett, *Thought and Reality*, 106).

101. Chapp, *The God of Covenant*, 88. That god can be described also as "the first mover in the clunky sense of the first domino in a series of falling dominos" (ibid.).

102. Chapp, *The God of Covenant*, 2.

103. Craig, "The Origin and Creation," 233.

104. Spitzer, *New Proofs*, 45.

and with "a transcendent power outside of physical space and time."[105] For Spitzer, "transcendent" means "independent of the universe and beyond it."[106] Accordingly, these theologians locate God "outside" the universe. Notwithstanding, I cannot simply say that their image of God is extrinsic just because they place God "outside" the universe. The terms "inside" and "outside" are both spatial metaphors that are not strictly applicable to God. It is admissible by way of analogy to talk about God as being outside the world, but only if we keep in mind that what we mean by "outside" at the same time makes God radically interior to the world, and that being radically interior to the world has a bearing on what the world is. It is crucial to highlight that the image of God inherent in the *kalam* cosmological argument is extrinsic because God's transcendent otherness to the order of creation is lost. As already said, the being of God and the being of the world are completely different. They are not different species of the same genus. The concept of being has to be understood in an analogical way and not in a univocal way, as extrinsicism does.[107]

The classical concept of analogy attempts to give expression to God's transcendence or otherness to the world. The idea of analogy emphasizes "the unsurpassability of the *analogia entis*, the ever greater dissimilarity to God no matter how great the similarity to Him."[108] In the analogy, "Unlikeness remains infinitely greater than likeness, yet not to the point of abolishing analogy and its language."[109] When the infinite difference between God and the world is lost, analogy becomes a simple parallelism between two beings, a greater and a lesser. For the promoters of the *kalam* cosmological argument who believe in God, he is the first efficient cause (the greater) among many efficient causes (the lesser). Therefore, God is, in the end, a particular being (although a very important one) within the comprehensive order of being, which is described in physical terms

---

105. Spitzer, "Cosmology."

106. Spitzer, "Cosmology."

107. Remember that Craig rejects the analogical understanding of being in favor of the univocal understanding of being.

108. Balthasar, *Glory of the Lord V*, 548. Balthasar referred here to this teaching from Lateran Council IV: "Between the Creator and the creature so great a likeness cannot be noted without the necessity of noting a greater dissimilarity between them [*Inter creatorem et creaturam non potest similitudo notari, quin inter eos maior sit dissimilitudo notanda*]" (Denzinger, *Sources of Catholic Dogma*, n. 432).

109. Benedict XVI, "The Regensburg Address," 170.

such as power and force.[110] Because being is not understood in analogical terms, because God is not described as *ipsum esse subsistens*, the concept of *nihil* cannot be apprehended properly. For example, Craig says that the *nihil* of *creatio ex nihilo* is the initial singularity of the Big Bang model, which is a mathematical concept—a point having infinite density.[111] Again, the philosophical theologian is not able to think properly about *nihil* (which is understood as something, i.e., a mathematical concept) because he is not able to think of God's transcendence radically and thoroughly enough. Indeed, Craig finds the Thomistic idea of God as *ipsum esse subsistens* as "just unintelligible,"[112] "enormously implausible,"[113] and "wholly obscure."[114]

When God's transcendence is lost, the image of God is distorted. As an illustration, Craig affirms that God begins to exist because the universe begins to exist. According to the philosophical theologian, the exercise of God's "causal power in order for the universe to be created . . . entails, of course, an intrinsic change on God's part which brings Him into time at the moment of creation. For that reason He must be temporal since creation, even if He is timeless sans creation."[115] For Craig, God "en-

---

110. "A super-intelligent, transcendent, creative *power* that stands at the origin of our universe" (Spitzer, *New Proofs*, 1); "A *causative power* transcending universal space and time" (ibid, 3); "A creative *power* transcending universal space-time asymmetry" (ibid., 105); "Creative *power*" (ibid., 107); "A *causative force* outside of universal space-time asymmetry" (ibid., 215); "A transcendent *powerful* creative *force*" (Spitzer, "Cosmology.") All emphases are mine.

111. Craig, "Professor Mackie," 374 and Craig, "God and the Initial," 241.

112. Craig, "Divine Simplicity."

113. Craig, *Proofs for God*.

114. Craig, "The Cosmological Argument," 130n9. "To say that God is His essence seems to make God into a property (or a property instance), which is incompatible with His being a living, concrete being. Moreover, if God is not distinct from His essence, then God cannot know or do anything different than what He knows and does, in which case everything becomes necessary. To respond that God is perfectly similar in all logically possible worlds which we can imagine but that contingency is real because God stands in no real relations to things is to make the existence or non-existence of creatures in various possible worlds independent of God and utterly mysterious. To say that God's essence just is His existence seems wholly obscure, since then there is in God's case no entity that exists; there is just the existing itself without any subject" (ibid.). Obviously, it might be said in response to Craig that God is not *a* living concrete being, because he is not a thing among things.

115. Craig and Sinclair, "The Kalam Cosmological Argument," 194n101. "Senor has dubbed such a model of divine eternity 'accidental temporalism' (Senor, 1993)" (Craig, "Ultimate Question of Origins," 736n10). See Senor, "Divine Temporality."

ters time at the moment of creation in virtue of His causal relation to the temporal universe."[116] Behind this misconception, there is a mechanical conception of time as a succession of lineal instants. In agreement with this notion, the eternal God is reduced to a God who has existed for a very long time and will exist indefinitely in the future. In this extrinsic theology, time and eternity are understood as opposites. However, we saw in the second chapter that God's eternity, understood as indivisible actuality, is the primal image of time. A creature participates in eternity by the mere act of existing. This is so because existence is a participation in the actuality of being that is ultimately from God. The now of time is a kind of participation in the fullness of actuality that is being.

Because theological extrinsicism is unable to properly understand divine transcendence, it is also unable to understand the distinction between primary and secondary causality. In this extrinsic scenario, creation, understood as a mechanical event, is in a position of rivalry with natural processes. For this reason, Craig and Spitzer situate God in a place where there is no available scientific explanation.[117] The *kalam* cosmological argument presupposes that God can only act in the world by initiating the expansion of the universe, which is ultimately void of the divine presence (as a consequence of the loss of divine transcendence). The god defended by the *kalam* cosmological argument is a god who has a right to appear as an explanation for the beginning of the natural world, as long as there is no current scientific explanation for the beginning. A god located at the unknown frontier of science is a god of the gaps.[118] The agnostic Jastrow conceded the possibility of a creator as an explanation of the beginning of the universe[119] because he held "fast to the view that

116. Craig and Sinclair, "The Kalam Cosmological Argument," 196.

117. Craig and Sinclair, "The Kalam Cosmological Argument," 193 and 196; Spitzer, *New Proofs*, 43.

118. Ernan McMullin pointed out that "the appeal is not to a 'gap' in scientific explanation but to a different order of explanation that leaves scientific explanation intact, that explores the conditions of possibility of there being *any* kind of scientific explanation" (McMullin, "Natural Science and Belief," 74). The doctrine of *creatio ex nihilo* leaves intact any scientific explanation, except those negating an absolute beginning of the universe. "With respect to the *creatio ex nihilo*, theologians can note that the Big Bang theory does not contradict this doctrine insofar as it can be said that the supposition of an absolute beginning is not scientifically inadmissible" (International Theological Commission, "Communion and Stewardship," 342 (paragraph 67)).

119. "We cannot tell by scientific methods whether the birth of the Universe is the work of a Creator or some force outside the domain of science, or is instead the product of physical forces, that is, a part of natural law" (Jastrow, "The Astronomer

science will not be able to decipher the cause of the cosmic explosion as long as it appears that the Universe was infinitely hot and dense in its first moments."[120] That possible creator would be, again, a god of the gaps.

The extrinsic image of God goes hand in hand with an extrinsic relation of science to theology and metaphysics. For example, Spitzer considers that "God is not an object or phenomenon or regularity within the physical universe; so science cannot say anything about God."[121] He is unable to realize that science always tacitly presupposes an image of God, since the world's intrinsic relation to God is reflected in science's intrinsic relation to theology and metaphysics, as previously discussed in the first chapter. An extrinsicist scholar, whether a theologian or a scientist, defends a science that is neutral regarding theology and metaphysics. These two subjects are placed outside the realm of scientific knowledge. There is no surprise when Spitzer declares: "When we speak of a beginning (a point prior to which there is no physical reality), we stand at the threshold of physics and metaphysics (beyond physics)."[122] In this matter, Jastrow was more explicit:

> At this moment it seems as though science will never be able to raise the curtain on the mystery of creation. For the scientist who has lived by his faith in the power of reason, the story ends like a bad dream. He has scaled the mountains of ignorance, he is about to conquer the highest peak; as he pulls himself over the final rock, he is greeted by a band of theologians who have been sitting there for centuries.[123]

As already said, theological extrinsicism does not correctly understand God's transcendence so that, in the end, God becomes an external agent who is in competition with natural processes.[124] At the same time, creation ceases to be about the generation of being and becomes a worldly mechanism. We saw in the first chapter that the concepts of God and creation are intrinsically related to the metaphysical structure

---

and God," 19). It seems that for the astronomer there is no difference between a creator and a force unknown by science.

120. Jastrow, "The Astronomer and God," 17.

121. Spitzer, *New Proofs*, 22.

122. Spitzer, *New Proofs*, 23.

123. Jastrow, *God and the Astronomers*, 116.

124. "Creation should be thought of, not according to the model of a craftsman who makes all sorts of objects, but rather in the manner in which thought is creative" (Ratzinger, *Dogma and Preaching*, 140).

of reality. When God's otherness is lost and when creation ceases to be about the transition from non-being to being, God and creation have no bearing on the ontological constitution of the creature. Therefore, theology does not inform the world in any essential way. In fact, the defective concepts of creation and God leave the mechanical understanding of nature unaffected.

In this section, I have dealt with theologians who use the *kalam* cosmological argument (based on the beginning of the universe) to defend the existence of God. I have also shown that the image of God whose existence they defend is an extrinsic one. The problem with the *kalam* cosmological argument is not the affirmation that every effect must have a cause, nor even that this leads to God. The real problem is the positivism and the neglect of the question of being built into the argument. As we have seen, the defenders of the *kalam* argument exhibit a reduced understanding of causality that only requires an object called God, and thus they are unable to understand the radical nature of the absoluteness of God. As a result, they can only apprehend an extrinsic image of God.

When atheistic cosmologists deny the existence of God on the basis of their science, they are assuming the same extrinsic God. In this regard, Craig recognizes that Hawking accepted the *kalam* cosmological argument: "Hawking repeatedly states that on the classical GTR Big Bang model of the universe an initial space-time singularity is unavoidable, and he does not dispute that the origin of the universe must therefore require a supernatural cause. He points out that one could identify the Big Bang as the instant at which God created the universe."[125] Moreover, "on Hawking's view, . . . given the classical Big Bang model, the inference to a Creator or temporally First Cause seems natural and unobjectionable."[126] When Hawking accepted the *kalam* cosmological argument, he was accepting the extrinsic image of God implicit in it. This extrinsic image is the one that he rejected by using his science, as I am going to show in the next section. Indeed, the task for the next section is to explain that the God rejected by atheistic cosmologists is the same one defended by extrinsicist theologians and scientists. I will continue focusing on the cosmological topic of the beginning of the universe.

---

125. Craig, "What Place for Creator?" 477; Hawking, *Brief History of Time* (1988), 9. GTR stands for General Theory of Relativity.

126. Craig, "What Place for Creator?" 477.

Alternatives to the Beginning of the Universe

The affirmation that atheistic cosmologists harbor an extrinsic image of God is evidenced by the fact that these cosmologists unequivocally associate the unexplained beginning of the universe of the Big Bang model with a creator. Because of this, they offer different cosmological models to avoid the initial singularity and thus the creator. The atheistic cosmologist Vilenkin explains that the initial singularity, also known as the Big Bang, is the point "where the mathematics of general relativity breaks down. At the singularity, matter is compressed to infinite density, and the solutions cannot be extended to earlier times."[127] And this is his conclusion:

> Thus, taken literally, the big bang should be interpreted as the beginning of the universe. Was that the creation of the world? Could it be that the whole universe began in a singular event a finite time ago? For most physicists this was too much to take. A singular jump-starting of the universe looked like a divine intervention, for which they thought there should be no place in physical theory. But although the "beginning of the world" was—and to a large degree remains—a source of discomfort for most scientists, it also has some benefits to offer.[128]

The beginning of the universe implicit in the Big Bang model is a source of discomfort for scientists because, as we have seen, they think that the initial singularity unequivocally points to a creator. As pointed out in the second chapter, the choice of atheistic cosmologists "between a divine intention for the world and the world's unfolding in its proper freedom . . . is a false dilemma rooted in defective notions of God, creation, and causality."[129] From Vilenkin's words, we can notice how creation is misapprehended as an event within the positivity of being, if not indeed in time, which cannot yet be fully described by physics because of the Big Bang singularity. We already know that the question of creation is not fundamentally a question of the temporal origin of the universe but rather "a question of the ontological structure of the world . . . at every moment of its existence."[130] The key issue is that a temporal beginning is always anteceded by an ontological beginning—not horizontally, in time,

127. Vilenkin, *Many Worlds in One*, 24.
128. Vilenkin, *Many Worlds in One*, 24.
129. Hanby, *No God, No Science?* 345.
130. Hanby, *No God, No Science?* 324.

but vertically, as a matter of existence—which transforms what a temporal beginning is. Nevertheless, atheistic cosmologists reduce creation to a mere temporal beginning of the world. From Vilenkin's words, we can realize how God is conceived as the mechanical cause of the beginning of the universe. A cause that is outside the range of scientific knowledge and whose transcendence is utterly lost. This is the case because being is taken for granted, and the analogy of being is replaced with a clumsy parallelism between a greater and a lesser. Although this god is situated outside the realm of science, he is ultimately a cause among causes. This god of the gaps is the god avoided by atheistic cosmologists when they propose their different cosmological models. In this section, I will investigate those cosmological models as a way to show the extrinsicist theology imbued in them.

Before discussing the cosmological models that avoid the singularity, it is necessary to explain some cosmological concepts that will appear in the rest of the chapter, especially in this section. As formerly discussed, the Big Bang model is a cosmological model in which the universe expands from an initial singularity known as the Big Bang. This model, also known as the hot Big Bang model, has been modified in the past decades in order to adjust it to astronomical observations. The modifications introduced are dark matter, which was added in the 1930s, inflation, which was added in the 1980s, and dark energy, which was added in the 1990s. The modified Big Bang model is what constitutes the inflationary model.[131] This model assumes that "just after the bang, a small region of the universe underwent a dramatic process called inflation, during which it expanded a googol (10^{100}) times or more within a billionth of a billionth of a trillionth (10^{-30}) of a second." After the astonishingly short period of inflation finished, "the energy causing the inflation was transformed into a dense gas of hot radiation. The gas cooled and the expansion slowed, allowing atoms and molecules to clump into galaxies and stars."[132] Because the amount of luminous matter, or normal matter, was insufficient to explain the formation of galaxies, the concept of dark matter was introduced into the model to provide the gravitational attraction necessary for galaxies to form and not disintegrate once they were formed.[133] The inflationary model also assumes that after the formation of galaxies, "9

---

131. Steinhardt and Turok, *Endless Universe*, 6 and 66.

132. Steinhardt and Turok, *Endless Universe*, 6.

133. Liddle and Loveday, *Oxford Companion to Cosmology*, 89.

billion years after the big bang, a mysterious force called dark energy took over and started to accelerate the expansion again. In the standard picture, the expansion of the universe will accelerate forever, turning all of space into a vast and nearly perfect vacuum."[134]

It is commonly held by scientists that inflation is an eternal process. Andrei Linde, one of the fathers of inflationary cosmology, affirms that "instead of being an expanding ball of fire the universe is a huge, growing fractal. It consists of many inflating balls that produce new balls, which in turn produce more balls, ad infinitum."[135] This model is known as the eternal inflationary model or the self-reproducing inflationary universe. In accordance with this model, "One inflationary universe sprouts other inflationary bubbles, which in turn produce other inflationary bubbles." In the eternal inflation scenario, "the universe as a whole is immortal," and there is "no end for the evolution of the entire universe."[136] Linde notices that "the possibility that the universe eternally re-creates itself in all its possible forms does not necessarily solve the problem of creation, but pushes it back into the indefinite past."[137] It is necessary to add one more thing about inflation. It has the property of explaining the current

134. Steinhardt and Turok, *Endless Universe*, 6. It is interesting to note that the nature of dark matter, "apart from its gravitational influence . . . is unknown" (Liddle and Loveday, *Oxford Companion to Cosmology*, 89). This seems to make dark matter a lot like ordinary matter. In a similar way, "The term 'dark energy' is covering the fact that although it is quite well established that the expansion of the Universe is accelerating, the cause of this is presently unknown" (ibid., 86). As it is frequently said, the terms "dark matter" and "dark energy" are placeholders for our ignorance. The situation gets worse when we realize that, according to recent measurements by the Planck satellite, dark matter and dark energy add up to 95 percent of the content of the universe. According to the Planck collaboration, dark energy constitutes 69 percent of the universe; dark matter, 26 percent; and normal matter only 5 percent. (Ade et al., "Planck 2013 Results," 10, table 2, *Planck+WP* column). Notice that physics considers matter and energy equivalent because matter can convert into energy and vice versa. Einstein's famous equation expresses the equivalence mathematically: $E=mc^2$, where E is energy, m is mass, and c is the speed of light. By the way, the nature of light is unknown as well.

135. Linde, "Self-Reproducing Inflationary Universe," 48.

136. Linde, "Self-Reproducing Inflationary Universe," 54.

137. Linde, "Universe, Life, and Consciousness," 196. Certainly, the eternal inflation scenario does not solve the problem of creation, not because it pushes creation back into the past, but because it reduces creation to its first temporal instant. The problem of creation is the problem of *being*—why there is something rather than nothing at all—and the problem of the *structure* of being—the novelty that characterizes each existing being.

universe without the necessity of having to specify the initial conditions of the universe. This is so because "the whole point of inflation was to avoid having to assume finely tuned initial conditions when the universe emerged from the big bang."[138] In a later section of this chapter, I will explore more deeply this issue of inflation and fine-tuning.

As already said, the goal of this section is to review the cosmological models that try to avoid the initial singularity, as a way to show the extrinsicist theology inherent in these models. I will begin with the old-fashioned cosmological model known as the steady-state model. This model was proposed in 1948 by the atheistic astronomer Fred Hoyle, and also by Hermann Bondi and Thomas Gold, as an alternative to the Big Bang model. According to the steady-state model:

> The universe has always remained unchanged in its broad features, so that it looks more or less the same at all places and at all times. This view seems to be in glaring contradiction with the expansion of the universe: If the distances between the galaxies grow, how can the universe remain unchanged? To compensate for the expansion, Hoyle and his friends postulated that matter is being continuously created out of the vacuum. This matter fills the voids opened by the receding galaxies, so that the new galaxies can be formed in their places.[139]

The steady-state model wanted to avoid the initial singularity of the Big Bang. Hoyle opined that "the big bang theory requires a recent origin of the Universe that openly invites the concept of creation."[140] He also "found the big bang abhorrent because he was vehemently antireligious and he thought the cosmological picture was disturbingly close to the biblical account."[141] The astrophysicist admitted that the development of the steady-state model "sought to avoid the conceptual difficulties associated with an 'origin' by dispensing with the need for it."[142] In this regard, Craig asks: "But why would a man who proposes a theory requiring the continuous generation of matter *ex nihilo* have conceptual difficulties with the beginning of the universe from nothing?" And this is his own answer: "I get the strong impression that it is because Hoyle, unlike the

138. Steinhardt and Turok, *Endless Universe*, 95.
139. Vilenkin, *Many Worlds in One*, 27–28.
140. Hoyle, *The Intelligent Universe*, 237.
141. Steinhardt and Turok, *Endless Universe*, 179.
142. Hoyle, "Origin of the Universe," 278.

vast majority of scientists, realizes the metaphysical and theological implications of such a beginning, and he recoils from these implications."[143]
Notice here the confusion between temporal origin and ontological origin for both Craig the philosophical theologian and Hoyle the atheist.

In the same way as Craig, Hoyle considered unavoidable a connection between the beginning of the universe and the existence of a creator.
Both Craig and Hoyle share the reasoning of the *kalam* cosmological argument and the extrinsic image of God inherent in it. The former uses it
to affirm the existence of God and the latter to avoid it. This is how Hoyle
saw the connection between the initial singularity and a creator:

> The abrupt beginning is regarded as *metaphysical*—i.e., *outside*
> physics. The physical laws are therefore considered to break
> down at $\tau = 0$, *and to do so inherently*. To many people this
> thought process seems highly satisfactory because a "some-
> thing" outside physics can then be introduced at $\tau = 0$. By a
> semantic manoeuvre, the word "something" is then replaced by
> "god," except that the first letter becomes capital, God, in order
> to warn us that we must not carry the enquiry any further.[144]

Notice that Hoyle thought that God is "something," a being in the all-
inclusive order of being. Apparently, this "something" is a being whose
name must begin with a capital letter. For the astrophysicist, God appeared at the end of the chain of scientific questions. However, God is
not "a mechanism for the being of the world." In fact, God is the beginning of questions, not the end. This is why "the existence of the world
becomes almost *more* mysterious when God is admitted than when he
is denied."[145]

It is very interesting to note how Hoyle himself witnessed the inevitability of science having theological presuppositions, even though
scientists try to avoid them: "I have always thought it curious that, while

---

143. Craig and Smith, *Theism, Atheism,* 45.

144. Hoyle, *Astronomy and Cosmology,* 684–85.

145. Hanby, "Trinity, Creation," 51. "Why in fact is there something rather than
nothing? The question remains open regardless of whether one affirms or denies the
existence of an absolute being. If there is no absolute being, what reason could there
be that these finite, ephemeral things exist in the midst of nothing, things that could
never add up to the absolute as a whole or evolve into it? But on the other hand, if
there is an absolute being, and if this being is sufficient unto itself, it is almost more
mysterious why there should exist something else. Only a philosophy of freedom and
love can account for our existence, though not unless it also interprets the essence of
finite being in terms of love" (Balthasar, *Love Alone Is Credible,* 143).

most scientists claim to eschew religion, it actually dominates their thoughts more than it does the clergy."[146] Remember that, as shown in the first chapter, science and theology are intrinsically related. Hoyle also recognized that the desire of some scientists to accept the Big Bang had a theological motivation: "The passionate frenzy with which the big-bang cosmology is clutched to the corporate scientific bosom evidently arises from a deep-rooted attachment to the first page of Genesis, religious fundamentalism at its strongest."[147]

The steady-state model lost its battle against the Big Bang model when the latter received experimental confirmation in 1965, with the discovery of the cosmic microwave background. This is "the relic radiation left over from earlier stages of the hot big bang . . . , and is currently the most important way of understanding the properties of the young Universe."[148] The cosmic microwave background "is a snapshot of the oldest light in our Universe, imprinted on the sky when the Universe was just 380,000 years old."[149] In spite of the experimental confirmation of the Big Bang model, Hoyle defended a modified version of his steady-state model (the quasi-steady-state model) until his death, in 2001.[150] Seemingly, his theological convictions were stronger than his commitment to science.

146. Hoyle, "The Universe," 23.

147. Hoyle, "The Universe," 23.

148. Liddle and Loveday, *Oxford Companion to Cosmology*, 56.

149. ESA and Planck Collaboration, "Planck Reveals." The cosmic microwave background "shows tiny temperature fluctuations that correspond to regions of slightly different densities, representing the seeds of all future structure: the stars and galaxies of today" (ibid.).

150. The quasi-steady-state cosmology (QSSC) was developed by Fred Hoyle, Geoffrey R. Burbidge, and Jayant V. Narlikar in the 1990s to get around the problems of the steady-state cosmology. "In this model, a single big bang event is replaced with a series of mini big bangs: the sources of energy in quasars and active galaxy nuclei result from mini creation events. One can think of a QSSC Universe as undergoing long-term, steady-state expansion interspersed with short term oscillations" (Liddle and Loveday, *Oxford Companion to Cosmology*, 289). The steady-state theory was "conceptually founded on the 'perfect cosmological principle'—the postulate that the universe in its large-scale features is not only spatially but also temporally homogenous" (Halvorson and Kragh, "Physical Cosmology," 245). The QSSC "does not satisfy the perfect cosmological principle, but it assumes an indefinite cosmic time scale during which matter is continually created. In this respect it is an alternative to the big-bang theory and its supposed association with the divine creation" (ibid., 246). For further information about the QSSC, see Hoyle et al., *Different Approach to Cosmology*, chapters 15 and 16.

In 1970, the singularity of the Big Bang received theoretical confirmation from the Penrose-Hawking singularity theorem.[151] This theorem defended that "there must have been a big bang singularity provided only that general relativity is correct and the universe contains as much matter as we observe."[152] Hawking pointed out the resistance that their singularity theorem generated, mostly not for scientific reasons: "There was a lot of opposition to our work, partly by the Russians because of their Marxist belief in scientific determinism, and partly from people who felt that the whole idea of singularities was repugnant and spoiled the beauty of Einstein's theory. However, one cannot really argue with a mathematical theorem."[153] The cosmologist also recognized the pleasure among religious leaders regarding the singularity theorem: "It delighted those religious leaders who believed in an act of creation, for here was scientific proof."[154] Obviously, Hawking had in mind those religious leaders who shared with him the same extrinsicist image of God, such as Craig or Spitzer.

Although the Penrose-Hawking singularity theorem implied a beginning for an expanding universe, following Einstein's theory of general relativity, cosmologists, including Hawking himself, found a way to avoid this theorem: a new theory of gravitation known as quantum gravity. This theory was intended to reconcile Einstein's theory of general relativity (a theory of gravity) and quantum mechanics (a theory of the microscopic).[155] Scientists claimed that, in the very early universe, when it was extremely small and dense, Einstein's theory of gravity should take into account the effects of quantum mechanics. In other words, the force of gravity should be described as a quantum force in the very early universe. The theory of quantum gravity seeks to describe that quantum

151. Hawking and Penrose, "Singularities of Gravitational Collapse."

152. Hawking, *Brief History of Time* (1988), 50.

153. Hawking, *Brief History of Time* (1988), 50. Note how mathematics was the ultimate source of truth for Hawking.

154. Hawking, *Universe in a Nutshell*, 41.

155. Craig and Sinclair, "The *Kalam* Cosmological Argument," 158. "The basic precept of quantum mechanics is that physics on microscopic scales becomes probabilistic in nature. Rather than having a definite location, an electron exists in a state where it may be at any number of different positions, each with its own probability. Only the act of measurement can determine where it actually is. Further, objects have complementary properties which cannot be known simultaneously, an example being their position and velocity. This is known as Heisenberg's Uncertainty Principle" (Liddle and Loveday, *Oxford Companion to Cosmology*, 242).

force.[156] The new theory of gravitation would avoid the initial singularity. Hawking recognized that "we do not yet have a complete consistent theory that unifies general relativity and quantum mechanics, but we do know a number of features it should have."[157] In this situation, "there are several candidate quantum gravity theories but no established consensus on which is likely to be correct."[158]

Current cosmological models make use of the different approaches to quantum gravity to avoid the initial singularity. The cosmological models that incorporate quantum gravity "can be divided into two types: 'beginning' cosmologies, in which there is a first moment of time, and 'eternal' cosmologies, where time stretches to the past without limit." The beginning cosmologies "typically attempt to replace the Big Bang singularity of classical general relativity with some sort of quantum-mechanical event. . . . These models imagine that spacetime is a classical approximation to some sort of quantum mechanical structure. In particular, time may be just an approximate notion, useful in some regimes but not others." These cosmologies suggest that a "mental journey backwards in time will ultimately reach a point past which the concept of 'time' is no longer applicable."[159] In this section, I will consider the two major beginning cosmologies: the no-boundary proposal of James Hartle and Stephen Hawking, and the "creation out of nothing" model of Alexander Vilenkin.[160] The eternal cosmologies use a theory of quantum gravity to "replace the singularity by a transitional stage in an eternal universe."[161] In this section, I will deal with the most prominent eternal cosmology: the cyclic universe, defended by Paul Steinhardt and Neil Turok.

Let us begin now with the Hartle-Hawking no-boundary model for the universe.[162] This model uses the concept of space-time. In accordance with Einstein's theory of relativity, "There are no separate concepts of space and time. . . . Instead, space and time must be united into a

156. Craig and Sinclair, "The *Kalam* Cosmological Argument," 158.

157. Hawking, *Brief History of Time* (1988), 61.

158. Liddle and Loveday, *Oxford Companion to Cosmology*, 241.

159. Sean Carroll, "Does the Universe?" 188.

160. Sean Carroll, "Does the Universe?" 188.

161. Sean Carroll, "Does the Universe?" 189.

162. Hartle and Hawking, "Wave Function." "The no boundary condition, is the statement that the laws of physics hold everywhere" (Hawking, "Beginning of the Universe," 135). Therefore, if there is no boundary, there is no singularity in the beginning where the physical laws break down.

single entity, space-time. . . . The geometry of space-time is described by the metric, which measures the distance between neighbouring space-time points."[163] The metric of the ordinary space-time (also known as Lorentzian metric) is given be the following formula: $ds^2 = -c^2dt^2 +dx^2+dy^2+dz^2$, where ds is the distance between two spatial-temporal points, c is the speed of light, dt is the difference in time, dx is the difference in the x-coordinate, and likewise with the rest of the spatial coordinates, y and z. The minus sign in the Lorentzian metric formula indicates "the special character in the time dimension."[164] The no-boundary model uses the concept of imaginary time to "describe how quantum theory shapes time and space."[165] By changing the time coordinate, t, with the imaginary time coordinate, τ (which defined as $\tau \equiv it$), in the Lorentzian metric formula, it is obtained that $ds^2 = +c^2d\tau^2+dx^2+dy^2+dz^2$. This is a Euclidean metric, where all the coordinates, temporal and spatial, have the same positive sign. Consequently, "A Euclidean metric . . . treats time the same as it does space dimensions."[166] As Hawking said, "In the Euclidean space-time there is no difference between the time direction and directions in space. On the other hand, in real space-time, in which events are labeled by ordinary, real values of the time coordinate, it is easy to tell the difference [between time and space]."[167] The no-boundary model uses a Euclidean metric, which would describe the Planck era, the period of the universe before the Planck time, where quantum effects are no longer negligible with respect to gravitational effects.[168] In line with the model,

163. Liddle and Loveday, *Oxford Companion to Cosmology*, 275.

164. Craig and Sinclair, "The *Kalam* Cosmological Argument," 177–78.

165. Hawking, *Universe in a Nutshell*, 59. Imaginary time "is a well-defined mathematical concept: time measured in what are called imaginary numbers" (ibid.). Imaginary numbers are numbers whose square is negative. Imaginary numbers are represented by the product of a real number and the imaginary unit i, which is defined as the square root of -1. From the scientific point of view, the concept of imaginary time is a "real cause for concern" because it "lacks any asymmetry or arrow of time" (Jaroszkiewicz, "Analysis of the Relationship," 164).

166. Craig and Sinclair, "The *Kalam* Cosmological Argument," 178; Hartle and Hawking, "Wave Function."

167. Hawking, *Brief History of Time* (1988), 134.

168. Remember that Planck time is the extremely small time of 5.391×10^{-44} seconds. Hawking regarded his "use of imaginary time and Euclidean space-time as merely a mathematical device (or trick) to calculate answers about real space-time" (Hawking, *Brief History of Time* (1988), 134–35). Hawking also suggested that "the so-called imaginary time is really the real time, and that what we call real time is just a figment of our imaginations. In real time, the universe has a beginning and an end

"The Universe appears to exist in imaginary time only during the Planck era (i.e., at times close to 10^{-43} sec. and radii close to 10^{-33} cm.). Shortly after this, however, the Universe is no longer a Euclidean four-space, but instead exists as a classical GTR (Lorentzian) spacetime, with three spatial dimensions and a real temporal dimension."[169]

According to the no-boundary model, the Big Bang ceases to be "an 'edge' at which spacetime runs into a wall; it could be more like the North Pole, which is as far north as you can possibly go, without actually representing any sort of physical boundary of the globe."[170] In the no-boundary model, "The boundary conditions of the universe are that it has no boundary."[171] In accordance with this model, "Time ceases to be well defined in the very early universe [Planck era] just as the direction "north" ceases to be well defined at the North Pole of the earth. Asking what happens before the Big Bang is like asking for a point one kilometer north of the North Pole." To be sure, "The quantity that we measure as time had a beginning, but that does not mean spacetime has an edge, just as the surface of the earth does not have an edge at the North Pole."[172] In other words, "According to the Hartle/Hawking proposal the past of the universe is finite (as it is in the Big Bang model) but, unlike the path of the Big bang, it is *unbounded* (there is no singularity, t=o)."[173]

---

at singularities that form a boundary to space-time and at which the laws of science break down. But in imaginary time, there are no singularities or boundaries. So maybe what we call imaginary time is really more basic, and what we call real is just an idea that we invent to help us describe what we think the universe is like" (ibid., 139). In this regard, Craig forthrightly states: "I can think of no more egregious example of self-deception than this. One employs mathematical devices (tricks) such as . . . changing the sign of the time coordinate in order to construct a model space-time, a model which is physically unintelligible, and then one invests that model with reality and declares that the time in which we live is in fact unreal" (Craig, "What Place for Creator?" 483). Here one is tempted to wonder whether Hawking is indulging in science fiction with his invention of imaginary time to avoid eternity and God. The primitive theology and metaphysics that accompanies Hawking's cosmology (and not only his) occasion a return to mythos without logos.

169. Deltete and Guy, "Emerging from Imaginary Time," 189–90. See also Hawking, "The Edge of Spacetime," 68.

170. Sean Carroll, "Why Cosmologists Are Atheists," 630.

171. Hawking, "The Edge of Spacetime," 68–69. Boundary conditions are the conditions at the boundary, edge or singularity. (Hawking, *Brief History of Time* (1988), 148).

172. Hawking, "The Edge of Spacetime," 69.

173. Russell, "Does Creation Have?" 181.

In the classical theory of gravity, which is based on real space-time, there are only two possible ways the universe can behave: either it has existed for an infinite time, or else it had a beginning at a singularity at some finite time in the past. In the quantum theory of gravity, on the other hand, a third possibility arises. Because one is using Euclidean space-times, in which the time direction is on the same footing as the direction in space, it is possible for space-time to be finite in extent and yet to have no singularities that formed a boundary or edge. Space-time would be like the surface of the earth, only with two more dimensions. The surface of the earth is finite in extent but it doesn't have a boundary or edge: if one sails off into the sunset, he will not fall off the edge or run into a singularity.[174]

As already discussed, Hawking defended that in the very early universe there are "effectively four dimensions of space and none of time. That means that when we speak of the 'beginning' of the universe, we are skirting the subtle issue that as we look backward toward the very early universe, time as we know it does not exist!"[175] There is no $t = 0$ in the universe because as one goes backwards in time, the temporal dimension disappears, to become a spatial dimension. The affirmation of the atemporal character of the Planck era is highly problematic because "time is a condition of the creature, a sign of dependence. It is created *with* the creature; by bringing a changing world to be, God brings time."[176] In this regard, Augustine affirmed that "time and the world were created simultaneously,"[177] and Joseph Ratzinger says that "being *is* time, it does not merely *have* time."[178] The atemporal character of the Planck era is also problematic from the point of view of physics. For example, motion cannot be explained without time.[179]

174. Hawking, *Brief History of Time* (1988), 135–36.

175. Hawking and Mlodinow, *The Grand Design*, 134.

176. McMullin, "Evolutionary Contingency," 105.

177. Augustine, *The City of God* (1998), 456 (XI, 6).

178. Ratzinger, *Dogma and Preaching*, 138.

179. In an effort to overcome this problem, Heller suggests that "a generalized dynamics is possible even in the absence of the usual notion of time. . . . One of the essential features of this generalization consists in replacing all local elements with their global counterparts (if they exist)" (Heller, "Cosmological Singularity," 681). Heller points out: "Theologians would certainly notice an analogy between this generalization process and the way of forming concepts referring to God in the traditional theology. I have in mind especially the so-called *via emminentiae*, a concept that is known from everyday usage [and] is ascribed to God, but only after it has been purified from all

Claiming that there is no initial singularity in the universe, Hawking derived the theological conclusion that God is superfluous. These are his famous words:

> The quantum theory of gravity has opened up a new possibility, in which there would be no boundary to space-time and so there would be no need to specify the behavior at the boundary. There would be no singularity at which the laws of science broke down and no edge of space-time at which one would have to appeal to God or some new law to set the boundary conditions for space-time. One could say: "The boundary condition of the universe is that it has no boundary." The universe would be completely self-contained and not affected by anything outside of itself. It would neither be created nor destroyed. It would just BE.[180]

The previous paragraph is very revelatory regarding Hawking's positivism toward being. The fact that the universe is not created is not a *consequence* of Hawking's cosmology but one of its *premises*. As the philosopher and bishop Joseph Życiński appropriately pointed out, the no-boundary model "tacitly introduces the thesis that the universe exists."[181] When Hawking said the universe just IS, he disregarded the mystery of being and gave himself permission to stop thinking. This

---

negative connotations and after all of its positive connotations have been strengthened to their possible maximum" (ibid., 684n13). The priest also affirms that "macroscopic physics is only the result of some 'averaging' of what happens on the noncommutative, fundamental level." That is to say, what we observe in our macroscopic everyday world is the averaging of what really happens on the microscopic probabilistic world of quantum mechanics. In this scenario, Heller defends that "[ordinary] time is but an epiphenomenon of timeless existence" (ibid., 683). Therefore, time would not have real ontological significance. To know more about scientific problems of time in quantum gravity, see Edward Anderson, "The Problem of Time."

180. Hawking, *Brief History of Time* (1988), 136.

181. Życiński, "Metaphysics and Epistemology," 278. This is the whole paragraph: "The Hawking-Hartle model in its original version also implies methodological presuppositions. They deal, for instance, with the so-called normalization procedure. To determine the wave function of the universe, the authors assume that there is a probability equal to 1 of having a metric at a three-dimensional spacelike surface. This procedure requires at least two methodological assumptions: (1) Analogies from quantum physics can be used at a cosmological level to describe the universe, which has been *ex definitione* the only and unique object in its class; (2) the normalization of the wave function of quantum objects requires that the integral of the probabilities over the whole space must yield probability equal to 1 at any moment *t*. In such normalization practice, the very assumption that the outcome is set to 1 tacitly introduces the thesis that the universe exists" (ibid.).

shows the unreasonable dimension of scientism. As a fervent follower of scientism, Hawking took being for granted. Due to his positivism, creation was not considered as a transition from non-being to being but as the first mechanical process of the universe, which could be explained by science. Obviously, this first change presupposes the existence of the universe. Hawking was unable to establish any relation between creation and being. He could only reason from his positivistic point of view, which blinded him to the crucial question of creation, i.e., being. Therefore, when this cosmologist was denying creation, he was not denying what creation *really is* but he was just denying a mechanical change.

According to Hawking, God had a place as the initiator of the universe as long as the universe had a beginning. However, after the no-boundary proposal removes a beginning (remember, in imaginary time), there is no place for God:

> With the success of scientific theories in describing events, most people have come to believe that God allows the universe to evolve according to a set of laws and does not intervene in the universe to break these laws. However, the laws do not tell us what the universe should have looked like when it started—it would still be up to God to wind up the clockwork and choose how to start it off. So long as the universe had a beginning, we could suppose it had a creator. But if the universe is really completely self-contained, having no boundary or edge, it would have neither beginning nor end: it would simply be. What place, then, for a creator?[182]

Karl Giberson and Mariano Artigas fittingly asserted that "Hawking conflates two different issues, a universe with no edges in space and time; and a self-contained universe. He links them by suggesting that if the universe has no edges in space and time, then it is self-contained and not created." As already explained, creation is not fundamentally a question of temporal origins but a question of *ontological* origins. Creation refers ultimately to a dependence in being not only at the beginning of the existence of a creature, but throughout its whole existence. "God's role is not confined to creaturely 'beginnings' or 'space-time edges,' to use Hawking's terminology. God is the only 'self-contained' Being, not dependent on any other being, and is the source of all created beings."

---

182. Hawking, *Brief History of Time* (1988), 140–41.

Hence, "claiming that the universe is self-sufficient [uncreated] because it has no boundaries in space and time makes no sense."[183]

Aquinas had already addressed the question of an eternal created world. He defended that there is no "contradiction between these two ideas, that something is created by God and that it, nevertheless, always existed."[184] This is precisely "the problem that Hawking thinks his work has created."[185] An eternal created world could be possible because (1) "God produces effects instantaneously, not through motion, and therefore it is not necessary that He precedes His effect in duration," and because (2) creation out of nothing does not require non-being to *temporally* precede being. In other words, "There is no need that the thing first be nothing and later be something."[186] Accordingly, Giberson and Artigas concluded that "Aquinas would reject Hawking's confident assertion that a proof that the universe has no boundaries would have 'profound implications for the role of God as Creator.'"[187] Thomas Aquinas' affirmation that the world would still be creation, even if it were eternal, points to the distinction between *esse* and *essentia*. An eternal world would exist only by participation in God's being because every *ens* (being) is a composite of *esse* (being) and *essentia* (essence), even if that *ens* is eternal. God is the only *ipsum esse subsistens*. When we conflate, as the positivistic Hawking did, *esse* and *essentia*, every *ens* exists necessarily and the world does not have a beginning or end; it simply exists, as Hawking claimed.[188] The distinction between *esse* and *essentia* only makes sense if there is a difference between being and history. Indeed, the distinction between *esse* and *essentia* tacitly presupposes the aforesaid difference between being and history.

As pointed out in the previous section, positivism towards being is closely associated with an extrinsic image of God. This extrinsicist god is intrinsic to the thought of the atheistic Hawking. As mentioned before, the positivistic Hawking could only see mere brute facticity. For him, there was no difference between the being of God, *ipsum esse subsistens*,

183. Giberson and Artigas, *Oracles of Science*, 105.

184. Aquinas, "Eternity of the World," 115.

185. Giberson and Artigas, *Oracles of Science*, 106.

186. Giberson and Artigas, *Oracles of Science*, 106; Aquinas, "Eternity of the World," 116–19.

187. Giberson and Artigas, *Oracles of Science*, 106. The inside quotation is Hawking, *Brief History of Time* (1988), 174.

188. Hawking, *Brief History of Time* (1988), 141.

and the being of the world, *esse commune*. They belonged to the same order, to the order of positivistic being. Therefore, the infinite divine transcendence (and the intimate divine immanence) were lost, and God became a mechanical cause among mechanical causes. For Hawking, God was an "efficient cause producing an absolutely first temporal effect."[189] Hawking's extrinsic theology was unable to properly understand divine transcendence. Therefore, the distinction between primary and secondary causality disappeared and divine causality was in a position of rivalry with natural processes. In other words, "Hawking sets God and scientific explanation in opposition—we can use one or the other to explain things, but not both."[190]

For Hawking, God was confined to those areas that are not yet understood by science.[191] This is clearly a god of the gaps. The creator has a place in the universe only "when the natural sciences reach a boundary in their explanatory procedures, in the well-known manner characteristic of the deus ex machina."[192] After several centuries of modern science, the last space granted to God was the beginning of the universe. But once this beginning is supposedly understood scientifically, there is no place for a creator. In this regard, Hawking said: "Over the centuries many . . . believed the universe had a beginning, and used it as an argument for the existence of God. The realization that time behaves like space presents a new alternative. It . . . means that the beginning of the universe was governed by the laws of science and doesn't need to be set in motion by some god."[193] This god of the gaps who is discarded is the same one who is defended by the adherents of the *kalam* cosmological argument.

Hawking, using his no-boundary model, concluded that God was an unnecessary hypothesis. However, that affirmation was not a conclusion that came from the cosmological model; on the contrary, it was its inspiration. As the philosopher Phil Dowe explains, "The whole rationale

---

189. Craig, "What Place for Creator?" 474.

190. Giberson and Artigas, *Oracles of Science*, 104.

191. Hawking, *Brief History of Time* (1988), 172. "Laplace's determinism was incomplete in two ways. It did not say how the laws should be chosen, and it did not specify the initial configuration of the universe. These were left to God. God would choose how the universe began and what laws it obeyed, but he would not intervene in the universe once it had been started. In effect, God was confined to the areas that nineteenth-century science did not understand" (ibid.).

192. Życiński, "Metaphysics and Epistemology," 270.

193. Hawking and Mlodinow, *The Grand Design*, 135.

for the no-boundary model is to avoid the conclusion that there is a God."[194] Hawking addressed this matter very bluntly in this interview:

> WEBER: Why is it so important whether there is or is not an edge to space-time?
>
> HAWKING: It obviously matters because if there is an edge somebody has to decide what should happen at the edge. You would really have to invoke God.
>
> WEBER: Why does that follow?
>
> HAWKING: If you like, it would be a tautology. You could define God as the edge of the universe, as the agent who was responsible for setting all this into motion.
>
> WEBER: You are invoking God because we need an explanatory principle for the edge.
>
> HAWKING: Yes, if you want a complete theory, then we would have to know what happens at the edge. Otherwise, we cannot solve the equations.[195]

Hawking certainly recognized the hypothetical nature of his model: "I'd like to emphasize that this idea that time and space should be finite without boundary is just a *proposal*: it cannot be deduced from some other principle. Like any other scientific theory, it may initially be put forward for aesthetic or metaphysical reasons, but the real test is whether it makes predictions that agree with observation." And he added that experimental confirmation "is difficult to determine in the case of quantum gravity."[196] To date, there has not yet been any experimental confirmation.[197] How-

194. Dowe, *Galileo, Darwin, and Hawking*, 147.

195. Hawking and Weber, "Interview with Stephen Hawking," 214.

196. Hawking, *Brief History of Time* (1988), 136–37.

197. "Experimental data casting light on this cosmological epoch [Planck epoch] has been scant or non-existent until now [2015], but recent results from the WMAP probe have allowed scientists to test hypotheses about the universe's first trillionth of a second (although the cosmic microwave background radiation observed by WMAP originated when the universe was already several hundred thousand years old). Although this interval is still orders of magnitude longer than the Planck time, other experiments currently coming online including the Planck Surveyor probe, promise to push back our 'cosmic clock' further to reveal quite a bit more about the very first moments of our universe's history, hopefully giving us some insight into the Planck epoch itself. Data from particle accelerators provides meaningful insight into the early universe as well. Experiments with the Relativistic Heavy Ion Collider have allowed physicists to determine that the quark-gluon plasma (an early phase of matter) behaved

ever, Hawking dealt with the no-boundary model as if it were real, and concluded categorically from his model the theological affirmation we have been dealing with until now: science has made God dispensable. Let us remember Hawking's words: "The realization that time behaves like space . . . removes the age-old objection to the universe having a beginning, but also means that the beginning of the universe was governed by the laws of science and doesn't need to be set in motion by some god."[198] The dispensable god that Hawking had in mind was an extrinsic one. This extrinsic god is the same one who is affirmed by the supporters of the *kalam* cosmological argument. When Hawking denied both creation and God, he was not denying them at all, but rather "a projection of his own [positivistic] theory, rooted in a theological extrinsicism" that he shared "with his opponents."[199]

We have seen that the Hartle-Hawking no-boundary model claims to avoid the initial singularity predicted by general relativity. Another way to avoid the singularity is proposed by Vilenkin, with his "creation out of nothing" model. As already discussed, both cosmological models are beginning cosmologies, which advocate for a beginning of the universe. Before discussing Vilenkin's cosmological model, it is interesting to note his effort to defend a beginning of the universe. Vilenkin, along with Arvind Borde and Alan Guth, proposed in 2003 a singularity theorem that defends that the universe should have a beginning.[200] More concretely, the Borde-Guth-Vilenkin singularity theorem concludes that "past-eternal inflation without a beginning is impossible." Note that this theorem is more general than the Penrose-Hawking singularity theorem. As Vilenkin recognizes, "A remarkable thing about the theorem is its sweeping generality." Borde, Guth, and Vilenkin "made no assumptions about the material content of the universe." They "did not even assume that gravity is described by Einstein's equations." The only assumption made by Borde, Guth, and Vilenkin "was that the expansion rate of the universe never gets below some nonzero value, no matter how small."[201] It is important to notice that Vilenkin claims that both the eternal inflation

---

more like a liquid than a gas, and the Large Hadron Collider at CERN will probe still earlier phases of matter, but no accelerator (current or planned) will be capable of probing the Planck scale directly" (Rupert Anderson, *The Cosmic Compendium*, 99).

198. Hawking and Mlodinow, *The Grand Design*, 135.

199. Hanby, *No God, No Science?* 412n61.

200. Borde et al., "Inflationary Spacetimes."

201. Vilenkin, *Many Worlds in One*, 175.

model and the cyclic model, which we will see later, fall under the general range of applicability of the Borde-Guth-Vilenkin singularity theorem.[202] In other words, the eternal inflation model and the cyclic model, which is an example of eternal cosmologies, cannot avoid a beginning. Although Vilenkin thinks that the evidence for the beginning is inescapable, he does not consider it a proof God's existence. For the cosmologist, "This view would be far too simplistic."[203] Let us now see his cosmological model and the extrinsic image of God supporting it.

Vilenkin proposes a cosmological model with a beginning in which the universe is created from nothing. This creation from nothing is very different from what we have already seen in the second chapter. The mechanism that would explain the creation from nothing is called quantum tunneling. According to this phenomenon, a particle has a probability of tunneling through an energy barrier. This is a phenomenon predicted by quantum mechanics, but forbidden in classical mechanics. "In classical, or Newtonian, physics, if you put a ball in a cup, it will not get out. It will sit there forever. But quantum mechanically, objects can tunnel through. If I sit here long enough, there is some probability I will tunnel through this wall, and then I will be in the corridor. Of course the probability is very small, but it is 'non-zero.'"[204] This weird prediction of quantum mechanics has been experimentally confirmed in the alpha decay, which is a kind of radioactive decay of atomic nuclei.

Vilenkin explains that the quantum tunneling happens from a zero-size universe, which he identifies with "nothing," to a finite radius universe that begins to inflate. Therefore, he concludes, there is no need for an initial universe.[205] "The initial state prior to tunneling is a universe of vanishing radius, that is, no universe at all. There is no matter and no space in this very peculiar state. Also, there is no time. Time has meaning only if something is happening in the universe."[206] Vilenkin recognizes that "the state of 'nothing' cannot be identified with *absolute* nothingness. The tunneling is described by the laws of quantum mechanics, and thus 'nothing' should be subjected to these laws. The laws of physics must

202. Vilenkin, *Many Worlds in One*, 173–75.

203. Vilenkin, *Many Worlds in One*, 177.

204. Vilenkin, *In the Beginning*.

205. Vilenkin, *Many Worlds in One*, 180.

206. Vilenkin, *Many Worlds in One*, 180–81.

have existed, even though there was no universe."[207] Notice that Vilenkin refers to "nothing" in quotation marks because the nothing he refers to is "the absence of matter, space and time. That is as close to nothing as you can get, but what is still required here is the laws of physics. So the laws of physics should still be there, and they are definitely not nothing."[208]

Interestingly enough, Vilenkin distinguishes between "nothing" and vacuum. As is already known, "nothing" is for this cosmologist "a state with no matter, no space, and no time,"[209] but subject to the laws of physics. On the contrary, vacuum has space and time. As Vilenkin states, "Vacuum, or empty space, has energy and tension, it can bend and warp, so it is unquestionably something."[210] The cosmologist also acknowledges that vacuum "is a physical object, endowed with energy density and pressure, and can be in a number of different states. Particle physicists refer to these states as different vacua. The properties and the types of elementary particles differ from one vacuum to another."[211] The primordial state of Vilenkin's model is not vacuum, but "nothing." As a result of the quantum tunneling, "a finite-sized universe, filled with a false vacuum, pops out of nowhere ('nucleates') and immediately starts to inflate. The radius of the newborn universe is determined by the vacuum energy density: the higher the density, the smaller the radius."[212] Therefore, vacuum appears from "nothing."

According to Vilenkin, "nothing" is more fundamental than vacuum. In fact, he criticizes Edward Tryon's cosmological model, which explains the universe as "a quantum fluctuation of the vacuum."[213] Vilen-

---

207. Vilenkin, *Many Worlds in One*, 181. With his affirmation that the physical laws must have existed without a universe, Vilenkin seems to imply a transcendent order of being different from material reality. If this is the case, it would seem that the cosmologist cannot not help taking recourse to tacit principles of being otherwise excluded from his cosmology, principles which point toward a more comprehensive sense of creation.

208. Vilenkin, *In the Beginning*.

209. Vilenkin, *Many Worlds in One*, 186.

210. Vilenkin, *Many Worlds in One*, 185.

211. Vilenkin, "The Principle of Mediocrity," 5.33.

212. Vilenkin, *Many Worlds in One*, 181. The true vacuum is "the lowest-energy vacuum" (ibid., 49). "High-energy vacua are called 'false' because, unlike our true vacuum, they are unstable. After a brief period of time, typically a small fraction of a second, a false vacuum decays, turning into true vacuum, and its excess energy is released in a fireball of elementary particles" (ibid., 50).

213. Vilenkin, *Many Worlds in One*, 185; Tryon, "Is the Universe?" 396. "The

kin affirms that Tryon's scenario "does not really explain the origin of the universe. A quantum fluctuation of the vacuum assumes that there was a vacuum of some pre-existing space. And we know that 'vacuum' is very different from 'nothing.'"[214] In this regard, Vilenkin agrees with Guth, who says: "A proposal that the universe was created from empty space is no more fundamental than a proposal that the universe was spawned by a piece of rubber. It might be true, but one would still want to ask where the piece of rubber came from."[215] Vilenkin is clear about vacuum being something. However, he is not so clear about his "nothing" being something. Vilenkin thinks that he can avoid the question about the origin of the state prior to the quantum tunneling by calling it "nothing." Because there is "nothing," one does not have to go backwards in the sequence of causality. "Nothing" does not need to be caused.[216] Moreover, there is no need for a creator to explain the beginning of the universe because the quantum tunneling from "nothing" is uncaused.

> If there was nothing before the universe popped out, then what could have caused the tunneling? Remarkably, the answer is that no cause is required. In classical physics, causality dictates what happens from one moment to the next, but in quantum mechanics the behavior of physical objects is inherently unpredictable and some quantum processes have no cause at all. Take, for example, a radioactive atom. It has some probability of decaying, which is the same from this minute to the next. Eventually, it will decay, but there will be nothing which causes it to decay at that particular moment. Nucleation of the universe is also a quantum process and does not require a cause.[217]

---

vacuum is anything but dull or static; it is a site of frantic activity. Electric, magnetic, and other fields are constantly fluctuating on subatomic scales because of unpredictable quantum jerks. The spacetime geometry is also fluctuating, resting in a frenzy of spacetime foam at the Planck distance scale. In addition, the space is full of *virtual* particles, which spontaneously pop out here and there and instantly disappear. The virtual particles are very short-lived, because they live on borrowed energy. The energy loan needs to be paid off, and according to Heisenberg's uncertainty principle, the larger the energy borrowed from the vacuum, the faster is has to be repaid" (Vilenkin, *Many Worlds in One*, 184). The Planck distance is 1.616×10^{-35} m.

214. Vilenkin, *Many Worlds in One*, 185.

215. Guth, *The Inflationary Universe*, 273.

216. Vilenkin, *In the Beginning*.

217. Vilenkin, *Many Worlds in One*, 181.

Because there is no need for a cause, there is no need for a creator. In this regard, Vilenkin recognizes that "for many physicists [including him], the beginning of the universe is uncomfortable, because it suggests that something must have caused the beginning, that there should be some cause outside the universe. In fact, we now have models where that's not necessary—the universe spontaneously appears, quantum mechanically."[218] Ultimately, this is the underlying purpose of Vilenkin's model: the rejection of an outside cause of the universe. Nevertheless, Vilenkin acknowledges that his model of quantum creation from "nothing" cannot be the last step in the explanation of the universe. Although he recognizes that the quantum creation from nothing seems to avoid the question about the previous state before the Big Bang, "the description of the creation of the universe from nothing is given in terms of the laws of physics. . . . If the laws describe the creation of the universe, that suggests they existed prior to the universe. The question that nobody has any idea how to address is where these laws come from and why these laws in particular?"[219]

Because there is no answer from science for this question, that means for Vilenkin that God can be placed there, as the origin of physical laws. We have again the god of the gaps:

> Earlier cosmological models suggested a Creator meticulously designing and fine-tuning the universe. Every detail of particle physics, each constant of nature, and all the primordial ripples had to be set just right. One can imagine the volumes and volumes of specifications the Creator handed down to his assistants to complete the job. The new worldview evokes a different image of the Creator. After some thought, he comes up with a set of equations for the fundamental theory of nature. This initiates the process of runaway creation. No further instructions are needed: the theory describes quantum nucleation of universes from nothing, the process of eternal inflation, and the creation of regions with every possible type of particle physics, ad infinitum. Any specific member of this ensemble of universes is incredibly complicated and would take an enormous amount of

218. Vilenkin, *In the Beginning*.

219. Vilenkin, *In the Beginning*. We can clearly see here how scientism leads to metaphysical and theological primitivism. This primitivism makes a real dialogue between science and theology impossible.

information to describe. But the entire ensemble can be codified in a relatively simple set of equations.[220]

God has ceased to be the initiator of the Big Bang because this process is now understood by science. His sole remaining role is to set up the physical laws that describe the universe. If the previous deistic god could only interact with the universe in the beginning, to set it in motion, in this new theory offered by cosmology, God has no possibility of interacting at all with the universe. Nevertheless, he has a role, a minimal one, but a role: to choose a set of physical equations. The existence of that god of the gaps is guaranteed as long as science is not able to answer the question about the origin of physical laws. That god is safe in the outskirts of the scientific realm.

What would happen if there were no need to choose a set of physical equations for the universe? In this case, the last role for God would disappear. In this regard, the cosmologist Max Tegmark proposes that there are as many universes as there are sets of physical equations.[221] Vilenkin thinks that if Tegmark's proposal were correct, this "would drive the Creator entirely out of the picture. Inflation relieved him of the job of setting up the initial conditions of the big bang, quantum cosmology unburdened him of the task of creating space and time and starting up inflation, and now he is being evicted from his last refuge—the choice of the fundamental theory of nature."[222] Again, Vilenkin is evidencing his theological presupposition of a god of the gaps whose role disappears as science finally explains everything. That image of God is directly related to a comprehension of theology and metaphysics as being outside of the

220. Vilenkin, *Many Worlds in One*, 200.

221. See Tegmark, "Parallel Universes (2003)" and Tegmark, *Our Mathematical Universe*. This multitude of universes, each one having different physical equations, is what Tegmark calls the "Level IV Multiverse" (ibid., 319–57). These are the four levels of multiverse described by Tegmark: "Level I: Other Hubble volumes have different initial conditions. Level II: Other post-inflation bubbles may have different effective laws of physics (constants, dimensionality, particle content). Level III: Other branches of the quantum wave function add nothing qualitatively new. Level IV: Other mathematical structures have different fundamental equations of physics" (Tegmark, "Parallel Universes (2004)," 486).

222. Vilenkin, *Many Worlds in One*, 203. "Tegmark's proposal, however, faces a formidable problem. The number of mathematical structures increases with increasing complexity, suggesting that 'typical' structures should be horrendously large and cumbersome. This seems to be in conflict with the simplicity and beauty of the theories describing our world. It thus appears that the Creator's job security is in no immediate danger" (ibid.).

realm of (scientific) truth. These are Vilenkin's words: "If I claim that the universe ends abruptly beyond the horizon, or that it is filled with water and inhabited by intelligent goldfish, how can anyone prove me wrong? Cosmologists, therefore, focus mostly on the observable part of the universe, leaving it to philosophers and theologians to argue about what lies beyond."[223] It is ironic that Vilenkin appeals to observation to differentiate quantum mechanics from metaphysics or theology when he recognizes that "quantum cosmology is not about to become an observational science. The dispute between different approaches [such as the Hartle-Hawking no-boundary model and Vilenkin's quantum-tunneling-from-nothing model] will probably be resolved by theoretical considerations, not by observational data."[224] Moreover, "any predictions that quantum cosmology could make about the initial state of the universe cannot be tested observationally."[225] As we can see, Vilenkin's proposal is scientifically unreasonable, to the point of being more science fiction than real science. In general, there is a real inconsistency in modern cosmology because it is permeated with scientism. Vilenkin's model clearly reveals a lack of understanding of the world and a lack of understanding of science's own nature and limits.

Having explored the model proposed by Vilenkin to explain the beginning of the universe, I am able to provide two points of criticism about it. First, the positivistic assumption of the cosmologist is clear. As is normal for scientists, being is taken for granted. There is no recognition of the mystery of being, and so there is an evasion of rigorous metaphysical reflection. Consequently, science itself is replete with primitive metaphysical and theological assertions. In the positivistic mindset, the being of God, *ipsum esse subsistens*, and the being of the world, *esse commune*, belong to the same order of factual being. Therefore, the infinite divine transcendence—and the intimate divine immanence—are lost, and God becomes a mechanical cause among mechanical causes. Thus, the divine cause is in opposition with natural causes, and the result is a god of the gaps. Because of positivism, creation is not comprehended as the passage from *nihil* to being,[226] but as a mechanical process described as quantum tunneling from nothing.

223. Vilenkin, *Many Worlds in One*, 5.
224. Vilenkin, *Many Worlds in One*, 193.
225. Vilenkin, "Quantum Cosmology," 662.
226. In this regard, Craig asserts that "Vilenkin has not truly grasped how radical being's coming from non-being is" (Craig, "Vilenkin's Cosmic Vision," 237).

Second, Vilenkin's idea of "nothing" is totally different from the metaphysical idea of *nihil*, which is key to the understanding of *creatio ex nihilo*. As previously said, Vilenkin's "nothing" is a definitive something: a set of physical laws, which smuggles in metaphysical considerations through the back door.[227] The extrinsic image of God held by the cosmologist correlates with his defective idea of *nihil*. Vilenkin does not think properly about the idea of *nihil* because he does not think about God's transcendence and immanence radically enough. As Hanby notes, "The difficulty in thinking of the *nihil* is really but the reverse side of difficulty in thinking of God alone as *ipsum esse subsistens*."[228] Only when God is understood as the totally other and, at the same time, the one innermost present to every creature, can the concept of *nihil* be understood without being hypostasized and creation out of nothing be perceived as the radical and total gift of the universe to itself. Finally, the concept of cause is comprehended by Vilenkin in a mechanistic way, as "a temporal succession of predictable events."[229] As pointed out in the first chapter, the misconceptions of God and creation are closely related to a mechanistic understanding of nature.

My two points of criticism of Vilenkin—for his positivist ideas of being and nothing—have a logical connection. Because being is conceived as brute facticity, the cosmologist cannot think properly about nothing. He can only understand nothing as something positive. Since being is taken for granted, there is no consideration whatsoever of a transition from non-being (nothing) to being or of metaphysical principles distinct from time; being has always existed. Therefore, Vilenkin cannot talk about nothing without hypostasizing it, without converting nothing into a something.

227. Craig criticizes Vilenkin's "nothing" in his review of the cosmologist's book *Many Worlds in One*: "As Vilenkin's diagram on the same page illustrates [p. 180], the quantum tunneling is at every point a function from something to something. For quantum tunneling to be truly from nothing, the function would have to have a single term, the posterior term" (Craig, "Vilenkin's Cosmic Vision," 237).

228. Hanby, *No God, No Science?* 310.

229. William Carroll, "Big Bang Cosmology," 63n12. "There is a great deal of confusion in the philosophical interpretation of quantum mechanics: especially with respect to the meaning of Heisenberg's 'relation of uncertainty.' It is one thing to affirm that we are not able to provide a precise mathematical measure of both the velocity and the position of a subatomic particle. It is quite another thing either to deny the objective reality of the particle or to contend that there is a realm of 'causeless' effects. We might not be able to predict certain events; this does not mean that these events have no cause" (ibid.).

Now that I have dealt with the beginning cosmologies, let us study the most prominent example of eternal cosmologies, i.e., the cyclic model. Remember that eternal cosmologies are those without a beginning of time. As already discussed, the cyclic model is proposed by Steinhardt and Turok. These cosmologists make use of string theory to offer a cosmological model of the universe that avoids the initial singularity. Before explaining the cyclic model, some clarifications are required about string theory. This theory attempts to provide "a unified description for all particles and all their interactions. It is the most promising candidate we have ever had for the fundamental theory of nature. According to string theory, particles like electrons or quarks, which seem to be point-like and were thought to be elementary, are in fact tiny vibrating loops of string."[230] The theory of strings "requires that space should have nine dimensions instead of three."[231] Our universe is characterized in string theory as a braneworld, which is a three-dimensional volume residing in the higher-dimensional space predicted by string theory.[232]

Steinhardt and Turok adopt the representation of the observable universe as a braneworld. In their cyclic model, that braneworld "is separated by a tiny gap, perhaps 10^{-30} centimeters across, from a second 'hidden braneworld.'" The two cosmologists continue explaining that "all the particles and forces we are familiar with, and even light itself, are confined to our braneworld. We are stuck like flies on flypaper, and can never reach across the gap to the 'hidden' world, which contains a second set of particles and forces with different properties from those in our braneworld."[233] Steinhardt and Turok say that "the cyclic universe can be built from two braneworlds drawn together by a springlike force and colliding at regular intervals."[234] In each one of the cycles, "a big bang creates hot matter and radiation, which expand and cool to form the galaxies and stars observed today. Then the expansion of the universe speeds up, causing the matter to become so spread out that space approaches a nearly perfect vacuum. Finally, after a trillion years or so, a new big bang occurs and the cycle begins anew."[235] Steinhardt and Turok explain that the cyclic

230. Vilenkin, *Many Worlds in One*, 156.

231. Vilenkin, *Many Worlds in One*, 159. This problem is avoided by postulating that "the extra six dimensions are curled up or, as physicists say, *compactified*" (ibid.).

232. Liddle and Loveday, *Oxford Companion to Cosmology*, 36.

233. Steinhardt and Turok, *Endless Universe*, 139.

234. Steinhardt and Turok, *Endless Universe*, 155.

235. Steinhardt and Turok, *Endless Universe*, 8–9.

model can accommodate infinite cycles in the past, not requiring a beginning.[236] According to Turok, "The Big Bang represents just one stage in an infinitely repeated cycle of universal expansion and contraction." The cosmologist also thinks that "neither time nor the universe has a beginning or end."[237]

The cyclic model is not the first one to claim the possibility of an eternal universe, but it has the great asset of avoiding the main problem of the eternal universe models: the heat death.[238] Linde recognizes that the cyclic model is the best alternative to the inflationary model,[239] which is the dominant model among cosmologists. Note that both Hartle-Hawking's and Vilenkin's proposals assume the inflationary model. For Steinhardt and Turok, "The inflationary paradigm is fundamentally untestable, and hence scientifically meaningless."[240] Although they claim that their model is scientifically testable,[241] the only observational test that they propose is a test based on the detection of cosmic gravitational waves. This test would be able to determine which model (inflationary or cyclic) is the correct one because "the two models give vastly different predictions for the production of cosmic gravitational waves."[242] Nevertheless, Steinhardt and Turok recognize that the detection of cosmic

236. Steinhardt and Turok, *Endless Universe*, 244. Remember that this is in clear contradiction with the Borde-Guth-Vilenkin singularity theorem, which requires a beginning even for the cyclic model.

237. Turok, *Big Bang*.

238. The heat death is the state of the universe characterized by thermodynamic equilibrium. In this state the universe has reached its maximum entropy and, therefore, there is no available energy. "The problem of the heat death is also avoided, because the amount of expansion in a cycle is greater than the amount of contraction, so the volume of the universe is increased after each cycle. The entropy of our observable region is now the same as the entropy of a similar region in the preceding cycle, but the entropy of the entire universe has increased, simply because the volume of the universe is now greater. As time goes on, both the entropy and the total volume grow without bound. The state of maximum entropy is never reached, because there is no maximum entropy" (Vilenkin, *Many Worlds in One*, 172).

239. Linde, "Inflationary Theory," 832.

240. Steinhardt, "Big Bang Blunder," 9.

241. Steinhardt and Turok, "The Cyclic Model Simplified," 45.

242. Steinhardt and Turok, *Endless Universe*, 197–98. "Gravitational waves are ripples in space-time, which propagate as waves at the speed of light" (Liddle and Loveday, *Oxford Companion to Cosmology*, 151). Cosmic gravitational waves are the gravitational waves produced during the inflation period, which occurred right after the Big Bang and lasted for a tiny fraction of a second.

gravitational waves is very unlikely to be achieved at least "in the foresee-able future."[243]

To the previous, I have to add the fact that one of the main pillars of the cyclic model is string theory. This theory is highly hypothetical and there is no observational confirmation of it. "More than twenty years [thirty years by now] of intensive research by thousands of the best scientists in the world producing tens of thousands of scientific papers has not led to a single testable experimental prediction of the [string] theory."[244] The cosmologists George Ellis and Joe Silk describe string theory as a speculative and undermining of science because "it relies on extra dimensions that we can never observe."[245] Therefore, string theory is untestable and it has to be accepted on mostly fideistic grounds. This hypothetical theory is accepted because it "is supposedly the 'only game

243. Steinhardt and Turok, *Endless Universe*, 222. In 2014, a group of scientists claimed the first detection of cosmic gravitational waves. Max Tegmark hailed the discovery as "the first-ever experimental evidence for quantum gravity" (Cowen, "Telescope Captures View"; Tegmark's words are quoted on page 283). However, some months later, the discovery was put into question and finally scientifically rejected. (Cowen, "Gravitational Wave Discovery Faces"; Cowen, "Gravitational Waves Discovery Now.") On February 11, 2016, the physicists of the Advanced Laser Interferometer Gravitational-Wave Observatory (LIGO) announced the first detection ever of gravitational waves: "On September 14, 2015 at 09:50:45 UTC the two detectors of the Laser Interferometer Gravitational-Wave Observatory simultaneously observed a transient gravitational-wave signal. . . . It matches the waveform predicted by general relativity for the inspiral and merger of a pair of black holes and the ringdown of the resulting single black hole" (Abbott et al., "Observation of Gravitational Waves," 061102/1). The gravitational waves detected came from the collision of two black holes about 440 Mpc from us (about 1.4 billion light-years from us), and the source was named GW150914 (Abbott et al., "Improved Analysis of GW150914," 041014/5 and Abbott et al., "Observation of Gravitational Waves.") Afterward, several detections of gravitational waves have been announced. The sources of those gravitational waves are approximately between 0.13 and 3.3 billion light-years from us (Abbott et al., "Improved Analysis of GW150914"; Abbott et al., "GW151226"; Abbott et al., "GW170104": Abbott et al., "GW170608": Abbott et al., "GW170814"; Abbott et al., "GW170817.") Obviously, these first detections of gravitational waves open the possibility of detection of *cosmic* gravitational waves produced right after the Big Bang (about 13.8 billion years ago; see Ade et al., "Planck 2013 Results," 10). However, the detection of *cosmic* gravitational waves still appears as something only remotely possible in the distant future (think, for example, that the sources of the gravitational waves detected were 0.13–3.3 billion light-years away and the source of cosmic gravitational waves was 13.8 billion light-years away).

244. Woit, *Not Even Wrong*, 203. See also Smolin, *The Trouble with Physics*; Baggott, *Farewell to Reality*.

245. Ellis and Silk, "Defend the Integrity," 321.

in town' capable of unifying the four fundamental forces."[246] However, that assumption might be wrong. "There may be no need for an overarching theory of four fundamental forces and particles if gravity, an effect of space-time curvature, differs from the strong, weak and electromagnetic forces that govern particles."[247] According to Ellis and Silk, "It is a promissory note that there might be such a unified theory."[248]

The preceding discussion exposes the untestability of the cyclic model. In fact, current science cannot say anything testable before the Planck time.[249] Consequently, what happened at the Big Bang or even before it cannot be scientifically affirmed, because of the lack of experimental observation that can be obtained, even with our state-of-the-art technology. The cyclic model is distinctly speculative; it offers supposedly scientific answers to questions that present-day science is unable to provide. Again, we have a cosmological model that is more science fiction than real science. The unreasonable dimension of modern cosmology keeps appearing. The gap in scientific knowledge regarding the Big Bang is used by the inventors of the cyclic model to insert and justify their

---

246. Ellis and Silk, "Defend the Integrity," 321. "The standard view of physics is that Nature has four fundamental forces, namely electromagnetism, gravity, and the strong and weak nuclear forces. These forces, also known as interactions, govern the way in which particles respond to each other's presence. While only the first two of these impact directly on our day-to-day existence, the strong force is responsible for holding atomic nuclei together, and the weak force for nuclear reactions including those that power the Sun. All four forces are therefore vital to our existence" (Liddle and Loveday, *Oxford Companion to Cosmology*, 125).

247. Ellis and Silk, "Defend the Integrity," 321.

248. Ellis and Silk, "Defend the Integrity," 321.

249. As previously said, "Experimental data casting light on this cosmological epoch [Planck epoch] has been scant or non-existent until now [2015], but recent results from the WMAP probe have allowed scientists to test hypotheses about the universe's first trillionth of a second (although the cosmic microwave background radiation observed by WMAP originated when the universe was already several hundred thousand years old). Although this interval is still orders of magnitude longer than the Planck time, other experiments currently coming online including the Planck Surveyor probe, promise to push back our 'cosmic clock' further to reveal quite a bit more about the very first moments of our universe's history, hopefully giving us some insight into the Planck epoch itself. Data from particle accelerators provides meaningful insight into the early universe as well. Experiments with the Relativistic Heavy Ion Collider have allowed physicists to determine that the quark-gluon plasma (an early phase of matter) behaved more like a liquid than a gas, and the Large Hadron Collider at CERN will probe still earlier phases of matter, but no accelerator (current or planned) will be capable of probing the Planck scale directly" (Rupert Anderson, *The Cosmic Compendium*, 99).

metaphysical presupposition: a creator is unnecessary. In other words, the cyclic model is (at least implicitly) proposed to provide a replacement for a creator. The model's underlying strategy can be easily described by a term coined by the theologian Connor Cunningham: *the devil of the gaps*. The strategy of the devil of the gaps is to select "arbitrarily and parochially a subset of 'current science' and then . . . [forcing] it to yield a metaphysic that accommodates the radical deflation of reality."[250] The scientists using the devil of the gaps "look at current science (or some sample of it) and extrapolate a metaphysical position. This is wholly illegitimate and does science a great disservice,"[251] because "science must be understood to be an open and endless discipline, never extracting (or forcing) philosophical conclusions, since this would be to employ the very same logic of the God of the gaps (but in the name of the 'devil')."[252] The devil "lives in the gaps, that is, the absences of banished concepts."[253]

Implicitly, Steinhardt and Turok use the strategy of the devil of the gaps, also named as *atheism of the gaps* by Cunningham in his papers and lectures,[254] to assert the inexistence of a creator. Let us deal now with this

250. Cunningham, *Darwin's Pious Idea*, 50. "Parochially, because science is a necessarily open-ended activity; thus, to foreclose future developments is wrongheaded, to say the least, and in being so does science a great disservice" (ibid., 434n101). I will take the concept *devil of the gaps* as the exact mirror image of the concept *god of the gaps*. Notice that Cunningham considers the god of the gaps ultimately as the devil of the gaps. "Dawkins will point to, say, an apparent imperfection in the biological world; the absence of 'perfection' leads him to conclude that 'God' is absent. So also with the advocates of Intelligent Design, who point to a current gap of science, or the inequity of a mechanism to give full account of the biological world, and conclude that a designer exists. There too the devil lies in the gaps, for, as we pointed out earlier, any such designer is more Homeric than Abrahamic" (ibid., 279); "Intelligent Design is thus a misnomer. It should be asking not for an interference to design, but simply for more scientific work" (ibid., 277); "So-called Intelligent Design is scientifically wrong because it's not science: science asks for more science, not for religion (or atheism)" (ibid., 278); "The problem with I-D is that it is itself guilty of scientism—it too presumes that science is the sole criterion of truth" (ibid.); "For the ultra-Darwinist interpretation of natural selection is indeed the god of Intelligent Design, whom orthodox Christians would find diabolic" (ibid, 280). The fundamental claim of the Intelligent Design Movement is "that there are living organisms which are so complex that they could not have emerged through evolution but must have been designed by an intelligent being" (Coyne, "Evolution and Intelligent Design," 717).

251. Cunningham, *Darwin's Pious Idea*, 279.

252. Cunningham, *Darwin's Pious Idea*, 280.

253. Cunningham, *Darwin's Pious Idea*, 279.

254. Cunningham, e-mail to author, May 6, 2015.

issue. The cosmologists clearly state that their cyclic model avoids "the most disturbing feature of the inflationary model by far, . . . the idea that time has a 'beginning.'"[255] They recognize that nowadays many cosmologists interpret the initial singularity of the Big Bang model "as signifying the beginning of space and time." However, their "cyclic model of the universe challenges this point of view, suggesting that the big bang was not the beginning of time but was rather a violent transition between two stages of cosmic evolution, with a 'before' and an 'after.'"[256] The two cosmologists emphasize that, according to their model, "the big bang is not the beginning of space and time but, rather, an event that is, in principle, fully describable using physical laws."[257] After the necessity of a beginning is removed, there is no need for a creator. This is the atheism of the gaps: Steinhardt and Turok use a gap in science (the beginning) to propose an untestable scientific theory that accommodates their atheism. The god denied by the atheism of the gaps is, obviously, the god of the gaps.

It is important to note that the cyclic model presupposes the eternal existence of the universe. From this eternity, Steinhardt and Turok deny the existence of a creator. It is relevant to remember here Aquinas' argument that the world would still be a creation *even if it were eternal*. As already said, this argument points to the distinction between *esse* and *essentia*. An eternal world would exist only by participation in God's being because every *ens* is a composite of *esse* and *essentia*, even if that *ens* is eternal. God is the only *ipsum esse subsistens*. However, the positivistic Steinhardt and Turok conflate *esse* and *essentia* and, therefore, every *ens* exists necessarily and the world does not have a beginning or end;

---

255. Steinhardt and Turok, *Endless Universe*, 11. Another motivation for the cyclic model is to avoid "the contrived nature of the inflationary model and its failure, so far, to connect with fundamental physics in a simple way" (ibid.). For Steinhardt and Turok, "The odd design of the inflationary story is perhaps a reflection of the way it was developed. Cosmologists converged on the current version by 'stapling together' different ideas introduced over the course of a century: the big bang model from the 1920s, dark matter from the 1930s, inflationary theory from the 1980s, and dark energy, discovered in the 1990s. No overarching principle explains how or why any of these ideas requires the others. The big bang does not lead directly to inflation. Inflation does not require dark matter. Dark matter does not require dark energy. Each piece has been added independently and must be carefully adjusted to fit. . . . In contrast to the inflationary model, the cyclic story has an overarching principle that ties its components together: cosmic evolution is endlessly repeating with no beginning or end" (ibid., 66–67).

256. Steinhardt and Turok, *Endless Universe*, 38.

257. Steinhardt and Turok, *Endless Universe*, 8.

it simply exists throughout different cycles. As we know, positivism can only think of being as mere brute facticity. There is no difference between the being of God, *ipsum esse subsistens*, and the being of the world, *esse commune*. They belong to the same positivistic order of being. Therefore, divine transcendence (and thus intimate divine immanence) disappears and God becomes a mechanical cause among mechanical causes. Even more, creation is understood as a mechanism in competition with natural processes, with God as the extrinsic initiator of the process. Unsurprisingly, Turok thinks that the Big Bang is "a creation event," and that, in the cyclic model, God could only be accommodated as "a policeman to enforce the laws of physics."[258] In the end, we have again the same extrinsic image of God, which we have found in the previous atheistic cosmologists.

In this section we have seen different attempts of modern cosmology to avoid the initial singularity of the inflationary model. The different models that we have considered use conjectural ideas (quantum gravity and string theory) which are untestable. As Jim Baggott states, "The very beginning of the universe (if this is indeed the right word) is beyond the reach of science for the seeable future and, quite possibly, for all time."[259] Time and again, I have noted the unreasonable character of the different cosmological models proposed. They are highly speculative and are closer to science fiction than to properly done science. As stated above, modern cosmology suffers in its understanding of the world and in its self-understanding. The cosmological models that we have dealt with use the scientific gap about the beginning of the universe to avoid the initial singularity and, in this way, to disallow any divine intervention. The cosmologists who propose these models presuppose an extrinsic theology that reduces God to an object within the more comprehensive order of being. This order of being is taken for granted but never explicated by the cosmologists. Because being is taken for granted, they are unable to understand the main concern of creation: "the difference between nothing and something."[260] The cosmologists only see creation as *a mechanical event from something to something else*.

The cosmological accounts that we have considered misconstrue God and creation in such a way that whether God exists or not makes

258. Turok, *Big Bang*.

259. Baggott, *Origins*, 12.

260. Ratzinger, *Dogma and Preaching*, 133.

no difference to what remains an essentially mechanistic understanding of nature. As previously stated, this mechanistic understanding severely reduces the description of reality and entails massive gaps in its account of the world. Key concepts for the comprehension of nature, such as immanence, interiority, indivisible unity, and intelligibility, fall outside the mechanistic consideration of nature. The mechanistic presuppositions assumed by these cosmologists blind them to their own misconceptions. The atheistic cosmologists use the atheism of the gaps to deny the existence of an extrinsic god who is the same one defended by those using the beginning of the universe as evidence for the existence of God. Both defenders and opponents of the existence of God share not only an extrinsic image of god but also a flawed conception of creation. These scholars neither demonstrate nor deny creation, because what they demonstrate or deny is beside the point with respect to the question of creation. The mechanistic approach to creation held by those scholars fails to be metaphysically cogent, and it fails also to understand its own nature as thought. For instance, one of the implications of the atheism of the gaps as the reverse image of the god of the gaps is the fact that there is really no "atheist cosmology," except in the uninteresting sense that the cosmologists in question disbelieve in God.[261] As previously shown, the atheist cosmologies are extensively impregnated with thought about God, and their concept of God enters in a determinative way into their cosmologies, so these can be said in some way to depend upon the God they deny.[262]

Apart from the beginning of the universe, there is also a very important cosmological question used by both defenders of the existence of God and their opponents. This is the question of the fine-tuning of the universe. For some, the fine adjustment of physical constants constitutes a proof for the existence of God. Others offer scientific alternatives to the fine-tuning to avoid any theological conclusion. Once more, both groups share the same extrinsicist theology. In the remaining part of this chapter, I will discuss the cosmological issue of the fine-tuning of the universe

261. "'Atheism' too is a form of theology—even a form of Christian theology, historically speaking—inasmuch as it requires a determinate conception of God to reject" (Hanby, No God, No Science? 13). "Even atheism's dismissal of the subject of God is only apparent, that in reality it represents a form of man's concern with the question of God, a form that can express a particular passion about this question and not infrequently does" (Ratzinger, Introduction to Christianity, 104).

262. "Every atheism is parasitic upon the God which it rejects" (Hanby, No God, No Science? 299).

from the point of view of both defenders of the existence of God and their opponents, in order to criticize the extrinsic image of God that all of them presuppose.

The Finely Tuned Universe as Scientific Evidence for the Existence of God

"The fine-tuning argument is based on the fact that earthly life is very sensitive to the values of several fundamental physical constants. Making [sic] the tiniest change in any of these, and life as we know it would not exist. The delicate connections between physical constants and life are called the *anthropic coincidences*."[263] These are some examples of anthropic coincidences:

> If the gravitational attraction between protons in stars had not been many orders of magnitude weaker than their electrical repulsion, stars would have collapsed long before nuclear processes could build up the chemical periodic table from the original hydrogen and deuterium. Furthermore, the element-synthesizing reactions in stars depend sensitively on the properties and abundances of deuterium and helium produced in the early universe. Deuterium would not exist if the neutron-proton mass difference were just slightly displaced from its actual value; neutrons, unstable in a free state, were stored in deuterium for their later use in building the elements. The existing relative abundances of hydrogen and helium also implies a close balance of the relative strengths of the gravitational and weak nuclear forces. A slightly stronger weak force and the universe would be 100 percent hydrogen as all neutrons decayed away before assembling into deuterium and helium. A slightly weaker weak force and we would have a universe that is 100 percent helium; in that case neutrons would not have decayed and left the excess of protons that formed hydrogen. Neither of these extremes would have allowed for the existence of stars and life, as we know it, based on carbon chemistry.[264]

263. Stenger, "Anthropic Design," 41; Carter, "Large Number Coincidences"; Barrow and Tipler, *The Anthropic Cosmological Principle*.

264. Stenger, "Anthropic Design," 41. As is commonly known, the chemical elements are defined by the number of protons in their nucleus, i.e., the atomic number. All the atoms of the same chemical element have the same atomic number, but they can have different number of neutrons in their nucleus. Isotopes are atoms having the same atomic number but a different number of neutrons. The atomic number of

The philosophical theologian Craig uses the fine-tuning of the universe to demonstrate the existence of a designer, who is identified with God. Craig affirms that science has discovered that "the existence of intelligent, interactive life depends upon a complex and delicate balance of fundamental constants and quantities, such as the gravitational constant and the amount of entropy in the early universe, which are fine-tuned to a degree that is literally incomprehensible."[265]

This philosophical theologian recognizes that "there are three possibilities debated in the literature for explaining the presence of this remarkable fine-tuning: physical necessity, chance, or design."[266] Craig considers that the first alternative, physical necessity, "seems extraordinarily implausible because the constants and quantities are independent of the laws of nature. The laws of nature are consistent with a wide range of values for these constants and quantities." Regarding the second alternative, chance, he thinks that "the odds against the universe's being life-permitting are so incomprehensibly great that they cannot be reasonably faced." He adds that "in order to rescue the alternative of chance, its proponents have, therefore, been forced to adopt the hypothesis that there exists a sort of World Ensemble or multiverse of randomly ordered universes of which our universe is but a part."[267] The multiverse hypothesis supposes that all possible combinations of physical constants (including those allowing the appearance of life) are realized in different universes. Because every possible universe comes into existence, life will appear in some universes.[268] Craig dismisses the multiverse solution because of the Boltzmann Brain problem.[269] Because "the fine-tuning is not

---

hydrogen is 1 and its most common isotope has no neutrons. Its name is protium. The deuterium is an isotope of hydrogen which has a neutron. When Stenger refers to hydrogen, he is referring to protium. Helium is a chemical element whose atomic number is 2.

265. Sean Carroll and Craig, "God and Cosmology," 32.

266. Sean Carroll and Craig, "God and Cosmology," 32.

267. Sean Carroll and Craig, "God and Cosmology," 33.

268. Linde, "Inflation, Quantum Cosmology," 453. I will discuss more extensively the multiverse theory, which tries to avoid a divine designer, in the next section. Here, I am only interested in describing Craig's opinions about that theory.

269. Sean Carroll and Craig, "God and Cosmology," 34–35. "In order to be observable, the entire universe need *not* be fine-tuned for our existence. Indeed, it is vastly more probable that a random fluctuation of mass-energy would yield a universe dominated by Boltzmann Brain observers than one dominated by ordinary observers such as ourselves. In other words, the observer self-selection effect is explanatorily vacuous. As Robin Collins has noted, what needs to be explained is not just intelligent life, but

plausibly due to physical necessity or chance,"[270] Craig deduces that "the fine-tuning of the universe is due to . . . design."[271] According to him, "It is almost undeniable that God's existence is much more probable given the evidence that we have for the beginning of the universe and the fine-tuning of the universe. Therefore, contemporary cosmology is strongly confirmatory of theism."[272]

The Jesuit Spitzer also defends the fine-tuning of the universe as a proof for the existence of God. He sees only two possible explanations for the fine-tuning of the physical constants of the universe: "(1) A supernatural designing Intellect," or "(2) a multiplicity of universes."[273] Spitzer examines the "three major proposals for the many universes hypothesis over the last four decades,"[274] and he thinks that

> these proposals are subject to two or more of the following three problems which mitigate their reasonable likelihood:
> a. Running counter to the *canon of parsimony* or "Ockham's razor."
> b. Being *highly theoretical* (and likely to remain so in the indefinite future).
> c. Having significant problems of workability and consistency with cosmological observation.[275]

---

embodied, interactive, intelligent agents such as ourselves. Appeal to an observer self-selection effect accomplishes nothing because there's no reason whatever to think that most observable worlds or the most probable observable worlds are worlds in which that kind of observer exists. Indeed, the opposite appears to be true: most observable worlds will be Boltzmann Brain worlds. Since we presumably are not Boltzmann Brains, that fact strongly disconfirms a naturalistic World Ensemble or multiverse hypothesis" (ibid.). Craig is making reference to Collins' forthcoming book *The Well-Tempered Universe*. A Boltzmann Brain observer is a brain in an empty universe, able to observe its empty world. (Craig, "Invasion of Boltzmann Brains.")

270. Sean Carroll and Craig, "God and Cosmology," 35.

271. Sean Carroll and Craig, "God and Cosmology," 36 (figure 11).

272. Sean Carroll and Craig, "God and Cosmology," 66.

273. Spitzer, *New Proofs*, 50–51. As previously said, I will discuss the multiverse theory in the next section. Here, I am only interested in describing Spitzer's opinions about that theory.

274. Spitzer, *New Proofs*, 68. The "three major proposals for the many universes hypothesis" discussed by Spitzer are "the Everett-De Witt Quantum 'Many Worlds' Hypothesis," "Linde's Chaotic Inflationary Multiverse," and "the String Theory Landscape" (ibid.). The first proposal corresponds with Tegmark's Level III Multiverse and the second and third proposals correspond with Tegmark's Level II Multiverse. (See Tegmark, *Our Mathematical Universe*.)

275. Spitzer, *New Proofs*, 68.

The Jesuit concludes that there is "an inherent weakness in the multiverse hypothesis (in general) which makes the supernatural explanation (based on the evidence of a beginning of the universe) *more likely* than the naturalistic alternative."[276]

There are also some scientists who see in the finely tuned universe an evidence for the existence of an intelligent designer, who is identified with God in some cases. Remember that the astrophysicist Hoyle rejected the Big Bang model because of its theological implications. However, he could not help seeing a super intellect in the design of the universe. It was clear to him that some properties of the atoms were finely adjusted: "A common sense interpretation of the facts [the remarkable relation of the 7.65 MeV energy level in the nucleus of ^{12}C to the 7.12 MeV level in ^{16}O] suggests that a superintellect has monkeyed with physics, as well as with chemistry and biology, and that there are no blind forces worth speaking about in nature."[277] It was also clear for Hoyle that life was not the result of chance but of intelligent design:

> The difference between an intelligent ordering, whether of words, fruit into boxes, amino acids, or the Rubik cube, and merely random shufflings can be fantastically large, even as large as a number that would fill the whole volume of Shakespeare's plays with its zeros. So if one proceeds directly and straightforwardly in this matter, without being deflected by a fear of incurring the wrath of scientific opinion, one arrives at the conclusion that biomaterials with their amazing measure or order must be the outcome of intelligent design. No other possibility I have been able to think of in pondering this issue over quite a long time seems to me to have anything like as high a possibility of being true.[278]

276. Spitzer, *New Proofs*, 73.

277. Hoyle, "The Universe," 16. "Would you not say to yourself, in whatever language supercalculating intellects use, 'Some supercalculating intellect must have designed the properties of the carbon atom, otherwise the chance of my finding such an atom through the blind forces of nature would be less than 1 part in 10^{40000}.' Of course you would, and if you were a sensible superintellect you would conclude that the carbon atom is a fix" (ibid.).

278. Hoyle, *Evolution from Space*, 27–28. "Rather than accept a probability less than 1 in 10^{40000} of life having arisen through the 'blind' forces of nature, it seems better to suppose that the origin of life was a deliberate intellectual act. By 'better' I mean less likely to be wrong" (Hoyle, "The Universe," 14).

As stated above, the astrophysicist Jastrow used the singularity of the Big Bang to consider a divine causation at the beginning of the universe. The astrophysicist also pondered the anthropic principle as scientific evidence for the existence of a designer God: "The anthropic principle is the most interesting development next to the proof of creation, and it is even *more* interesting because it seems to say that science itself has proven, as a hard fact, that this universe was made, was designed, for man to live in. It's a very theistic result."[279] Jastrow later deepened his assessment by saying that the anthropic principle "is the most theistic result ever to come out of science, in my view."[280] Although Jastrow considered himself an agnostic, he recognized that the idea that someone created the universe came out of his own scientific knowledge.[281]

There are more explicit examples of physicists who infer the existence of God from the fine-tuning of the universe. It will suffice to mention two of them. According to Paul Davies, "The apparent 'fine-tuning' of the laws of nature necessary if conscious life is to evolve in the universe then carries the clear implication that God has designed the universe so as to permit such life and consciousness to emerge."[282] Even more explicit is Tony Rothman:

> It's not a big step from the SAP [Strong Anthropic Principle] to the Argument from Design: it says that the Universe was made very precisely, and were it ever so slightly different, man wouldn't be here. Therefore, Someone must have made it. Even as I write these words my pen balks, because as a twentieth-century physicist I know that the last step is a leap of faith, not a logical conclusion. When confronted with the order and beauty of the universe and the strange coincidences of nature, it's very tempting to take a leap of faith from science into religion. I am sure many physicists want to. I only wish they would admit it.[283]

Rothman remarks upon the order and beauty of the universe. This order and beauty of the universe is something evident to any unprejudiced intellect. It is no coincidence that the concepts of *universe* and *cosmos* are interchangeable. "The word Cosmos, which primitively . . .

279. Durbin and Jastrow, "A Scientist Caught," 17. Thinking the converse requires an immense degree of abstraction.

280. Jastrow, "The Astronomer and God," 22.

281. Durbin and Jastrow, "A Scientist Caught," 18.

282. Davies, *The Mind of God*, 213.

283. Rothman, "What You See," 99.

indicated an idea of order and harmony, was subsequently adopted in scientific language, where it was gradually applied to the order observed in the movements of the heavenly bodies, to the whole universe, and then finally to the world in which this harmony was reflected to us."[284] The agnostic scientist Carl Sagan, internationally known for his 1980 documentary television series named *Cosmos*, reflected on the importance of the idea of order attached to that word: "*Cosmos* is a Greek word for the order of the universe. It is, in a way, the opposite of *Chaos*. It implies the deep interconnectedness of all things. It conveys awe for the intricate and subtle way in which the universe is put together."[285] The naturalist Alexander von Humboldt maintained that the word cosmos not only conveys the order of the world but also its beauty.[286] In fact, "Κόσμος, in the most ancient, and at the same time most precise, definition of the word, signified *ornament* (as an adornment for a man, a woman, or a horse); taken figuratively for εὐταξία, it implied the order or adornment of a discourse." Later on, "It was Pythagoras who first used the word to designate the order of the universe, and the universe itself."[287]

Again, the order and beauty that we find in the world is not a negligible fact. In this regard, Balthasar said that "without any doubt the phenomenal world contains on all sides an objective order which is not imposed by man, and thus a beauty; the legitimacy of the premise is repeatedly confirmed for him that there is within Nature a greater objective ordering of things than he had previously recognized."[288] The objective order and beauty of the world is something unquestionable because there is no being without order and beauty. Indeed, the presence of order and beauty can be a true source of "genuine philosophical wonder at the question of Being"[289] and a powerful pointer to the divine. Nonetheless, the previous advocates of the fine-tuning of the universe as an evidence for the existence of God, both theologians and scientists, do not "wonder at the fact that there is something rather than nothing."[290] They only admire "that everything appears so wonderfully and 'beautifully' ordered within

284. Humboldt, *Cosmos*, 68.

285. Sagan, *Cosmos*, 18.

286. Walls, *The Passage to Cosmos*, 220–21. See Humboldt, *Cosmos*.

287. Humboldt, *Cosmos*, 69.

288. Balthasar, *Glory of the Lord V*, 613.

289. Hanby, *No God, No Science?* 152.

290. Balthasar, *Glory of the Lord V*, 613.

the necessity of Being."[291] This is because they consider "Being [as] . . . identical with the necessity to be."[292]

The scientific validation of the existence of God, in this case using the fine-tuning of the universe, entails the positivism inherent in modern science because it considers God as a being among beings. Due to their positivism, the defenders of the fine-tuning of the universe conflate creation and design. As repeatedly said, creation is the generation of being from nothing. On the other hand, *design is the rearranging of being that is already given.* In other words, design presupposes the existence of being and, therefore, there is no questioning about being itself. The conflation of creation and design brings the problems of extrinsicism: an extrinsic image of God and, inevitably, an extrinsic image of nature. As a consequence, there is never a real discussion of God and creation, and hence a genuine and fruitful dialogue is impossible.

The finely tuned universe argument uses "the model of a divine designer as . . . [its] default paradigm for order in the natural world."[293] However, as Aquinas stated, "The divine will does not remove contingency from things, nor does it impose absolute necessity on things."[294] The divine designer allegedly demonstrated by the finely tuned universe is not the Christian God, but an "atrophied and contorted notion of divinity."[295] In this matter, Życiński asked: "Should we recognize the existence of the Divine Designer when we acknowledge this cosmic design?" And this is his response: "My answer is negative when by the Divine Designer we understand the God of classical theism conceived as an omnipotent Person. I agree with John Leslie that to explain the nature of the cosmic design one can refer to a force or a form of energy imposing rational structures on the physical processes."[296] The design argument "is not an argument for the Christian God; it is at best an argument for a cosmic architect in a deistic sense, or for that matter several such architects."[297]

I agree with the atheistic physicist Victor Stenger in his assessment of the image of God that results when the anthropic coincidences are used

291. Balthasar, *Glory of the Lord V*, 613–14.

292. Balthasar, *Glory of the Lord V*, 613. See previous sections of this chapter regarding Craig's, Spitzer's, Jastrow's, and Hoyle's positivism.

293. Cunningham, *Darwin's Pious Idea*, 278.

294. Aquinas, *Summa Contra Gentiles*, lib. 1, cap. 85, n. 1.

295. Cunningham, *Darwin's Pious Idea*, 278.

296. Życiński, "Weak Anthropic Principle," 128. See Leslie, *Universes*, 165–74.

297. Halvorson and Kragh, "Physical Cosmology," 250.

as evidence for God: "The fine-tuning argument and other recent intelligent design arguments are modern versions of God-of-the-gaps reasoning, where a God is deemed necessary whenever science has not fully explained some phenomenon."[298] In fact, "Scientists consider fine-tuning to be a sign that a current theory is flawed or incomplete."[299] It could well happen that "the fine-tunings you think are there might go away once you understand the universe better. They might only be apparent."[300] In that situation, the designer God would be unnecessary. In the end, God is at the mercy of scientific results because he has become simply one being among beings—albeit a vast one.

Ultimately, the image of God shared by the supporters of the anthropic principle as evidence for God is a "Creator sitting at the control board of the universe and turning different knobs to adjust the value of the constants."[301] "Had the Creator adjusted the knobs slightly differently, the universe would be a strikingly different place. And most likely neither we, nor any other living creatures, would be around to admire it."[302] Notice how the universe is conceived as a machine whose knobs are adjusted in the beginning by someone external to it. Nature becomes a dumb reality without real interiority, i.e., an *artifice*. Without interiority, the artifact lacks any immanent finality. Teleological purpose is reduced to conscious intentionality and that intentionality is transferred "to an external artificer who imposes his purposes (laws) back on an inert nature."[303] As Hanby remarks, "The relation of a designer to his artifact . . . [is] the relation of one finite agent externally juxtaposed to another." The divine designer "is neither responsible for the whole being of the artifact nor immanent within it as the source of its being. Once made, the artifact

298. Stenger, "Is the Universe Fine-Tuned?" 184.

299. Steinhardt and Turok, *Endless Universe*, 232.

300. Sean Carroll and Craig, "God and Cosmology," 49–50. "The strong version of the anthropic principle . . . is philosophically deficient because it relies to a great extent on a large gap in present scientific knowledge. If it is to be based only on the current scientific inability to explain the tightly knit character of the cosmos, then it suffers from all the weaknesses of a kind of philosophical 'god of the gaps' remedy. And it must await in the history of science the development of more adequate theories that may or may not incorporate an anthropic principle" (Mooney, "The Anthropic Principle," 124).

301. Vilenkin, *Many Worlds in One*, 128–29. Vilenkin is referring here to Hogan, "Quarks, Electrons and Atoms," 223.

302. Vilenkin, *Many Worlds in One*, 130.

303. Hanby, *No God, No Science?* 163.

does not remain dependent upon its maker."[304] The role of the divine designer is to set the initial conditions of the universe by giving extremely adjusted values to the physical constants. Once the values are adjusted, the designer does not interact with the universe. As a matter of fact, the divine designer is neither immanent within the artifact nor transcendent to it. As previously explained, divine transcendence and divine immanence are intrinsically related. The divine designer, the image of God implicit in the design argument, is an extrinsic god. This extrinsic god is a "reduction of God from transcendent (and Trinitarian) Creator to finite (and unitarian) artisan extrinsically juxtaposed to his products."[305] This reduction of God implies a correlative "reduction of nature to art."[306] We can notice here that the design argument, as developed by the above-mentioned advocates of the fine tuning of the universe, does not contribute much to changing the defective images of God and nature entailed by modern science. God remains a cosmic artificer understood in a deistic sense, and thus nature continues being a mechanical artifact.

There are interesting connections between the anthropic principle and Paley's teleological argument for the existence of God, given in his 1802 book *Natural Theology*. In this book, Paley "imagines how finding a timepiece lying along the side of one's path would naturally lead one to suppose that this timepiece was *designed by someone* rather than just happened there by pure chance." In the same way, knowing that "the universe has a far more complex design than a timepiece," the "finding" of the universe would lead to the conclusion that "somebody (God) must have designed it."[307] Moreover, Craig, one of the advocates of the anthropic coincidences as evidence for the existence of God, claims that the scientific evidence of fine-tuning in the universe is "for the design argument in the twentieth century what Paley's *Natural Theology* was in the nineteenth, viz., a compendium of the data of contemporary science which point to a design in nature inexplicable in natural terms and therefore pointing to the Divine Designer."[308] Notice how Craig positions God in the area unknown by science.

304. Hanby, *No God, No Science?* 166.

305. Hanby, *No God, No Science?* 152.

306. Hanby, *No God, No Science?* 128.

307. Thomas, "Transcendence and Sentience," 166. See also Hanby, *No God, No Science?* 154.

308. Craig, "Barrow and Tipler," 393. The scientific evidence referred to by Craig is the one offered in Barrow and Tipler, *The Anthropic Cosmological Principle.*

Formally, the argument from design using the fine-tuning of physical constants is the same as Paley's teleological argument. The English theologian conceived creatures as artifacts, and "he transformed creation into manufacture, conceiving of God not as the interior source of the creature's act of being, but as an extrinsic object within a positivity of being reduced to brute facticity, who imposes his designs on matter whose 'essential' characteristic is to lack it." Every creature ceases "to be a *per se unum* and becomes an object juxtaposed to the world and in competition with it. This is evidenced by the fact that Paley . . . regarded supernatural 'design' and 'natural explanations' as mutually exclusive alternatives."[309] The extrinsic theology and mechanistic ontology of Paley are none other than the defective theological and ontological presuppositions inherent in modern science.[310] Ironically, the same presuppositions present in those who use the anthropic principle to give proof for God's existence are also present in those who, in an attempt to reject any theological implications, find scientific alternatives to the anthropic principle.

In the same way that there is an agreement between the Intelligent Design Movement and Neo-Darwinism at the ontological and theological level,[311] there is also ontological and theological agreement between supporters of the argument from design and those offering scientific explanations to avoid a cosmological designer. As we will see in the next section, the image of God inherent in those using the fine-tuning of the physical constants to offer evidence for the existence God is the same image of God inherent in those offering alternative explanations to the fine-tuning to exclude any divine intervention in nature. Both adherents and opponents of a cosmological designer share the same extrinsic image

---

309. Hanby, *No God, No Science?* 196.

310. Hanby, *No God, No Science?* 152.

311. "The apparent disagreement between Darwinism and ID" is "betrayed by a much more basic agreement at the ontological level" (Hanby, *No God, No Science?* 181n77). "The appearance of a fundamental disagreement between Intelligent Design and Neo-Darwinism is in fact an illusion, for what unites them is more profound than what divides them, and what unites them are certain deeply flawed metaphysical and even theological commitments that ground the science" (Hanby, "Much Ado about Nothing"); "ID is ostensibly for the truncated 'God' permitted by modern science; militant Darwinians are against" (ibid.); "Both Darwinian biology and ID . . . give us mirror images of the same bad metaphysics and bad theology, such that nature is collapsed into artifice, organisms are mere machines, creation is simply causation, and God might as well be a space alien" (ibid.).

of God because both assume the theological presuppositions of modern science.

Alternatives to the Finely Tuned Universe

The initial conditions of the early universe are among the main evidences of a finely tuned universe. In the hot Big Bang model, "there was not enough time in the early Universe for heat to have flowed from one region to another. This means that the initial state of the Universe would have to have had exactly the same temperature everywhere in order to account for the fact that the microwave background has the same temperature in every direction we look."[312] Moreover, "The initial rate of expansion also would have had to be chosen very precisely for the rate of expansion still to be so close to the critical rate needed to avoid recollapse."[313] Another finely tuned property of the universe is its flatness.[314] "While observations indicate that the Universe has a geometry which is either flat or very close to flat, the standard hot big bang cosmology . . . indicates that the flat geometry is unstable and that only very special choices of initial conditions for the Universe can lead to a present Universe matching our observations."[315]

According to Hawking, these considerations showed that "the initial state of the Universe must have been very carefully chosen indeed if the hot big bang model was correct right back to the beginning of time." From all of this, he concluded that "it would be very difficult to explain why the Universe should have begun in just this way, except as the act of a God who intended to create beings like us."[316] Again, Hawking was taking recourse to the god of the gaps. God could be used as an explanation because science was unable to explain something. Nevertheless, Hawking referred immediately to inflation as the way to avoid a theistic conclusion. For him, inflation was "an attempt to find a model of the universe

312. Hawking, *Brief History of Time* (1988), 126–27. This is known as the "horizon problem" (See Liddle and Loveday, *Oxford Companion to Cosmology*, 162).

313. Hawking, *Brief History of Time* (1988), 127.

314. "Einstein taught us that space-time is not flat, but curved. Because of this curvature, bodies seem to attract each other by the force we call gravity. However, it turns out that the space of our universe, if looked at on large enough scales of distance, is on average astonishingly flat" (Barr, "Anthropic Coincidences," 19).

315. Liddle and Loveday, *Oxford Companion to Cosmology*, 122.

316. Hawking, *Brief History of Time* (1988), 127.

in which many different initial configurations could have evolved to something like the present universe."[317] In this way, there is no need to justify an adjustment of the initial conditions. Linde, one of the fathers of inflationary cosmology, recognizes that "inflationary theory provides us with a unique possibility to construct a theory largely independent of any assumptions about the initial singularity."[318] Despite the fact that inflation is assumed as normative in current cosmological models, Steinhardt points out that "the inflationary paradigm is so flexible that it is immune to experimental and observational tests."[319] At any rate, as Steinhardt and Turok admit, "The whole point of inflation was to avoid having to assume finely tuned initial conditions when the universe emerged from the big bang."[320]

It is very interesting to note that Vilenkin considers the theory of inflation similar, in some ways, to the Darwinian theory of evolution. "Both theories proposed an explanation for something that was previously believed to be impossible to explain. The realm of scientific enquiry was thus substantially expanded. In both cases, the explanation was very compelling, and no plausible alternatives have ever been suggested."[321] Again, another scientist invokes inflation to negate God as explanation. We have here another example of atheism of the gaps. The god negated is a god of the gaps. Again, creation is misunderstood as design and God as a finite designer, neither transcendent nor immanent to the universe. In other words, God becomes an extrinsic god. This is the same god rejected by Darwin and the same god affirmed by Paley. As Hanby points out, "Darwin basically takes over Paley's theology in negative form, thus making the theological and ontological assumptions of Paley's theology

317. Hawking, *Brief History of Time* (1988), 127.

318. Linde, "Inflationary Theory," 826–27.

319. Steinhardt, "Big Bang Blunder," 9. "First, inflation is driven by a hypothetical scalar field, the inflation, which has properties that can be adjusted to produce effectively any outcome. Second, inflation does not end with a universe with uniform properties, but almost inevitably leads to a multiverse with an infinite number of bubbles, in which the cosmic and physical properties vary from bubble to bubble. The part of the multiverse that we observe corresponds to a piece of just one such bubble. Scanning over all possible bubbles in the multiverse, everything that can physically happen does happen an infinite number of times. No experiment can rule out a theory that allows for all possible outcomes. Hence, the paradigm of inflation is unfalsifiable" (ibid.).

320. Steinhardt and Turok, *Endless Universe*, 95.

321. Vilenkin, *Many Worlds in One*, 67.

endemic to the subsequent Darwinian tradition."[322] Those defective theological and ontological assumptions are present not only in the Darwinian tradition but in all those adopting the assumptions of modern science,
particularly the defenders of the anthropic principle as evidence for the
existence of God and those scientists invoking inflation to avoid carefully
adjusted initial conditions.

In summary, behind the decision to avoid the finely tuned initial
conditions of the universe, there is a desire to avoid a gap in scientific
knowledge, which would provide evidence for the existence of an external designer identified with God. There is thus a clear intention to
reject God as explanation. The god rejected by inflationary scientists is
an extrinsic god, a god of the gaps and a deistic god. Ultimately, the god
refused by scientists, because of their scientistic knowledge, is the god
who is presupposed by modern science.

In addition to inflation, cosmologists propose a multiverse as a way
to avoid the finely tuned physical constants of our universe. The multiverse consists of a multitude of completely disconnected universes (also
known as bubbles) where the physical constants take different values.[323]
"Intelligent observers exist only in those rare bubbles in which, by pure
chance, the constants happen to be just right for life to evolve. The rest
of the multiverse remains barren, but no-one is there to complain about
that."[324] The multiverse is a consequence of inflation and string theory. As
seen before, inflation produces universes able to reproduce other universes. "One inflationary universe sprouts other inflationary bubbles, which
in turn produce other inflationary bubbles."[325] The inflationary bubbles
or universes produce "a multiverse with an infinite number of bubbles, in
which the cosmic and physical properties vary from bubble to bubble. . . .
Scanning over all possible bubbles in the multiverse, everything that can
physically happen does happen an infinite number of times."[326] Remem-

322. Hanby, *No God, No Science?* 4.

323. Tegmark, "Parallel Universes (2004)," 467–68.

324. Vilenkin, "The Principle of Mediocrity," 5.34.

325. Linde, "Self-Reproducing Inflationary Universe," 54.

326. Steinhardt, "Big Bang Blunder," 9. This multiverse is what Tegmark calls the
"Level II Multiverse." See Tegmark, *Our Mathematical Universe*, 119–53. Initially,
Hawking was a defender of the conventional multiverse idea. Regarding this issue, he
stated that the "multiverse idea is not a notion invented to account for the miracle of
fine-tuning. It is a consequence of the no-boundary condition as well as many other
theories of modern cosmology" (Hawking and Mlodinow, *The Grand Design*, 164).
Hawking recognized that "the usual theory of eternal inflation predicts that globally

ber that the kernel of the design argument is the extremely small probability of having a finely tuned universe by chance. This is considered an indicator of a designer. By proposing infinite universes, every possible universe is realized by chance, even the unlikely finely tuned universe. Therefore, the need for a designer is eliminated.

The idea of a multiverse is a very controversial idea, even among scientists, because of its untestability. In this matter, Steinhardt and Turok point out that the multiverse "is neither predictive nor verifiable."[327] Moreover, bishop Życiński stated that "not only is there no empirical confirmation [of a multiverse], but in fact there can be none, since the neighboring worlds are supposed to be causally disjoint and thus inaccessible to direct observation."[328] He also denounced the concept of a multiverse as "contrary to the basic principles of the Popperian scientific methodology."[329] Even Vilenkin, one of the promoters of the multiverse hypothesis, recognizes that "there is not one iota of evidence to support this hypothesis. Even worse, it does not seem possible to *ever* confirm or disprove it."[330] Nevertheless, there are scientists who defend the multiverse theory as an unavoidable consequence of the current cosmological theories: "Given inflation and the string theory landscape (or other equivalent dynamical mechanisms), a multiverse happens, whether you like it or not."[331] The cosmologists George Ellis and Joseph Silk complain that the idea of a multiverse is not "robust, let alone testable" because it

---

our universe is like an infinite fractal, with a mosaic of different pocket universes, separated by an inflating ocean" (Hawking, *Interview*.) However, the astrophysicist nuanced his position on the multiverse idea in a posthumous article. In that article, Hawking (and Thomas Hertog) proposed a cosmological model that "implies a significant reduction of the multiverse to a much more limited set of possible universes" (Hawking and Hertog. "A Smooth Exit from Eternal Inflation?" 147/10). Hawking's cosmological model does not reduce the multiverse "to a single, unique universe, but . . . [it implies] a significant reduction of the multiverse, to a much smaller range of possible universes" (Hawking, *Interview*).

327. Steinhardt and Turok, *Endless Universe*, 231.

328. Życiński, "Weak Anthropic Principle," 126.

329. Życiński, "Weak Anthropic Principle," 127. "Karl Popper famously suggested the criterion of 'falsifiability': A theory is scientific if it makes clear predictions that can be unambiguously falsified" (Sean Carroll, "Falsifiability," 124).

330. Vilenkin, *Many Worlds in One*, 134.

331. Sean Carroll, "Does the Universe?" 191. "The string landscape is the set of possible physical laws that might arise within superstring theory" (Liddle and Loveday, *Oxford Companion to Cosmology*, 290). Note that *superstring theory* is the technical term for string theory.

"relies on string theory, which is as yet unverified, and on speculative mechanisms for realizing different physics in different sister universes."[332] Finally, Ellis strongly declares that "the multiverse theory cannot make any testable predictions because it can [sic] explain anything at all."[333]

The lack of testability of the multiverse theory worries the scientists defending it. These scientists try to nuance the scientific maxim of falsifiability. For example, the cosmologist Sean Carroll states that "the falsifiability criterion gestures toward something true and important about science, but it is a blunt instrument in a situation that calls for subtlety and precision."[334] The cosmologist recognizes that, "in the real world, the interplay between theory and experiment isn't so cut and dried. A scientific theory is ultimately judged by its ability to account for the data." Carroll admits that "we can't (as far as we know) observe other parts of the multiverse directly. But their existence has a dramatic effect on how we account for the data in the part of the multiverse we do observe."[335] Concerning this, the Jesuit Stoeger provided

> a criterion for testing theories which imply the existence of a multiverse. If such a theory successfully explains various aspects of what we see and measure in our universe, and continues to provide a secure basis for further cosmological understanding, then that strongly supports the existence of such universes, even though we may never be able to detect them directly. This criterion can be summarized as: Does the multiverse lead to a greater intelligibility of the reality around us?[336]

It is very interesting to notice how the idea of a multiverse is defended by scientists despite its lack of experimental confirmation. One is prone to think that the motivation behind the relentless defense of the multiverse idea is to reject the designer god associated with the anthropic principle. In this regard, Hanby states that "the true purpose" of the multiverse hypothesis is "providing comfort to the atheists."[337] The paleontologist Simon Conway Morris describes the multiverse theory as an "escape clause" for atheists:

332. Ellis and Silk, "Defend the Integrity," 322.
333. Ellis, "Opposing the Multiverse," 2.35.
334. Sean Carroll, "Falsifiability," 125.
335. Sean Carroll, "Falsifiability," 126.
336. Stoeger, "Are Anthropic Arguments?" 450.
337. Hanby, No God, No Science? 51.

Creatio ex nihilo might be an embarrassment, but it is only a potential stumbling-block; as already noted, given it is beyond scientific discourse, the scientists have nothing to contribute. Even so, no scientist can avoid being embedded in a metaphysical framework (even if it is ostensibly nihilistic or solipsistic), and it is not surprising that the apparent peculiarities of our universe (famously in terms of the apparent "fine tuning" of the physical constants) sharpen the desire to find an "escape clause" from the ominous sense of a world designed for our habitation and understanding. It is hardly surprising, therefore, if many scientists believe the best course of action is to appeal to multiverses, endlessly generated, with no ultimate beginning and without conceivable end.[338]

The concept of the multiverse is a *metaphysical* concept, and cosmologists do not grasp its correct meaning. For example, Vilenkin points out that "philosophers often define the universe as 'everything there is.' Then, of course, there cannot be any other universes. Physicists do not usually use the term in this broadest sense and refer to completely disjointed, self-contained spacetimes as separate universes."[339] Vilenkin's clarification shows his metaphysical confusion. There cannot be unrelated universes because if they ever existed, "they would belong to the one order of being (and causality) and thus would not truly be alternative universes, but simply heretofore unknown parts of the one universe."[340] In other words, if other alternative universes *were* at all, they would have to belong to the more basic order of being and, therefore, be part of the one universe. Evidently, the universe is one because of the unity of being-as-act.[341] The idea of a multiverse proposes the nonsensical existence of different orders of being that are somehow outside the sole order of being. "The very possibility of '*other* worlds' signals some loss of recognition that the world is not fundamentally a collection of *things* to which other such collections could always be added, but a unity of being (*esse commune*) which would include by definition any further additions even where commerce between them was lacking or impossible."[342]

338. Conway Morris, "What Is Written?" 176.
339. Vilenkin, *Many Worlds in One*, 133.
340. Hanby, *No God, No Science?* 44–45n83.
341. Hanby, *No God, No Science?* 107.
342. Hanby, *No God, No Science?* 109.

The notion of multiverse betrays science's positivism. Being is reduced from act to positive facticity. This positivistic approach makes the question of the act of being fall from scientific view. Therefore, the question of creation is not properly understood and erroneously comprehended as a mechanical event. Positivism reduces the universe to a collection of entities and the unity of the universe to "a unity of aggregation."[343] The idea of a multiverse is only intelligible within the positivism that, in taking being for granted, reduces the universe to a set of things. In this understanding, the question becomes how many sets there are. But the unity of the universe is most fundamentally a unity of being—the unity of being-as-act—and consequently, the multiverse is ultimately unintelligible. Honestly, the multiverse proposal is more science fiction than real science. The unreasonable dimension of modern cosmology continues showing up.

Because of their positivism, the proponents of a multiverse cannot think about God as *ipsum esse subsistens*. He becomes "a finite object juxtaposed to and in competition with the world."[344] This extrinsic image of God is inherently related to the image of the universe as a collection of unrelated pieces put together. Once God ceases to be the fullness of being, becoming a mere external designer, the universe loses its inner unity, and it becomes an artificial aggregate. Even more, creation has nothing to do with the transition from non-being to being, or the ontological structure of the world, and becomes mere design. Ultimately, the image of god rejected by the adherents of the multiverse theory is the same one accepted by the defenders of the design argument based on anthropic coincidences. This is not a coincidence, but the consequence of both having the same theological and ontological presuppositions.

Although the proponents of the multiverse hypothesis reject God, who is conceived as an extrinsic designer, they give the "creation" role to alien designers. According to Guth, one of the fathers of inflationary theory, "The laws of physics do indeed allow, in principle, that a sufficiently advanced technological civilization could create a universe, or more than one universe."[345] Linde explains that "one may need to have only a milligram of matter in a vacuum-like exponentially expanding state, and then the process of self-reproduction will create from this mat

343. Hanby, *No God, No Science?* 109.

344. Hanby, *No God, No Science?* 334.

345. Gribbin, *In Search of the Multiverse*, 193. Gribbin is referring here to Guth, *The Inflationary Universe*, 253–70.

ter not one universe but infinitely many!"[346] Moreover, he thinks that "we can't rule out the possibility that our own universe was created in a lab by someone in another universe who just felt like doing it." And he concludes that, "on the evidence, our universe was created not by a divine being, but by a physicist hacker."[347] The astrophysicist John Gribbin defends "the possibility that our Universe was made deliberately by a member or members of a technologically advanced civilization in another part of the Multiverse." Gribbin clarifies that those designers "may have been responsible for the Big Bang; but this still means that evolution by natural selection and all the other processes that produced our planet and the life on it have been at work in our universe since the Big Bang, with no need for outside intervention."[348] The proposals mentioned above about universe designers are strikingly unserious from the point of view of both metaphysics and theology. Moreover, these proposals clearly depart from the scientific method. In the end, these proposals are unreasonable.

The designers of the universe proposed by atheistic cosmologists are fundamentally the same reality as the extrinsic god they reject. These designers are neither transcendent nor immanent to the universe. They are *finite beings*, albeit superior to us. Moreover, they are *external* to our universe and they only intervene at the beginning of our universe. Their only duty is to set the universe in motion. Because the rest of the development of the universe is explained by science, there is no continuing need for designers. As Gribbin remarks, "There is no need for an intelligent designer to explain how we got to be the way we are, given the laws of physics that operate in our universe."[349] In this sense, the designer is used to cover the scientific gaps, those areas unexplained by science.[350] We can see that the role attributed to the external designers is the same as the role attributed to the extrinsic god rejected by the atheists. In the end, they are the same thing. When theologians and physicists defend the existence of God using the design argument, they are promoting an image of God similar to the alien designers.[351]

346. Linde, "Universe, Life, and Consciousness," 196.

347. Linde, *The Big Lab Experiment*.

348. Gribbin, *In Search of Multiverse*, 195.

349. Gribbin, *In Search of Multiverse*, 197.

350. Some of the gaps are created by what a reductive scientific account of nature ignores—e.g., the act of scientific theorizing.

351. For those theologians and physicists, it seems not to matter whether the designer of our universe is God or an intelligent designer from another universe. "It

The atheistic cosmologist Sean Carroll attacks the argument from design based on the finely tuned universe by affirming that "there are many features of the laws of nature which don't seem delicately adjusted at all, but seem completely irrelevant to the existence of life." For Carroll, "The most obvious example is the sheer vastness of the universe; it would hardly seem necessary to make so many galaxies just so that life could arise on a single planet around a single star." The atheist even asks: "Why do the constituents of nature exhibit this pointless duplication, if the laws of nature were constructed with life in mind?"[352] Carroll's comments show how far this scientist is from understanding God as the inexhaustible source of being. Because Carroll can only understand God as an external designer, he cannot understand "the grandiose excess represented by . . . the universe's hundred billion galaxies,"[353] or "why God would do so much more fine-tuning of the state of the universe than seems to have been necessary."[354] The grandiose excess of the universe can only be understood when the universe ceases to be an artifice and becomes "the epiphanic and sacramental representation of God."[355] Nature can only be properly understood when God is properly understood. In other words, when God is misconceived (as extrinsic designer), nature is unavoidably misunderstood (as an artifact).[356]

In this chapter I have criticized the extrinsicist image of God that is held by both theologians and scientists who use scientific evidence, such as the beginning of the universe or the finely tuned characteristics of the physical constants, either to affirm the existence of God or to

---

appears to be a matter of indifference to Paley's contemporary disciples in the so-called Intelligent Design school whether the designer be God or one of Francis Crick's space aliens" (Hanby, No God, No Science? 178n51). See Crick and Orgel, "Directed Panspermia."

352. Sean Carroll, "Why Cosmologists Are Atheists," 633.

353. Sean Carroll, "Does the Universe?" 192.

354. Sean Carroll, "Does the Universe?" 193.

355. Chapp, The God of Covenant, 214. See Schmemann, Life of the World.

356. In this matter, Balthasar asked: "How can someone who is blind to Being be other than blind to God?" (Balthasar, My Work, 85). As previously mentioned, this theologian characterized positivism as a "sick blindness" to the primal value of being. For him, positivism "arises from regarding reality as raising no questions, being 'just there'—for the phrase 'the given' already says too much, since there is no one who 'gives.' In fact, the only question that arises is: 'What can we do with this material? When men are blind to the further question, it signifies the death of philosophy and even more the death of theology" (Balthasar, Theo-Drama II, 286).

deny it. In spite of the clear disagreement between atheistic scientists, on the one hand, and extrinsicist theologians and theistic scientists, on the other hand, regarding the existence of God, they all share the same extrinsic image of God. According to that image, God is "a finite subject within the positivity of being who imposes his designs upon his passive objects." This god is not "the creator God of Christianity, intimately and interiorly present to creatures as the source of their being because he infinitely transcends them, . . . [but] an artisan."[357] This artisan is "the hypothetical thing outside or beyond nature who may have set the universe in motion."[358] Because of positivism, this god is understood as a thing among other things. Therefore, this extrinsic god is in competition with natural processes and creation is misconceived as a mechanical event in rivalry with natural processes. When dealing with creation, there is no consideration whatsoever of creation as the transition from non-being to being. Being is taken for granted and, inevitably, nature is emptied of interiority and becomes a dumb artifact. The theological extrinsicism inherent in modern cosmology fails to be adequate to the meaning of God and creation. Therefore, both theologians and scientists who use modern cosmology either to affirm the existence of God or to deny it, never get to a real debate about or understanding of God and creation.

Finally, I would like to point out that the purpose of revealing and criticizing the extrinsic theology inherent in modern cosmology is not simply to rescue theology by denouncing the deficient image of God implicit in modern cosmology. The purpose is also to remark that there is no such thing as a truly atheistic cosmology, because a concept of God always lies at the foundation of all of these cosmological theories. The fact that some of the cosmologists in question disbelieve in a defective image of God or construct their cosmologies so as to render him obsolete is beside the point. Rather, the point is this: given the impossibility of dispensing with God in thought, one would expect that the atheist cosmologists would think and write about God more responsibly. This is the essential condition for any genuine dialogue between science and theology.

357. Hanby, *No God, No Science?* 128.
358. Hanby, "Much Ado about Nothing."

Bibliography

Abbott, Benjamin P., et al. "GW151226: Observation of Gravitational Waves from a 22-Solar-Mass Binary Black Hole Coalescence." *Physical Review Letters* 116, no. 24 (June 15, 2016) 241103/1–241103/14.

———. "GW170104: Observation of a 50-Solar-Mass Binary Black Hole Coalescence at Redshift 0.2." *Physical Review Letters* 118, no. 22 (June 1, 2017) 221101/1–221101/17.

———. "GW170608: Observation of a 19 Solar-Mass Binary Black Hole Coalescence." *Astrophysical Journal Letters* 851, no. 2 (December 18, 2017) L35/1–L35/11.

———. "GW170814: A Three-Detector Observation of Gravitational Waves from a Binary Black Hole Coalescence." *Physical Review Letters* 119, no. 14 (October 6, 2017) 141101/1–141101/16.

———. "GW170817: Observation of Gravitational Waves from a Binary Neutron Star Inspiral." *Physical Review Letters* 119, no. 16 (October 16, 2017) 161101/1–161101/18.

———. "Improved Analysis of GW150914 Using a Fully Spin-Precessing Waveform Model." *Physical Review X* 6, no. 4 (October 21, 2016) 041014/1–041014/19.

———. "Observation of Gravitational Waves from a Binary Black Hole Merger." *Physical Review Letters* 116, no. 6 (February 11, 2016) 061102/1–061102/16.

Ade, Peter, et al. "Planck 2013 Results. XVI. Cosmological Parameters." *Astronomy & Astrophysics* 571, no. A16 (2014) 1–66.

Aertsen, Jan. *Nature and Creature: Thomas Aquinas's Way of Thought*. Translated by Herbert D. Morton. Leiden, Netherlands: Brill, 1988.

Anastopoulos, Charis. *Particle or Wave: The Evolution of the Concept of Matter in Modern Physics*. Princeton, NJ: Princeton University Press, 2008.

Anderson, Edward. "The Problem of Time in Quantum Gravity." In *Classical and Quantum Gravity: Theory, Analysis, and Applications*, edited by Vincent R. Frignanni, 213–56. Hauppauge, NY: Nova Science, 2011.

Anderson, Rupert W. *The Cosmic Compendium: The Big Bang and the Early Universe*. Morrisville, NC: Lulu, 2015.

Aquinas, Thomas. *Aquinas on Creation: Writings on the "Sentences" of Peter Lombard, Book 2, Distinction 1, Question 1*. Translated by Steven E. Baldner and William E. Carroll. Mediaeval Sources in Translation 35. Toronto: Pontifical Institute of Mediaeval Studies, 1997.

———. *Commentary on Aristotle's Physics*. Translated by Richard J. Blackwell, et al. Rev. ed. Aristotelian Commentary Series 1. Notre Dame, IN: Dumb Ox, 1999.

————. *The Division and Methods of the Sciences: Questions V and VI of His Commentary on the* De Trinitate *of Boethius*. Translated by Armand Augustine Maurer. 4th ed. Mediaeval Sources in Translation 3. Toronto: Pontifical Institute of Mediaeval Studies, 1986.

————. *An Exposition of the "On the Hebdomads" of Boethius*. Translated by Janice L. Schultz and Edward A. Synan. Washington, DC: Catholic University of America Press, 2001.

————. *On Being and Essence*. Translated by Armand Maurer. 2nd ed. Mediaeval Sources in Translation 1. Toronto: Pontifical Institute of Mediaeval Studies, 1968.

————. "On the Eternity of the World." In *Aquinas on Creation: Writings on the "Sentences" of Peter Lombard, Book 2, Distinction 1, Question 1*, translated by Steven E. Baldner and William E. Carroll, 114–22. Mediaeval Sources in Translation 35. Toronto: Pontifical Institute of Mediaeval Studies, 1997.

————. *On the Power of God*. Translated by the English Dominican Fathers. Westminster, MD: Newman, 1952.

————. *Quodlibetal Questions 1 and 2*. Translated by Sandra Edwards. Mediaeval Sources in Translation 27. Toronto: Pontifical Institute of Mediaeval Studies, 1983.

————. *Summa Contra Gentiles*. Translated by Anton C. Pegis, et al. Notre Dame, IN: University of Notre Dame Press, 1975.

————. *Summa Theologica*. Translated by Fathers of the English Dominican Province. 5 vols. Westminster, MD: Christian Classics, 1981.

————. *Truth*. Translated by James V. McGlynn. Vol. 2. 3 vols. Library of Living Catholic Thought. Eugene, OR: Wipf and Stock, 2008.

Aristotle. *The Basic Works of Aristotle*. Edited by Richard P. McKeon. Translated by Ella M. Egdhill, et al. New York: Modern Library, 2001.

Augustine. *The City of God*. Translated by Marcus Dods. Peabody, MA: Hendrickson, 2013.

————. *The City of God against the Pagans*. Translated by Robert W. Dyson. Cambridge: Cambridge University Press, 1998.

Auletta, Gennaro, and William R. Stoeger. "Highlights of the Pontifical Gregorian University's International Conference on Biological Evolution." *Theology and Science* 8, no. 1 (2010) 7–15.

Ayres, Lewis. *Augustine and the Trinity*. Cambridge: Cambridge University Press, 2010.

Bacon, Francis. *The New Organon*. Edited by Lisa Jardine and Michael Silverthorne. Cambridge: Cambridge University Press, 2000.

Baggott, Jim E. *Farewell to Reality: How Modern Physics Has Betrayed the Search for Scientific Truth*. New York: Pegasus, 2013.

————. *Origins: The Scientific Story of Creation*. New York: Oxford University Press, 2015.

Baldner, Steven E., and William E. Carroll. "An Analysis of Aquinas' Writings on the 'Sentences' of Peter Lombard, Book 2, Distinction 1, Question 1." In Aquinas, Thomas. *Aquinas on Creation: Writings on the "Sentences" of Peter Lombard, Book 2, Distinction 1, Question 1*, translated by Steven E. Baldner and William E. Carroll, 35–62. Mediaeval Sources in Translation 35. Toronto: Pontifical Institute of Mediaeval Studies, 1997.

Balthasar, Hans Urs von. *Cosmic Liturgy: The Universe according to Maximus the Confessor*. Translated by Brian E. Daley. San Francisco: Ignatius, 2003.

————. *Epilogue*. Translated by Edward T. Oakes. San Francisco: Ignatius, 2004.

———. *The Glory of the Lord IV: The Realm of Metaphysics in Antiquity*. Translated by Oliver Davies and Rowan Williams. San Francisco: Ignatius, 1989.

———. *The Glory of the Lord V: The Realm of Metaphysics in the Modern Age*. Edited by Brian McNeil and John Riches. Translated by Oliver Davies et al. San Francisco: Ignatius, 1991.

———. *Homo Creatus Est*. Einsiedeln, Switzerland: Johannes, 1986.

———. *Love Alone Is Credible*. Translated by D. C. Schindler. San Francisco: Ignatius, 2004.

———. *My Work: In Retrospect*. Translated by Brian McNeil, et al. San Francisco: Ignatius, 1993.

———. *Science, Religion and Christianity*. Translated by Hilda Graef. Westminster, MD: Newman, 1958.

———. *Theo-Drama II: The Dramatis Personae: Man in God*. Translated by Graham Harrison. San Francisco: Ignatius, 1990.

———. *Theo-Drama V: The Last Act*. Translated by Graham Harrison. San Francisco: Ignatius, 1998.

———. *Theo-Logic I: Truth of the World*. Translated by Adrian J. Walker. San Francisco: Ignatius, 2000.

———. *Theo-Logic II: Truth of God*. Translated by Adrian J. Walker. San Francisco: Ignatius, 2004.

Barbour, Ian G. *Issues in Science and Religion*. Englewood Cliffs, NJ: Prentice-Hall, 1966.

Barr, Stephen M. "Anthropic Coincidences." *First Things*, no. 114 (June 1, 2001) 17–23.

Barrow, John D., and Frank J. Tipler. *The Anthropic Cosmological Principle*. Oxford: Oxford University Press, 1986.

Benedict XVI. "The Regensburg Address." In *Ratzinger's Faith: The Theology of Pope Benedict XVI*, edited by Tracey Rowland, 166–74. Oxford: Oxford University Press, 2008.

Betz, Frederick. *Managing Science: Methodology and Organization of Research. Innovation, Technology, and Knowledge Management*. New York: Springer, 2011.

Bieler, Martin. "*Analogia Entis* as an Expression of Love according to Ferdinand Ulrich." In *The Analogy of Being: Invention of the Antichrist or the Wisdom of God?* edited by Thomas J. White, 314–37. Grand Rapids, MI: Eerdmans, 2011.

Bohm, David. *Causality and Chance in Modern Physics*. London: Routledge and Kegan Paul, 1957.

———. "The Implicate Order: A New Approach to the Nature of Reality." In *Beyond Mechanism: The Universe in Recent Physics and Catholic Thought*, edited by David L. Schindler, 13–37. Lanham, MD: University Press of America, 1986.

———. *Wholeness and the Implicate Order*. London: Routledge, 2002.

Borde, Arvind, et al. "Inflationary Spacetimes Are Incomplete in Past Directions." *Physical Review Letters* 90, no. 15 (April 15, 2003) 151301/1–151301/4.

Brown, Montague. "Aquinas and the Individuation of Human Persons Revisited." *International Philosophical Quarterly* 43, no. 2 (2003) 167–85.

Bunge, Mario. *Causality and Modern Science*. 3rd ed. New York: Dover, 2012.

Burtt, Edwin A. *The Metaphysical Foundations of Modern Science*. New York: Doubleday, 2003.

Cahan, David. *From Natural Philosophy to the Sciences: Writing the History of Nineteenth-Century Science*. Chicago: University of Chicago Press, 2003.

Carroll, Sean. "Does the Universe Need God?" In *The Blackwell Companion to Science and Christianity*, edited by Jim B. Stump and Alan G. Padgett, 185–97. Malden, MA: Blackwell, 2012.

———. "Falsifiability." In *This Idea Must Die: Scientific Theories That Are Blocking Progress*, edited by John Brockman, 124–27. Edge Question. New York: Harper Perennial, 2015.

———. "Why (Almost All) Cosmologists Are Atheists." *Faith and Philosophy* 22, no. 5 (2005) 622–35.

Carroll, Sean, and William L. Craig. "God and Cosmology: The Existence of God in Light of Contemporary Cosmology." In *God and Cosmology: William Lane Craig and Sean Carroll in Dialogue*, edited by Robert B. Stewart, 19–106. Grear-Heard Lectures. Minneapolis: Fortress, 2016.

Carroll, William E. "Aquinas and Contemporary Cosmology: Creation and Beginnings." *Science & Christian Belief* 24, no. 1 (2012) 5–18.

———. "Aquinas on Creation and the Metaphysical Foundations of Science." *Sapientia* 54, no. 205 (1999) 69–91.

———. "Big Bang Cosmology, Quantum Tunneling from Nothing, and Creation." *Laval Théologique et Philosophique* 44, no. 1 (1988) 59–75.

———. *Creation and Science: Has Science Eliminated God?* London: Catholic Truth Society, 2011.

———. "Two Creators or One? Thomistic Metaphysics and the Theology of Creation." In *God and World: Theology of Creation from Scientific and Ecumenical Standpoints*, edited by Tomasz Trafny and Armand Puig i Tàrrech, 117–47. STOQ Project Research 11. Vatican City: Libreria Editrice Vaticana, 2011.

Carter, Brandon. "Large Number Coincidences and the Anthropic Principle in Cosmology." In *Confrontation of Cosmological Theories with Observational Data*, edited by Malcolm S. Longair, 291–98. Symposium of the International Astronomical Union 63. Dordrecht, Netherlands: Reidel, 1974.

Chapp, Larry S. "*Gaudium et Spes* and the Intelligibility of Modern Science." *Communio* 39, no. 1–2 (Spring–Summer 2012) 269–93.

———. *The God of Covenant and Creation: Scientific Naturalism and Its Challenge to the Christian Faith*. London: T. & T. Clark, 2011.

———. "Review Essay: Alan G. Padgett, *Science and the Study of God: A Mutuality Model for Theology and Science.*" *Pro Ecclesia* 14, no. 3 (2005) 364–69.

Clarke, W. Norris. "Metaphysics as Mediator between Revelation and the Natural Sciences." *Communio* 28, no. 3 (2001) 464–88.

Conway Morris, Simon. "What is Written into Creation?" In *Creation and the God of Abraham*, edited by David B. Burrell et al., 176–91. Cambridge: Cambridge University Press, 2010.

Copan, Paul, and William L. Craig. *Creation out of Nothing: A Biblical, Philosophical, and Scientific Exploration*. Grand Rapids, MI: Baker Academic, 2004.

Cowen, Ron. "Gravitational Wave Discovery Faces Scrutiny." *Nature News*. Last modified May 16, 2014. http://www.nature.com/news/gravitational-wave-discovery-faces-scrutiny-1.15248.

———. "Gravitational Waves Discovery Now Officially Dead." *Nature News*. Last modified January 30, 2015. http://www.nature.com/news/gravitational-waves-discovery-now-officially-dead-1.16830.

————. "Telescope Captures View of Gravitational Waves." *Nature* 507, no. 7492 (March 20, 2014) 281–83.

Coyne, George V. "Evolution and Intelligent Design. What Is Science and What Is Not." *Revista Portuguesa de Filosofia* 66, no. 4 (2010) 717–20.

Craig, William L. "Barrow and Tipler on the Anthropic Principle vs. Divine Design." *The British Journal for the Philosophy of Science* 39, no. 3 (1988) 389–95.

————. "The Cosmological Argument." In *The Rationality of Theism*, edited by Paul Copan and Paul K. Moser, 112–31. London: Routledge, 2003.

————. *The Cosmological Argument from Plato to Leibniz*. New York: Barnes and Noble, 1980.

————. "Creation and Conservation Once More." *Religious Studies* 34, no. 2 (1998) 177–88.

————. "Divine Simplicity." Reasonable Faith. Question & Answer #111. Last modified June 1, 2009. https://www.reasonablefaith.org/writings/question-answer/divine-simplicity/.

————. "God and the Initial Cosmological Singularity: A Reply to Quentin Smith." *Faith and Philosophy* 9, no. 2 (1992) 238–48.

————. "Graham Oppy on the Kalam Cosmological Argument." *International Philosophical Quarterly* 51, no. 3 (2011) 303–30.

————. "Invasion of the Boltzmann Brains." Reasonable Faith. Question & Answer #285. Last modified September 30, 2012. https://www.reasonablefaith.org/writings/question-answer/invasion-of-the-boltzmann-brains/.

————. "Is God a Being in the Same Sense That We Are?" Reasonable Faith. Question & Answer #276. Last modified July 29, 2012. http://www.reasonablefaith.org/is-god-a-being-in-the-same-sense-that-we-are (the webpage is no longer available, but Craig's words can be found at http://analyticscholastic.blogspot.com.es/2012/07/william-lane-craig-on-god-and-analogy.html (last modified July 31, 2012)).

————. "J. Howard Sobel on the Kalam Cosmological Argument." *Canadian Journal of Philosophy* 36, no. 4 (2006) 565–84.

————. *The Kalām Cosmological Argument*. New York: Barnes & Noble, 1979.

————. "The Origin and Creation of the Universe: A Reply to Adolf Grünbaum." *The British Journal for the Philosophy of Science* 43, no. 2 (1992) 233–40.

————. "Professor Mackie and the *Kalām* Cosmological Argument." *Religious Studies* 20, no. 3 (1984) 367–75.

————. *Proofs for God, Foreknowledge, and Scientism*. Interview by Kevin Harris. Reasonable Faith Podcast. Last modified October 23, 2012. https://www.reasonablefaith.org/media/reasonable-faith-podcast/proofs-for-god-foreknowlege-and-scientism/.

————. *A Rabbi Looks at the Kalam Argument*. Interview by Kevin Harris. Reasonable Faith Podcast. Last modified March 21, 2013. https://www.reasonablefaith.org/media/reasonable-faith-podcast/a-rabbi-looks-at-the-kalam-argument/.

————. "The Ultimate Question of Origins: God and the Beginning of the Universe." *Astrophysics and Space Science* 269–70 (December 1, 1999) 723–40.

————. "Vilenkin's Cosmic Vision: A Review Essay of *Many Worlds in One*." *Philosophia Christi* 11, no. 1 (2009) 232–38.

————. "'What Place, Then, for a Creator?': Hawking on God and Creation." *The British Journal for the Philosophy of Science* 41, no. 4 (1990) 473–91.

Craig, William L., and James D. Sinclair. "The *Kalam* Cosmological Argument." In *The Blackwell Companion to Natural Theology*, edited by William L. Craig and James P. Moreland, 101–201. Malden, MA: Wiley-Blackwell, 2012.

Craig, William L., and Quentin Smith. *Theism, Atheism, and Big Bang Cosmology*. Oxford: Clarendon, 1995.

Crick, Francis H. C., and Leslie E. Orgel. "Directed Panspermia." *Icarus* 19, no. 3 (1973) 341–46.

Cunningham, Conor. *Darwin's Pious Idea: Why the Ultra-Darwinists and Creationists Both Get It Wrong*. Grand Rapids, MI: Eerdmans, 2010.

Davies, Paul C. W. *The Mind of God: The Scientific Basis for a Rational World*. New York: Simon & Schuster, 1992.

Dawkins, Richard. "The God Debate: Join Richard Dawkins, Ruth Gledhill and Hannah Devlin." *The Times*. Last modified September 2, 2010. http://www.thetimes.co.uk/tto/science/article2711400.ece.

———. *The God Delusion*. Boston: Houghton Mifflin, 2006.

Deltete, Robert J., and Reed A. Guy. "Emerging from Imaginary Time." *Synthese* 108, no. 2 (1996) 185–203.

Denzinger, Heinrich, ed. *The Sources of Catholic Dogma*. Translated by Roy J. Deferrari. St. Louis, MO: Herder, 1957.

Descartes, René. "Meditations on First Philosophy." In *The Philosophical Writings of Descartes*, translated by John Cottingham et al., 2:1–62. Cambridge: Cambridge University Press, 1985.

———. "Principles of Philosophy." In *The Philosophical Writings of Descartes*, translated by John Cottingham et al., 1:177–292. Cambridge: Cambridge University Press, 1985.

Dodds, Michael J. *Unlocking Divine Action: Contemporary Science and Thomas Aquinas*. Washington, DC: Catholic University of America Press, 2012.

Dodelson, Scott. *Modern Cosmology*. Amsterdam: Academic, 2003.

Doolan, Gregory T. *Aquinas on the Divine Ideas as Exemplar Causes*. Washington, DC: Catholic University of America Press, 2008.

Dowe, Phil. *Galileo, Darwin, and Hawking: The Interplay of Science, Reason, and Religion*. Grand Rapids, MI: Eerdmans, 2005.

Draper, Paul. "God, Science, and Naturalism." In *The Oxford Handbook of Philosophy of Religion*, edited by William J. Wainwright, 270–303. Oxford: Oxford University Press, 2004.

Dummett, Michael. *Thought and Reality*. Oxford: Oxford University Press, 2006.

Dupuy, Jean-Pierre. "Do We Shape Technologies or Do They Shape Us?" ftp://ftp.cordis.europa.eu/pub/foresight/docs/ntw_22_dupuy_text.pdf.

———. *The Mark of the Sacred*. Translated by M. B. DeBevoise. Stanford, CA: Stanford University Press, 2013.

Durbin, Bill, and Robert Jastrow. "A Scientist Caught between Two Faiths: Interview with Robert Jastrow." *Christianity Today* 26, no. 13 (August 6, 1982) 14–18.

Dyson, Freeman J. *A Many-Colored Glass: Reflections on the Place of Life in the Universe*. Charlottesville, VA: University of Virginia Press, 2007.

Einstein, Albert. *Ideas and Opinions*. Edited by Carl Seelig. Translated by Sonja Bargmann. New York: Bonanza, 1954.

Ellis, George F. "Opposing the Multiverse." *Astronomy & Geophysics* 49, no. 2 (April 1, 2008) 2.33–2.35.

Ellis, George F., and Joseph Silk. "Defend the Integrity of Physics." *Nature* 516, no. 7531 (December 18/25, 2014) 321–23.

Emery, Gilles. "Trinity and Creation." In *The Theology of Thomas Aquinas*, edited by Rik Van Nieuwenhove and Joseph P. Wawrykow, 58–76. Notre Dame, IN: University of Notre Dame Press, 2005.

ESA, and Planck Collaboration. "Planck Reveals an Almost Perfect Universe." Max-Planck-Gesellschaft. Last modified March 21, 2013. http://www.mpg.de/7044245/.

Francis. *Praise Be to You: Laudato Si'*. San Francisco: Ignatius, 2015.

Funkenstein, Amos. *Theology and the Scientific Imagination from the Middle Ages to the Seventeenth Century*. Princeton, NJ: Princeton University Press, 1986.

Gaine, Simon F. "God Is an Artificer: A Reply to Professor Edward Feser." *Nova et Vetera* 14, no. 2 (2016) 495–501.

Galilei, Galileo. "The Assayer." In Galilei, Galileo et al. *The Controversy on the Comets of 1618*, translated by Stillman Drake and Charles D. O'Malley, 151–336. Philadelphia: University of Pennsylvania Press, 1960.

———. *Dialogue Concerning the Two Chief World Systems, Ptolemaic and Copernican*. Translated by Stillman Drake. New York: Modern Library, 2001.

———. "Letter to the Grand Duchess Christina." In *Discoveries and Opinions of Galileo*, translated by Stillman Drake, 173–216. Garden City, NY: Doubleday, 1957.

———. *Le Opere di Galileo Galilei*. Edited by Eugenio Albèri and Celestino Bianchi. Vol. 4. 15 vols. Firenze: Società Editrice Fiorentina, 1844.

Giberson, Karl, and Mariano Artigas. *Oracles of Science: Celebrity Scientists versus God and Religion*. Oxford: Oxford University Press, 2007.

Gilson, Etienne. *The Philosophy of St. Bonaventure*. Translated by Illtyd Trethowan and Francis J. Sheed. Paterson, NJ: St. Anthony Guild, 1965.

Gleick, James. *Chaos: Making a New Science*. London: Heinemann, 1988.

Gould, Stephen J. "Nonoverlapping Magisteria." *Natural History* 106, no. 2 (1997) 16–22; 60–62.

———. *Rocks of Ages: Science and Religion in the Fullness of Life*. New York: Ballantine, 1999.

Grant, Edward. *A History of Natural Philosophy: From the Ancient World to the Nineteenth Century*. Cambridge: Cambridge University Press, 2007.

Gribbin, John. *In Search of the Multiverse: Parallel Worlds, Hidden Dimensions, and the Ultimate Quest for the Frontiers of Reality*. Hoboken, NJ: Wiley, 2010.

Guénon, René. *The Reign of Quantity and the Signs of the Times*. Translated by Lord Northbourne. London: Luzac, 1953.

Guth, Alan H. *The Inflationary Universe: The Quest for a New Theory of Cosmic Origins*. Reading, MA: Addison-Wesley, 1997.

Hahn, Roger. *Pierre Simon Laplace, 1749–1827: A Determined Scientist*. Cambridge, MA: Harvard University Press, 2005.

Halvorson, Hans, and Helge Kragh. "Physical Cosmology." In *The Routledge Companion to Theism*, edited by Charles Taliaferro et al., 241–55. New York: Routledge, 2013.

Hanby, Michael. "Creation without Creationism: Toward a Theological Critique of Darwinism." *Communio* 30, no. 4 (2003) 654–94.

———. "Much Ado about Nothing: Metaphysics and the Misleading Debate between Intelligent Design and Neo-Darwininan Biology." Paper presented at the meeting *Evolution: Science, Ideology, Reason and Faith*, Union Theological Seminary, New

York, May 31, 2006. Last modified January 5, 2009. http://www.crossroadsnyc. com/files/EvolutionHanby.pdf.

———. *No God, No Science? Theology, Cosmology, Biology.* Oxford: Wiley-Blackwell, 2013.

———. "Saving the Appearances: Creation's Gift to the Sciences." *Anthropotes* 26, no. 1 (2010) 65–96.

———. "Trinity, Creation, and Aesthetic Subalternation." In *Love Alone Is Credible: Hans Urs von Balthasar as Interpreter of the Catholic Tradition*, edited by David L. Schindler, 1.41–74. Grand Rapids, MI: Eerdmans, 2008.

Hankins, Thomas L. *Science and the Enlightenment.* Cambridge: Cambridge University Press, 1985.

Hartle, James B., and Stephen W. Hawking. "Wave Function of the Universe." *Physical Review D* 28, no. 12 (December 15, 1983) 2960–75.

Hawking, Stephen W. "The Beginning of the Universe." In *Primordial Nucleosynthesis and Evolution of the Early Universe: Proceedings of the International Conference "Primordial Nucleosynthesis and Evolution of Early Universe" Held in Tokyo, Japan, September 4–8, 1990*, edited by Katsuhiko Sato and Jean Audouze, 129–39. Astrophysics and Space Science Library 169. Dordrecht, Netherlands: Kluwer Academic, 1991.

———. *A Brief History of Time: From the Big Bang to Black Holes.* New York: Bantam, 1988.

———. *A Brief History of Time: From Big Bang to Black Holes.* 2nd ed. New York: Bantam, 1998.

———. "Does God Play Dice?" Lecture 1999. Accessed March 27, 2018. http://www. hawking.org.uk/does-god-play-dice.html.

———. "The Edge of Spacetime." In *The New Physics*, edited by Paul C. W. Davies, 61–70. Cambridge: Cambridge University Press, 1988.

———. *Interview*, 2017. In Collins, Sarah. "Taming the Multiverse: Stephen Hawking's Final Theory about the Big Bang." University of Cambridge, Research, News. Last modified May 2, 2018. https://www.cam.ac.uk/research/news/taming-the-multiverse-stephen-hawkings-final-theory-about-the-big-bang.

———. *The Universe in a Nutshell.* New York: Bantam, 2001.

Hawking, Stephen W., and Thomas Hertog. "A Smooth Exit from Eternal Inflation?" *Journal of High Energy Physics* 2018, no. 4 (2018) 147/0–147/13.

Hawking, Stephen W., and Leonard Mlodinow. *The Grand Design.* New York: Bantam, 2010.

Hawking, Stephen W., and Roger Penrose. "The Singularities of Gravitational Collapse and Cosmology." *Proceedings of the Royal Society of London. A. Mathematical and Physical Sciences* 314, no. 1519 (January 27, 1970) 529–48.

Hawking, Stephen W., and Renée Weber. "Interview with Stephen Hawking: If There's an Edge to the Universe, There Must Be a God." In *Dialogues with Scientists and Sages: Search for Unity in Science and Mysticism*, by Renée Weber, 201–14. London: Arkana, 1990.

Hawley, John F., and Katherine A. Holcomb. *Foundations of Modern Cosmology.* New York: Oxford University Press, 1998.

Healy, Nicholas J. *The Eschatology of Hans Urs von Balthasar: Being as Communion.* Oxford: Oxford University Press, 2005.

———. "The World as Gift." *Communio* 32, no. 3 (2005) 395–406.

Heeren, Fred, and Robert Jastrow. *Evidence for God? Fred Heeren Interviews Today's Top Space Scientists*. VHS video. Show Me God—Part 1. Kansas City, KS: Day Star Productions, 1997. Transcript taken from http://evidenceforchristianity.org/interview-with-robert-jastrow-ph-d/ (last modified May 5, 2005).

Heidegger, Martin. "What Is Metaphysics?" In *Pathmarks*, edited by William McNeill, translated by David F. Krell, 82–96. Cambridge: Cambridge University Press, 1998.

Heller, Michael. "Cosmological Singularity and the Creation of the Universe." *Zygon* 35, no. 3 (2000) 665–85.

———. *Creative Tension: Essays on Science and Religion*. Radnor, PA: Templeton Foundation, 2003.

Henry, Michel. *Barbarism*. Translated by Scott Davidson. London: Continuum, 2012.

Herschel, William. *The Herschel Chronicle: The Life-Story of William Herschel and His Sister Caroline Herschel*. Edited by Constance A. Lubbock. Cambridge: Cambridge University Press, 2013.

Hogan, Craig J. "Quarks, Electrons and Atoms in Closely Related Universes." In *Universe or Multiverse?* edited by Bernard Carr, 221–30. Cambridge: Cambridge University Press, 2007.

Hoyle, Fred. *Astronomy and Cosmology: A Modern Course*. San Francisco: Freeman, 1975.

———. *Evolution from Space (the Omni Lecture) and Other Papers on the Origin of Life*. Hillside, NJ: Enslow, 1982.

———. *The Intelligent Universe*. New York: Holt, Rinehart, and Winston, 1984.

———. "The Origin of the Universe." *Quarterly Journal of the Royal Astronomical Society* 14 (1973) 278–87.

———. "The Universe: Past and Present Reflections." *Annual Review of Astronomy and Astrophysics* 20 (1982) 1–35.

Hoyle, Fred, et al. *A Different Approach to Cosmology: From a Static Universe through the Big Bang towards Reality*. Cambridge: Cambridge University Press, 2000.

Humboldt, Alexander von. *Cosmos: A Sketch of a Physical Description of the Universe*. Translated by Elise C. Otté. Vol. 1. 5 vols. New York: Harper & Brothers, 1856.

Hutchinson, Ian. *Monopolizing Knowledge: A Scientist Refutes Religion-Denying, Reason-Destroying Scientism*. Belmont, MA: Fias, 2011.

International Theological Commission. "Communion and Stewardship: Human Persons Created in the Image of God (2004)." In *Texts and Documents, 1986–2007*, edited by Michael Sharkey and Thomas Weinandy, 2.319–51. San Francisco: Ignatius, 2009.

Jardine, Lisa. "Introduction." In Francis Bacon, *The New Organon*, edited by Lisa Jardine and Michael Silverthorne, vii–xxviii. Cambridge: Cambridge University Press, 2000.

Jaroszkiewicz, George. "Analysis of the Relationship between Real and Imaginary Time in Physics." In *The Nature of Time: Geometry, Physics, and Perception*, edited by R. Buccheri et al., 153–64. NATO Science Series 95. Dordrecht, Netherlands: Kluwer Academic, 2003.

Jastrow, Robert. "The Astronomer and God." In *The Intellectuals Speak Out about God: A Handbook for the Christian Student in a Secular Society*, edited by Roy A. Varghese, 15–22. Chicago: Regnery Gateway, 1984.

———. *God and the Astronomers*. New York: Norton, 1978.

Jennings, Byron K. *In Defense of Scientism: An Insider's View of Science*. Vancouver, Canada: Byron Jennings, 2015.

Jonas, Hans. "Philosophical Aspects of Darwinism." In *The Phenomenon of Life: Toward a Philosophical Biology*, 38–63. Evanston, IL: Northwestern University Press, 2001.

———. "The Practical Uses of Theory." In *The Phenomenon of Life: Toward a Philosophical Biology*, 188–210. Evanston, IL: Northwestern University Press, 2001.

Kerr, Fergus. *After Aquinas: Versions of Thomism*. Malden, MA: Blackwell, 2002.

Koninck, Charles de. *The Hollow Universe*. Whidden Lectures 4. London: Oxford University Press, 1960.

Kovach, Francis J. "Divine Art in Saint Thomas Aquinas." In *Arts Libéraux et Philosophie au Môyen Age: Actes du Quatrième Congrès International de Philosophie Médiévale*, 663–71. Montreal: Institut d'Études Médiévales, 1969.

Koyré, Alexandre. "Galileo and Plato." *Journal of the History of Ideas* 4, no. 4 (1943) 400–428.

———. "The Origins of Modern Science: A New Interpretation." *Diogenes* 16, no. 4 (1956) 1–22.

Kuhn, Thomas S. *The Structure of Scientific Revolutions: 50th Anniversary Edition*. 4th ed. Chicago: University of Chicago Press, 2012.

Leibniz, Gottfried W. *Leibniz: Selections*. Edited by Philip P. Wiener. New York: Scribner's Sons, 1951.

Lemaître, Georges. "The Primaeval Atom Hypothesis and the Problem of the Clusters of Galaxies." In *La Structure et l'Évolution de l'Univers: Onzième Conseil de Physique Solvay*, edited by R. Stoops, 1–32. Brussels: Stoops, 1958.

Leslie, John. *Universes*. London: Routledge, 1989.

Liddle, Andrew R. *An Introduction to Modern Cosmology*. Chichester, UK: Wiley, 1999.

Liddle, Andrew R., and Jon Loveday, eds. *The Oxford Companion to Cosmology*. Oxford: Oxford University Press, 2008.

Lindberg, David C. *The Beginnings of Western Science: The European Scientific Tradition in Philosophical, Religious, and Institutional Context, Prehistory to A.D. 1450*. 2nd ed. Chicago: University of Chicago Press, 2008.

Linde, Andrei. *The Big Lab Experiment: Was Our Universe Created by Design?* Interview by Jim Holt. Last modified May 19, 2004. http://www.slate.com/articles/arts/egghead/2004/05/the_big_lab_experiment.single.html.

———. "Inflation, Quantum Cosmology and the Anthropic Principle." In *Science and Ultimate Reality: Quantum Theory, Cosmology, and Complexity*, edited by John D. Barrow et al., 426–58. Cambridge: Cambridge University Press, 2004.

———. "Inflationary Theory Versus the Ekpyrotic/Cyclic Scenario." In *The Future of Theoretical Physics and Cosmology: Celebrating Stephen Hawking's Contributions to Physics*, edited by Gary W. Gibbons et al., 801–38. Cambridge: Cambridge University Press, 2003.

———. "The Self-Reproducing Inflationary Universe." *Scientific American* 271, no. 5 (November 1994) 48–55.

———. "The Universe, Life, and Consciousness." In *Science and the Spiritual Quest: New Essays by Leading Scientists*, edited by W. Mark Richardson et al., 188–202. London: Routledge, 2002.

Locke, John. *An Essay concerning Human Understanding*. Amherst, NY: Prometheus, 1995.

Lockwood, Michael. *The Labyrinth of Time: Introducing the Universe*. Oxford: Oxford University Press, 2005.

Marion, Jean-Luc. "The Other First Philosophy and the Question of Givenness." Translated by Jeffrey L. Kosky. *Critical Inquiry* 25, no. 4 (1999) 784–800.

Mascall, Eric L. *He Who Is: A Study in Traditional Theism*. London: Longmans, Green and Company, 1943.

May, Gerhard. *Creatio ex Nihilo: The Doctrine of "Creation out of Nothing" in Early Christian Thought*. Translated by A. S. Worrall. London: T. & T. Clark, 2004.

McDermott, Timothy. "Introduction." In Thomas Aquinas, *Existence and Nature of God (Ia. 2–11)*, translated by Timothy McDermott, 2.xx–xxvii. St. Thomas Aquinas *Summa Theologiae*. Cambridge: Cambridge University Press, 2006.

McMullin, Ernan. "Evolutionary Contingency and Cosmic Purpose." In *The Interplay between Scientific and Theological Worldviews (Part I)*, edited by Niels H. Gregersen et al., 91–112. Studies in Science and Theology 5. Geneva, Switzerland: Labor et Fides, 1999.

———. "Natural Science and Belief in a Creator: Historical Notes." In *Physics, Philosophy, and Theology: A Common Quest for Understanding*, edited by Robert J. Russell et al., 49–79. Vatican City: Vatican Observatory, 1988.

———. "Plantinga's Defense of Special Creation." *Christian Scholar's Review* 21, no. 1 (1991) 55–79.

Meyerson, Émile. *De l'Explication dans les Sciences*. Vol. 1. 2 vols. Paris: Payot, 1921.

———. *Explanation in the Sciences*. Translated by Mary-Alice Sipfle and David A. Sipfle. Boston Studies in the Philosophy and History of Science 128. Dordrecht, Netherlands: Kluwer Academic, 1991.

Mithani, Audrey, and Alexander Vilenkin. "Did the Universe Have a Beginning?" In *Gravitation, Astrophysics and Cosmology: Proceedings of the Xth International Conference on Gravitation, Astrophysics and Cosmology (ICGAC10). Quy Nhon, December 17–22, 2011*, edited by Roland Triay et al., 173–77. Hanoi: Gioi, 2013.

Mooney, Christopher F. "The Anthropic Principle in Cosmology and Theology." *Horizons* 21, no. 1 (1994) 105–29.

Morales, José. *Creation Theology*. Translated by Michael Adams and Dudley Cleary. Portland, OR: Four Courts, 2001.

Moreland, James P., and William L. Craig. *Philosophical Foundations for a Christian Worldview*. Downers Grove, IL: InterVarsity, 2003.

Newton, Isaac. *The Principia: Mathematical Principles of Natural Philosophy*. Translated by I. Bernard Cohen and Anne M. Whitman. Berkeley: University of California Press, 1999.

———. *Unpublished Scientific Papers of Isaac Newton: A Selection from the Portsmouth Collection in the University Library, Cambridge*. Edited by A. Rupert Hall and Marie B. Hall. Cambridge: Cambridge University Press, 1962.

Oliver, Simon. *Philosophy, God and Motion*. London: Routledge, 2005.

———. "Physics, Creation and the Trinity." *Anthropotes* 26, no. 1 (2010) 181–205.

———. "Trinity, Motion and Creation *ex Nihilo*." In *Creation and the God of Abraham*, edited by David B. Burrell et al., 133–51. Cambridge: Cambridge University Press, 2010.

Orr, H. Allen. "Gould on God: Can Religion and Science Be Happily Reconciled?" *Boston Review* 24, no. 5 (1999) 33–38.

Owens, Joseph. "Thomas Aquinas." In *Individuation in Scholasticism the Later Middle Ages and the Counter-Reformation (1150–1650)*, edited by Jorge J. E. Gracia, 173–94. Albany, NY: State University of New York Press, 1994.

Padgett, Alan G. *Science and the Study of God: A Mutuality Model for Theology and Science*. Grand Rapids, MI: Eerdmans, 2003.

Paley, William. *Natural Theology, Or, Evidences of the Existence and Attributes of the Deity, Collected from the Appearances of Nature*. Cambridge: Cambridge University Press, 2009.

Pannenberg, Wolfhart. "Theological Questions to Scientists." *Zygon* 16, no. 1 (1981) 65–77.

———. *Toward a Theology of Nature: Essays on Science and Faith*. Edited by Ted Peters. Louisville, KY: Westminster John Knox, 1993.

Pieper, Josef. *The Silence of St. Thomas: Three Essays*. Translated by John Murray and Daniel O'Connor. South Bend, IN: St. Augustine's, 1999.

Pigliucci, Massimo. "Personal Gods, Deism, and the Limits of Skepticism." *Skeptic* 8, no. 2 (2000) 38–45.

Plantinga, Alvin. "Methodological Naturalism?" In *Intelligent Design Creationism and Its Critics: Philosophical, Theological, and Scientific Perspectives*, edited by Robert T. Pennock, 339–62. Cambridge, MA: Massachusetts Institute of Technology Press, 2001.

Polanyi, Michael. *Personal Knowledge: Towards a Post-Critical Philosophy*. 2nd ed. Chicago: University of Chicago Press, 1974.

Polkinghorne, John C. *Faith, Science and Understanding*. New Haven, CT: Yale University Press, 2001.

———. *From Physicist to Priest: An Autobiography*. London: SPCK, 2007.

———. *One World: The Interaction of Science and Theology*. 2nd ed. Philadelphia: Templeton, 2007.

———. "Physics and Metaphysics in a Trinitarian Perspective." *Theology and Science* 1, no. 1 (June 2003) 33–49.

———. *Theology in the Context of Science*. New Haven, CT: Yale University Press, 2009.

Pontifical Council of Justice and Peace. *Compendium of the Social Doctrine of the Church*. Vatican City: Libreria Editrice Vaticana, 2004.

Popper, Karl R. *The Logic of Scientific Discovery*. 2nd ed. London: Routledge, 2002.

Ratzinger, Joseph. *Dogma and Preaching: Applying Christian Doctrine to Daily Life*. Edited by Michael J. Miller. Translated by Michael J. Miller and Matthew J. O'Connell. 2nd ed. San Francisco: Ignatius, 2011.

———. *"In the Beginning . . .": A Catholic Understanding of the Story of Creation and the Fall*. Translated by Boniface Ramsey and Helen A. Saward. Grand Rapids, MI: Eerdmans, 2005.

———. *Introduction to Christianity*. Translated by J. R. Foster and Michael J. Miller. Rev. ed. San Francisco: Ignatius, 2004.

Ratzsch, Delvin L. *Science and Its Limits: The Natural Sciences in Christian Perspective*. 2nd ed. Downers Grove, IL: InterVarsity, 2000.

Ravasi, Gianfranco. "Foreword." In *God and World: Theology of Creation from Scientific and Ecumenical Standpoints*, edited by Tomasz Trafny and Armand Puig i Tàrrech, 11–19. STOQ Project Research 11. Vatican City: Libreria Editrice Vaticana, 2011.

Rey, Olivier. *Itinéraire de l'Égarement: du Rôle de la Science dans l'Absurdité Contemporaine*. Paris: Seuil, 2003.

———. "Science in the Twenty-First Century." *Queen's Quarterly* 117, no. 1 (2010) 41–54.

Rosheger, John P. "Augustine and Divine Simplicity." *New Blackfriars* 77, no. 901 (1996) 72–83.

Rothman, Tony. "A 'What You See Is What You Beget' Theory." *Discover* 8, no. 5 (1987) 90–99.

Russell, Robert J. "Does Creation Have a Beginning?" *Dialog: A Journal of Theology* 36, no. 3 (1997) 180–89.

Sachs, Joe. *Aristotle's Physics: A Guided Study.* New Brunswick, NJ: Rutgers University Press, 1995.

Sagan, Carl. *The Backbone of the Night.* VHS video. Cosmos TV Series. Los Angeles: KCET, 1980.

———. *Cosmos.* New York: Random House, 2002.

Sagan, Carl, and Ann Druyan. *The Demon-Haunted World: Science as a Candle in the Dark.* New York: Ballantine, 1997.

Schindler, D. C. *Hans Urs von Balthasar and the Dramatic Structure of Truth: A Philosophical Investigation.* Perspectives in Continental Philosophy 34. New York: Fordham University Press, 2004.

———. "Historical Intelligibility: On Creation and Causality." *Anthropotes* 26, no. 1 (2010) 15–44.

———. "Truth and the Christian Imagination: The Reformation of Causality and the Iconoclasm of the Spirit." *Communio* 33, no. 4 (2006) 521–39.

———. "What's the Difference? On the Metaphysics of Participation in a Christian Context." *The Saint Anselm Journal* 3, no. 1 (2005) 1–27.

Schindler, David L. "Beyond Mechanism: Physics and Catholic Theology." *Communio* 11, no. 2 (1984) 186–92.

———. "The Given as Gift: Creation and Disciplinary Abstraction in Science." *Communio* 38, no. 1 (2011) 52–102.

———. "The Person: Philosophy, Theology, and Receptivity." *Communio* 21, no. 1 (1994) 172–90.

———. "Time in Eternity, Eternity in Time: On the Contemplative-Active Life." In *Heart of the World, Center of the Church: Communio Ecclesiology, Liberalism and Liberation,* 221–36. Grand Rapids, MI: Eerdmans, 2001.

———. "Trinity, Creation, and the Order of Intelligence in the Modern Academy." *Communio* 28, no. 3 (2001) 406–28.

Schmemann, Alexander. *For the Life of the World: Sacraments and Orthodoxy.* Crestwood, NY: St. Vladimir's Seminary, 2005.

Schmitz, Kenneth L. *The Gift: Creation.* The Aquinas Lecture 46. Milwaukee, WI: Marquette University Press, 1982.

———. *The Texture of Being: Essays in First Philosophy.* Edited by Paul O'Herron. Studies in Philosophy and the History of Philosophy 46. Washington, DC: Catholic University of America Press, 2007.

Scott, Eugenie C. "Darwin Prosecuted: Review of Johnson's Darwin on Trial." *Creation/Evolution* 13, no. 2 (1993) 36–47.

Senor, Thomas D. "Divine Temporality and Creation *ex Nihilo.*" *Faith and Philosophy* 10, no. 1 (1993) 86–91.

Shanley, Brian J. "Divine Causation and Human Freedom in Aquinas." *American Catholic Philosophical Quarterly* 72, no. 1 (1998) 99–122.

Smedes, Taede A. "Beyond Barbour or Back to Basics? The Future of Science-and-Religion and the Quest for Unity." *Zygon* 43, no. 1 (2008) 235–58.

———. *Chaos, Complexity, and God: Divine Action and Scientism.* Leuven, Belgium: Peeters, 2004.

———. "Religion and Science: Finding the Right Questions." *Zygon* 42, no. 3 (2007) 595–98.

———. "Streams of Wisdom or Signs of Confusion? A Philosophical and Theological Exploration of 'Conflict' and 'Independence' in Religion and Science." In *Streams of Wisdom? Science, Theology and Cultural Dynamics,* edited by Hubert Meisinger et al., 87–103. Studies in Science and Theology 10. Lund, Sweeden: Lund University, 2005.

Smolin, Lee. *The Trouble with Physics: The Rise of String Theory, the Fall of a Science, and What Comes Next.* Boston: Houghton Mifflin, 2006.

Speyr, Adrienne von. *The Gates of Eternal Life.* Translated by Corona Sharp. San Francisco: Ignatius, 1983.

———. *The Word Becomes Flesh: Meditations on John 1–5.* Translated by Lucia Wiedenhöver and Alexander Dru. San Francisco: Ignatius, 1994.

Spitzer, Robert J. "Cosmology." Magis God Wiki. Last modified July 26, 2011. http://magisgodwiki.org/index.php?title=Cosmology.

———. *New Proofs for the Existence of God: Contributions of Contemporary Physics and Philosophy.* Grand Rapids, MI: Eerdmans, 2010.

Steinhardt, Paul J. "Big Bang Blunder Bursts the Multiverse Bubble." *Nature* 510, no. 7503 (2014) 9.

Steinhardt, Paul J., and Neil Turok. "The Cyclic Model Simplified." *New Astronomy Reviews* 49, no. 2–6 (2005) 43–57.

———. *Endless Universe: Beyond the Big Bang.* New York: Doubleday, 2007.

Stenger, Victor J. "Anthropic Design." *The Skeptical Inquirer* 23, no. 4 (1999) 40–43.

———. "Is the Universe Fine-Tuned for Us?" In *Why Intelligent Design Fails: A Scientific Critique of the New Creationism,* edited by Matt Young and Taner Edis, 172–84. New Brunswick, NJ: Rutgers University Press, 2004.

Stenmark, Mikael. *How to Relate Science and Religion: A Multidimensional Model.* Grand Rapids, MI: Eerdmans, 2004.

———. *Scientism: Science, Ethics and Religion.* Burlington, VT: Ashgate, 2001.

Stodolna, Aneta S., et al. "Hydrogen Atoms under Magnification: Direct Observation of the Nodal Structure of Stark States." *Physical Review Letters* 110, no. 21 (2013) 213001/1–213001/5.

Stoeger, William R. "Are Anthropic Arguments, Involving Multiverses and Beyond, Legitimate?" In *Universe or Multiverse?* edited by Bernard Carr, 445–57. Cambridge: Cambridge University Press, 2007.

———. "The Big Bang, Quantum Cosmology and *Creatio ex Nihilo.*" In *Creation and the God of Abraham,* edited by David B. Burrell et al., 152–75. Cambridge: Cambridge University Press, 2010.

———. "The Origin of the Universe in Science and Religion." In *Cosmos, Bios, Theos: Scientists Reflect on Science, God, and the Origins of the Universe, Life, and Homo Sapiens,* edited by Henry Margenau and Roy A. Varghese, 254–69. La Salle, IL: Open Court, 1992.

———. "Reductionism and Emergence: Implications for the Interaction of Theology with the Natural Sciences." In *Evolution and Emergence: Systems, Organisms,*

Persons, edited by Nancey Murphy and William R. Stoeger, 229–47. Oxford: Oxford University Press, 2007.

———. "Responses to Questions on Science and Religion." In *Can Science Dispense with Religion?* edited by Mehdi Golshani, 201–5. Tehran: Institute for Humanites and Cultural Studies, 1998.

Tegmark, Max. *Our Mathematical Universe: My Quest for the Ultimate Nature of Reality.* New York: Knopf, 2014.

———. "Parallel Universes." In *Science and Ultimate Reality: Quantum Theory, Cosmology, and Complexity*, edited by John D. Barrow et al., 459–91. Cambridge: Cambridge University Press, 2004.

———. "Parallel Universes." *Scientific American* 288, no. 5 (May 2003) 40–51.

Thomas, Jesse J. "Transcendence and Sentience in Science and Religion." *Journal of Interdisciplinary Studies* 24, no. 1/2 (2012) 159–76.

Timmons, Todd. *Makers of Western Science: The Works and Words of 24 Visionaries from Copernicus to Watson and Crick.* Jefferson, NC: McFarland, 2012.

Tryon, Edward P. "Is the Universe a Vacuum Fluctuation?" *Nature* 246 (December 1, 1973) 396–97.

Turok, Neil. *Physicist Neil Turok: Big Bang Wasn't the Beginning.* Interview by Brandon Keim. Last modified February 19, 2008. http://archive.wired.com/science/discoveries/news/2008/02/qa_turok.

Veatch, Henry B. *Two Logics: The Conflict between Classical and Neo-Analytic Philosophy.* Evanston, IL: Northwestern University Press, 1969.

Velde, Rudi A. te. *Aquinas on God: The "Divine Science" of the* Summa Theologiae. Farnham, UK: Ashgate, 2006.

———. *Participation and Substantiality in Thomas Aquinas.* Leiden, Netherlands: Brill, 1995.

Vilenkin, Alexander. *In the Beginning Was the Beginning.* Interview by Jacqueline Mitchell. Last modified May 29, 2012. http://now.tufts.edu/articles/beginning-was-beginning.

———. *Many Worlds in One: The Search for Other Universes.* New York: Hill and Wang, 2007.

———. "The Principle of Mediocrity." *Astronomy & Geophysics* 52, no. 5 (2011) 5.33–5.36.

———. "Quantum Cosmology and Eternal Inflation." In *The Future of Theoretical Physics and Cosmology: Celebrating Stephen Hawking's Contributions to Physics*, edited by Gary W. Gibbons et al., 649–66. Cambridge: Cambridge University Press, 2003.

Villemaire, Diane E. D. *E.A. Burtt, Historian and Philosopher: A Study of the Author of The Metaphysical Foundations of Modern Physical Science.* Boston Studies in the Philosophy of Science 226. Dordrecht, Netherlands: Kluwer Academic, 2002.

Waldrop, M. Mitchell. "Religion: Faith in Science." *Nature* 470, no. 7334 (February 17, 2011) 323–25.

Walker, Adrian J. "Personal Singularity and the *Communio Personarum*: A Creative Development of Thomas Aquinas' Doctrine of *Esse Commune*." *Communio* 31, no. 3 (2004) 457–80.

———. "*Wo Aber Gefahr Ist, Wächst Das Rettende Auch*: Four Sets of Theses on Scientism." Unpublished text based on conference delivered by the author presented at the "The Nature of Experience: Issues in Science, Culture, and

Theology," Pontifical John Paul II Institute for Studies on Marriage and Family at The Catholic University of America, December 2009.

Walls, Laura D. *The Passage to Cosmos: Alexander von Humboldt and the Shaping of America*. Chicago: University of Chicago Press, 2009.

Weinberg, Stephen. *Dreams of a Final Theory: The Scientist's Search for the Ultimate Laws of Nature*. New York: Vintage, 1994.

Wilhelmsen, Frederick D. "Creation as a Relation in Saint Thomas Aquinas." *Modern Schoolman* 56, no. 2 (1979) 107–33.

———. *The Paradoxical Structure of Existence*. Irving, TX: University of Dallas Press, 1970.

Wippel, John F. *The Metaphysical Thought of Thomas Aquinas: From Finite Being to Uncreated Being*. Washington, DC: Catholic University of America Press, 2000.

Woit, Peter. *Not Even Wrong: The Failure of String Theory and the Search for Unity in Physical Law*. New York: Basic, 2006.

Życiński, Joseph M. "Metaphysics and Epistemology in Stephen Hawking's Theory of the Creation of the Universe." *Zygon* 31, no. 2 (1996) 269–84.

———. "The Weak Anthropic Principle and the Design Argument." *Zygon* 31, no. 1 (1996) 115–30.

General Index

Abbott, Benjamin P., 157n243
actus essendi. See being: act of
actus purus. See God: as pure act
Ade, Peter, 133n134, 157n243
analogatum princeps, 84
analogy of being. *See* being: analogy of
Anastopoulos, Charis, 23nn61–62
Anderson, Edward, 142n179
Anderson, Rupert W., 146n197, 158n249
anthropic coincidences, 163, 169, 171, 179
anthropic principle, 106, 106n14, 108, 167, 170, 170n300, 171–72, 175, 177
Aquinas, Thomas, 6–7, 19n41, 53, 58, 58n3, 59–63, 65, 67–68, 68nn68–70, 69, 69n71, 70, 72–73, 74n103, 79–82, 82n148, 83, 85n172, 86–87, 87n181, 88–89, 95, 95n224, 96–97, 107, 107nn18–20, 108n21, 114, 114n50, 115, 115n51, 116–17, 122, 127, 144, 160, 169
argument, cosmological. *See* cosmological argument
Aristotle, 11nn4–5, 12, 12n8, 13, 13nn11–12, 14, 14n17, 15, 19n41, 24–25, 25n75, 26n79, 53, 82n150, 99, 99n247, 110n30, 114n50, 119–20
artifice. *See* nature: as artifact

Artigas, Mariano, 11n4, 143–44, 144nn185–86, 145n190
atheism, x, 2, 4n10, 28, 28n90, 42n165, 43n167, 159n250, 160, 162nn261–62
atheism of the gaps, 159–60, 162, 174. *See also* devil of the gaps
atheistic cosmologists, ix, 7–8, 55, 57, 63, 87, 99, 105–6, 108, 130–32, 161–62, 180, 182
atheistic cosmology, 8, 162, 182
Augustine, 65, 65n48, 66n56, 70, 70n82, 97, 141
Auletta, Gennaro, 41n163
autonomy
  of creatures, 38, 81, 85
  of science, 37, 50n195
Ayres, Lewis, 70n81

Bacon, Francis, 12, 12n10, 13n11, 17n31, 19n42, 25, 25n73
Baggott, Jim E., 157n244, 161
Baldner, Steven E., 83n154, 84n157, 85n171, 97nn239–40, 122nn88–89
Balthasar, Hans Urs von, 22n52, 28, 28n91, 44n170, 59, 67, 69, 69n71, 71n84, 73n95, 74–76, 76n110, 77, 77n118, 77nn120–22, 78, 78n126, 79, 79n129, 80, 84–85, 85n167, 87, 89, 89n192, 90, 90n196, 91n198, 91n201, 92, 92n206,

inflation, 132–33, 133n137, 134,
147, 151–52, 152n221,
156n242, 160n255, 173–74,
174n319, 175–76
Intelligent Design, 159n250, 172,
172n311, 180n351
International Theological
Commission, 128n118
ipsum esse subsistens. See God:
ipsum esse subsistens

Jardine, Lisa, 12n9
Jaroszkiewicz, George, 139n165
Jastrow, Robert, 109, 113, 120,
120n78, 123, 128, 128n119,
129, 167
Jennings, Byron K., 3n5
Jesus, 69–70, 93. *See also* Christ;
Incarnation; hypostatic
union
Jonas, Hans, 17, 18n34, 22n53,
79n130, 96n231

Kerr, Fergus, 116n55, 116n57,
117n58
knowledge
and "know-how," 17
and power, 17n31
Koninck, Charles de, 99n247
Kovach, Francis J., 107n19
Koyré, Alexandre, 13, 15n21, 16,
16nn26–27, 17, 17n28,
17n30
Kragh, Helge, 136n150, 169n297
Kuhn, Thomas S., 1, 45, 45n174

Laplace, Pierre Simon, 2, 3n5, 4n10,
145n191
Leibniz, Gottfried W., 110, 110n30
Lemaître, Georges, 50, 50n194,
105n11, 111
Leslie, John, 169, 169n296
Liddle, Andrew R., 5n11, 103n6,
104nn7–8, 106n14,
132n133, 133n134, 136n148,
136n150, 137n155, 138n158,
139n163, 155n232, 156n242,

158n246, 173n312, 173n315,
176n331
Lindberg, David C., 12n7, 13,
13n13, 14n15
Linde, Andrei, 133, 133n136, 156,
164n268, 165n274, 174,
175n325, 179, 180n347
Locke, John, 16, 42n166
Lockwood, Michael, 98n242
Loveday, Jon, 5n11, 103n6, 104nn7–
8, 106n14, 132n133,
133n134, 136n148, 136n150,
137n155, 138n158, 139n163,
155n232, 156n242, 158n246,
173n312, 173n315, 176n331

Marion, Jean-Luc, 19n41
Mascall, Eric L., 102n2
matter
coeval, 62, 85
dark, 132, 133n134, 160n255
and externality, 21–24
and form, 21–22, 22n55, 45,
47, 49
indifferent to God, 39
and intelligibility, 22, 39
and measurability, 23
mechanistic understanding of,
22n55
positivity of, 21–22, 22n55, 27,
34, 39, 45
May, Gerhard, 61, 61nn19–20,
61n23
McDermott, Timothy, 116n57
McMullin, Ernan, 40n159, 42n165,
128n118, 141n176
mechanistic ontology, xi, 6, 14, 21,
56, 120, 172. *See also* matter:
mechanistic understanding
of; nature: mechanistic
understanding of; time:
mechanistic understanding
of; universe: mechanical
understanding of the
metaphysics, as mediator between
science and theology, 38–39

CPSIA information can be obtained
at www.ICGtesting.com
Printed in the USA
LVHW020253220321
682052LV00008B/299